IMAGES
*of America*

# BERLIN

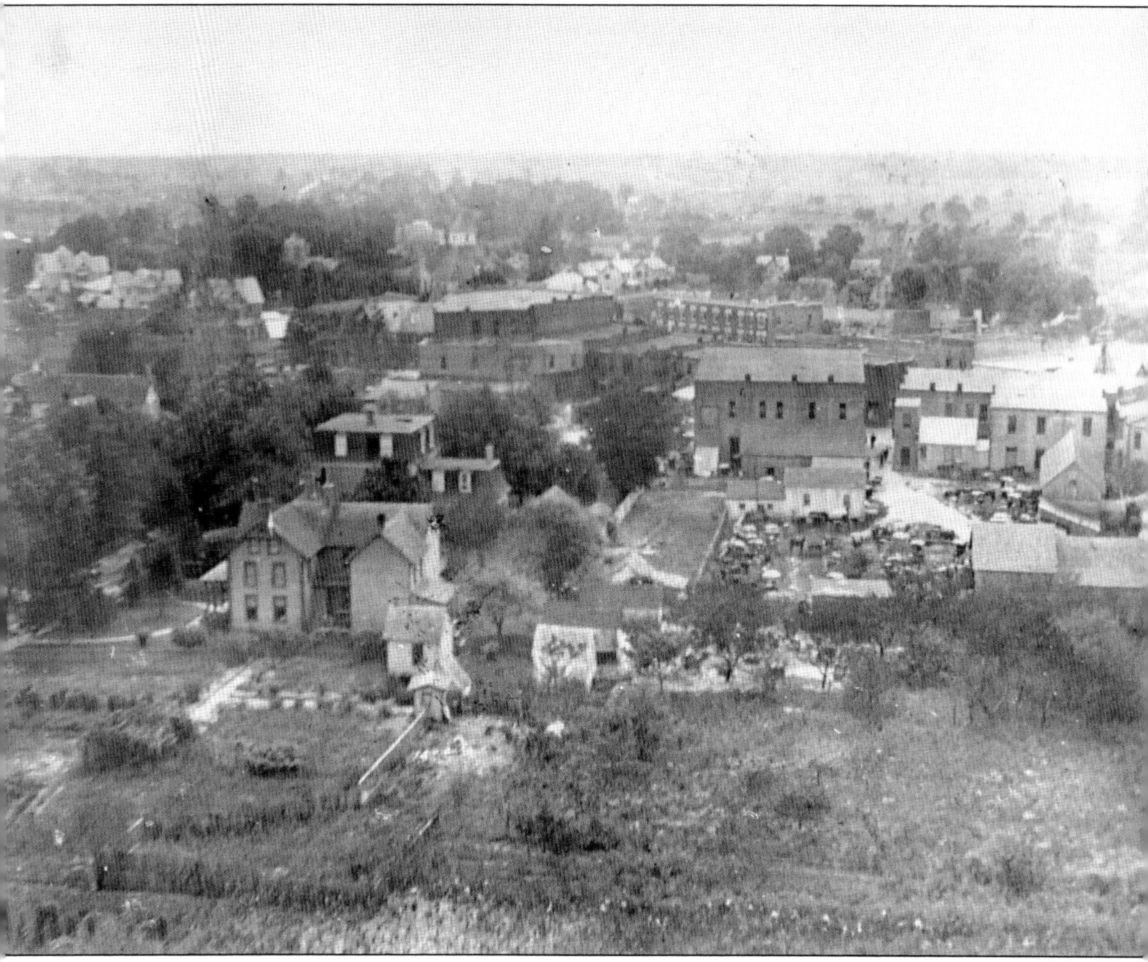

This photograph was taken in 1910 from the newly erected standpipe. At right center is the early stockyard, located where the public parking lot between Main and William Streets is today. The windows of the Atlantic Hotel can be seen at upper center. Also visible are the bell tower of Buckingham School (no longer there) and the steeple of the then newly constructed Buckingham Presbyterian Church. The earlier church had been destroyed in the 1904 fire.

**ON THE COVER:** This is the only known photograph of the second Berlin Milling Company, which was built to replace an older building. This mill burned in 1945. From left to right are (first row) unidentified, Bo Quillin, Joe Harrison, Orlando Harrison, and J. D. Quillin Jr.; (second row) Reese Harmon, Clinton E. Quillin, and Lull Hickman; (upstairs window) Nick Carroll. The mill has served the agricultural interest of the community for 100 years. (Taylor Museum Collection.)

IMAGES
*of America*

# BERLIN

Susan Taylor on behalf of
the Berlin History Foundation, Inc.

ARCADIA
PUBLISHING

ISBN 978-0-7385-4425-0

Published by Arcadia Publishing
Charleston, South Carolina

Printed in the United States of America

Library of Congress Catalog Card Number: 2006939377

For all general information contact Arcadia Publishing at:
Telephone 843-853-2070
Fax 843-853-0044
E-mail sales@arcadiapublishing.com
For customer service and orders:
Toll-Free 1-888-313-2665

Visit us on the Internet at www.arcadiapublishing.com

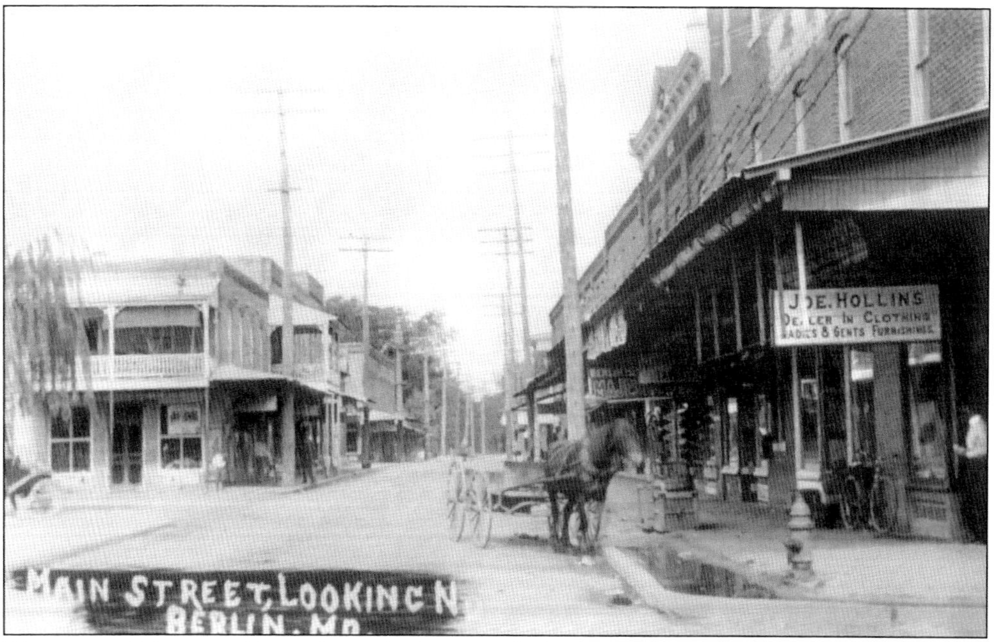


This early-1900s view of Main Street looking north shows the Joe. Hollins clothing store on the right and today's Rayne's Reef on the left. This historic image has now been re-created as a mural on the outside wall of Boomer's Restaurant on South Main Street.

# CONTENTS

# ACKNOWLEDGMENTS

If it takes a community to raise a child, this book is a true child of the Berlin community. The Berlin History Foundation, Inc., first undertook this project thinking to use photographs in the collections of the Calvin B. Taylor House Museum, but we soon realized we might be missing some really great images stored away in private collections throughout the community. We put the word out, and as a result, we were offered many more wonderful early images of our town. We would especially like to thank Mabel Rogers, Ellis Wainwright, and Katie and Bill Matthews for sharing their amazing postcard collections.

To all those who graciously provided photographs for this project and to the many other individuals who have donated images and memorabilia to the Calvin B. Taylor House Museum throughout the years, thank you for sharing your memories. All of the images in these pages not otherwise credited are from the collections of the Calvin B. Taylor House Museum. We have tried to arrange our chapters in a logical order, and it is interesting to note that chapter titles three through five are also town slogans.

Although we have only one name on the cover, a committee of interested and dedicated individuals, all of them volunteers, some of whom are listed here, assembled this book. Our writers—Katie Matthews, Tom Range, and Ed Hammond—faced the daunting task of choosing only a few images from the hundreds in our collections and organizing these images in the eight chapters you see here. Bill Matthews and Cheryl Holland were available to research anything we threw at them. Debbie Speier kept us all on track with her organizational abilities and her constant encouragement: "It will be alright." Thank you also to Mary Humphreys and Marieta Jacobs who proofed our final efforts and to Margaret Coyman who loaned her scanner for the entire project.

Finally, I would like to thank Lauren Bobier, our editor at Arcadia Publishing, for first approaching us with this project and for her quick responses to any questions and concerns we had along the way.

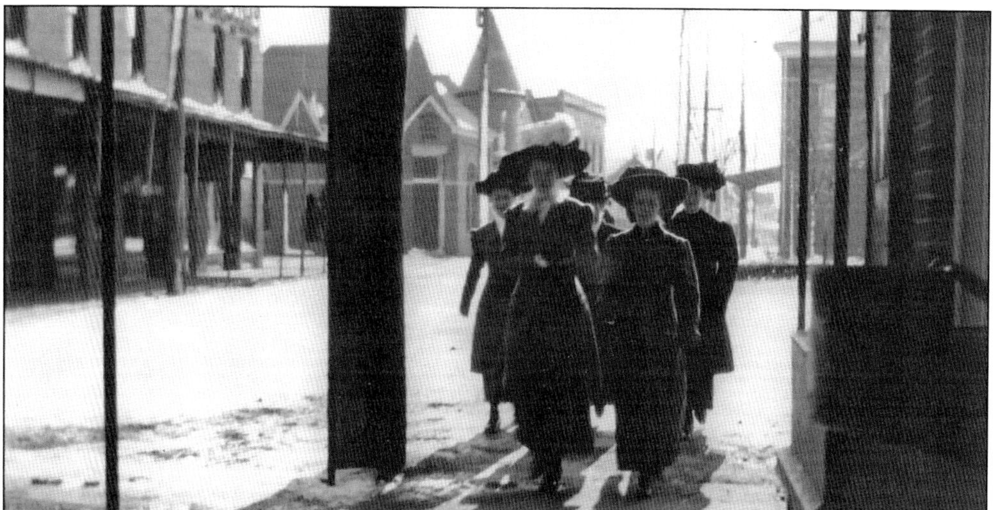

Taken between 1890 and 1910, this photograph of Main Street looking south shows a group of ladies walking north from the Atlantic Hotel. The Exchange and Savings Bank and First National Bank are on the left behind the ladies as they walk along the sidewalk in front of today's Rayne's Reef soda fountain.

# INTRODUCTION

"Make our past your present." So reads the recently adopted slogan of the town of Berlin in Worcester County, Maryland. Its past is rich in the 330-year-old tradition of the Eastern Shore.

Berlin began with an ink stroke on a sheet of parchment. In 1677, a tract of land was patented and named Burley. By 1683, Burley Inn had been established near the crossroads of the North-South road (the Philadelphia Post Road) and a road going toward the sea (the Sinepuxent Road), now the intersection of Berlin's South Main Street and Bay Street. In the imprecise spelling of the 17th century, the actual patent document dated July 12, 1683, spells the tract name "Bourly" in one place, but the predominant spelling in the instrument is "Burley." The town, which was known first as "Stevenson's Crossroads" became known for its inn. The name "Burley Inn" was later contracted to "Berlin."

The earliest credible record of European settlers in the region is that of Henry Norwood and his fellow passengers of the *Virginia Merchant*, who were marooned on Fenwick Island beginning in January 1649. Theirs is one of the most harrowing experiences ever recorded of our country's early times, a first-person experience written by Norwood in *A Voyage To Virginia*. The ship's course was from Gravesend, England, via the West Indies to Jamestown in the Virginia colony. The *Virginia Merchant* was blown off course in a northerly direction. With little food and water, and the ship storm-tossed, they put in on Fenwick Island. While Henry Norwood and other able-bodied passengers were searching for food and water on land, the wind shifted, and the master took his ship south, stranding the searchers.

The group elected Norwood leader, and after a period of freezing temperatures, lack of physical protection, and starvation, the ones who were able set out to find Native Americans to help them. Within a few days, friendly Native Americans were found. With much gesturing and repeated use of the word *Achomat*, it was decided that the white people needed to go south. The Native Americans provided great hospitality to the unfortunates, moving them to the "palace of the werowence" (the chief or king of the tribe) near Turville Creek, then on to the homes of two of his queens, both in the vicinity of Berlin. They were met at the last home by Jenkin Price, a white hunter and trapper, who had been told by a Native American messenger sent south by the werowence of their plight. He had come to guide them to Virginia. This saga of great suffering had a happy ending when the white men arrived in Accomack, Virginia. Henry Norwood went on to become a distinguished member of the Virginia colony.

During the late 17th and early 18th centuries, as plantations and churches were established, the area remained predominantly agrarian, depending upon indentured servants and slaves for working the land. The planters built sturdy brick houses and most kept their own boats, using the small streams and rivers as their thoroughfares. Small planters also contributed to the establishment of the area, building small cabins in the wilderness. Tobacco was grown on the plantations and used as legal tender, not only for goods, but for services as well.

In 1779, during the Revolutionary War, Stephen Decatur, later a hero of the Barbary Wars, was born just east of Berlin. His father, a patriot privateer, had fled from British-held Philadelphia, bringing his family to the Eastern Shore, as it was known to have a secure anchorage in the Sinepuxent Bay for his privateering ships. A historical marker stands on Route 113 North near the site of the Decatur home.

Berlin's location at a crossroads served the town well. In the early 19th century, the town became a rail junction for the north-south line, the Breakwater, Frankford and Worcester Rail Road (later shortened to Worcester Rail Road), and the east-west line, the Wicomico and Pocomoke Rail Road, which extended to Ocean City. In the second quarter of the 19th century, the town flourished.

During the War Between the States, virtually nothing happened in Berlin. Young white men so inclined (and there were many) "went south." The first mayor of the incorporated town

(1868) was Dr. John Pitts, a veteran of the 1st Virginia Cavalry C.S.A. Black counterparts of the young white soldiers joined the Union Army. The last surviving black veteran of the Grand Army of the Republic of the United States, Isaiah Fassett, lived in Berlin. About that time, a son was born to a slave near Berlin. Charles Albert Tindley was taught to read and write by lawyer and banker Calvin B. Taylor, for whom the town museum is named. Tindley became a respected Methodist minister in Philadelphia and was the writer of several hymns still published in Methodist hymnals. A counter-culture folk musician, Pete Seeger, took Reverend Tindley's hymn "I'll Overcome Someday" and with a few changes came up with "We Shall Overcome," which became the anthem of the 20th century's civil rights movement.

In 1895, 1901, and 1904, the town suffered devastating fires that completely destroyed the old downtown area. After the first fire, the mayor and council passed an ordinance requiring that all new structures in the downtown area be built of brick. Today's entire downtown area, with the exception of a 1925 storefront, was built between 1895 and 1905 and is on the National Register of Historic Places. By 1905, the town with its rail junction was flourishing as the hub of northern Worcester.

As the modern era arrived, automobiles replaced trains, telephones were everywhere, highways were being built, and a strip of sand became the nationally known resort of Ocean City, Maryland. Berlin remained a typical small town in rural America. The 1960s and 1970s were a slow period in the town's growth and development.

By the 1980s, some Berlin locals had made fortunes in Ocean City; however, they had never lost their sense of place. They began to realize the potential of the town they loved. Between 1980 and 2000, groups of Berliners researched their old photographs and memorabilia. They recorded the memories of their senior citizens. The restorers put their money on the line because they loved the town where they, in many cases, were born and raised. They realized that, if restored, Berlin could be a gem of a tourist attraction, drawing sunburned beachgoers away from the honky-tonk Boardwalk of Ocean City to spend a day walking through history.

These citizens have faithfully restored Berlin to its present-day appearance. The group created the Calvin B. Taylor House Museum in the early 1980s to serve as a historical depository as an adjunct to the restored town center. The story of the restoration of the small town is significant and inspiring, prompting Hollywood to find "just what it was looking for" as the setting for two major motion pictures. The story of Berlin, with a year-round population of about 3,000, has become the story of its restoration and preservation.

# *One*

# "On a Road going along the Seaside"

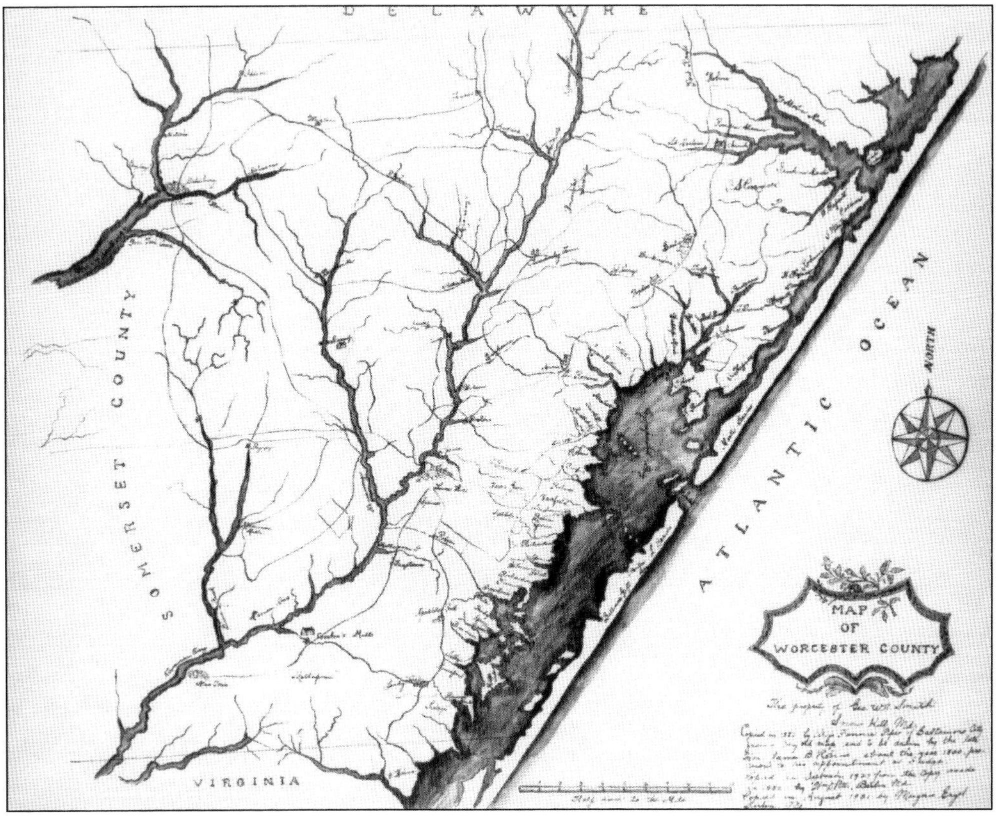


Worcester County was erected in 1742 from the Seaside of Old Somerset. It was part of an early Maryland land grant to George Calvert, first Lord Baltimore, from Charles I, King of England. George Calvert died before the final papers were signed, so it was his son, Cecilius Calvert, second Lord Baltimore, who began the settlement of Maryland. On the official grant, Maryland is named *Terra Maria*, Mary's Land, for the queen of Charles I, Henrietta Maria. As the population of the Seaside grew upwards of 12,000, Charles Calvert, third Lord Baltimore, was encouraged by the citizenry to petition the Assembly for another county. The Assembly agreed and separated the Seaside from Somerset County. In a 1697 Somerset sheriff's report, Worcester was described as "on a Road going [up] along the Seaside." Lord Baltimore named it for the Earl of Worcester.

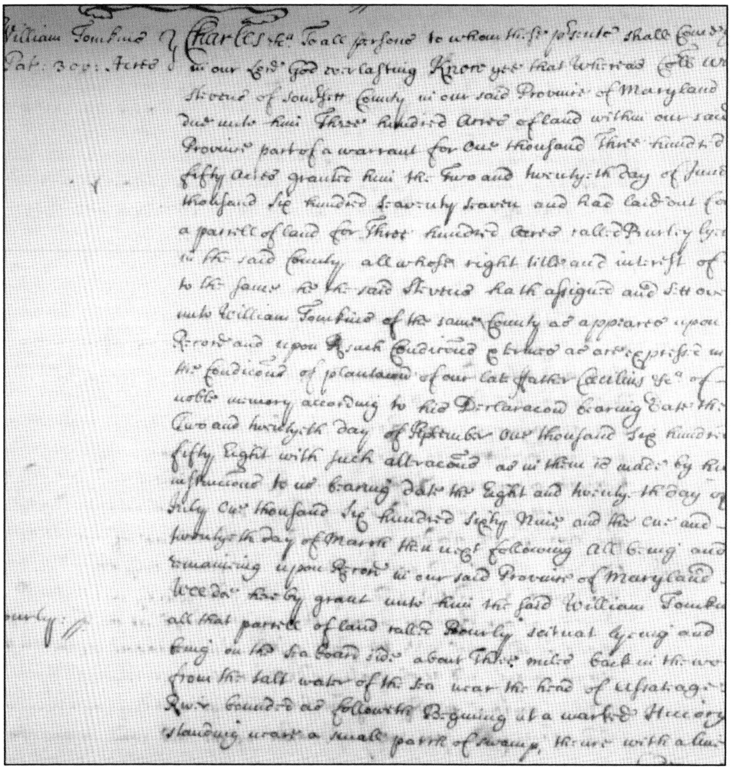

According to this original land patent, Col. William Stevens of Somerset County was deeded 300 acres, part of a warrant for 1,350 acres granted to him on June 22, 1677, by Charles II, King of England. Colonel Stevens assigned these 300 acres to William Tomkins in this patent dated July 12, 1683. The patent describes the 300 acres as "lying on the Seaboard side about three miles back in the woods from the salt water of the sea near the head of Assateague River." This tract was called "Burley" and later became the site of the town of Berlin.

**"BOURLY" PATENT**

William Tomkins — Charles Ve[a] To all persons to whom these presents shall come greeting

Pat. 300:acres — in our Lord God everlasting Know yee that whereas Coll William Stevens of Somersett County in our said Province of Maryland had deed unto him Three hundird acres of land within our said Province part of a warrant for one thousand Three hundred and fifty acres granted him the Two and twenty=th day of June one thousand Six hunderd Seaventy Seaven and had laid out for him a parcell of land for Three hundred acres called Burley lying in the said County all whose right title and interest of ______ to the same as the said Stevens hath assigned and sitt over unto William Tomkins of the same County as appeared upon Record and upon such condicons ______ as are expressed in the condicons of plantacon of our late father Cecilius Ve[a] noble memory according to his Declaracon bearing Date the Two and twenty=th Day of September one thousand Six hundred fifty eight with such alteracons as in them is made by his instrucions to us bearing date the Eight and twenty=th day of July one thousand Six hundred sixty nine and the one and twenty=th Day of March then next following all being and remaining upon Record in our said Province of Maryland

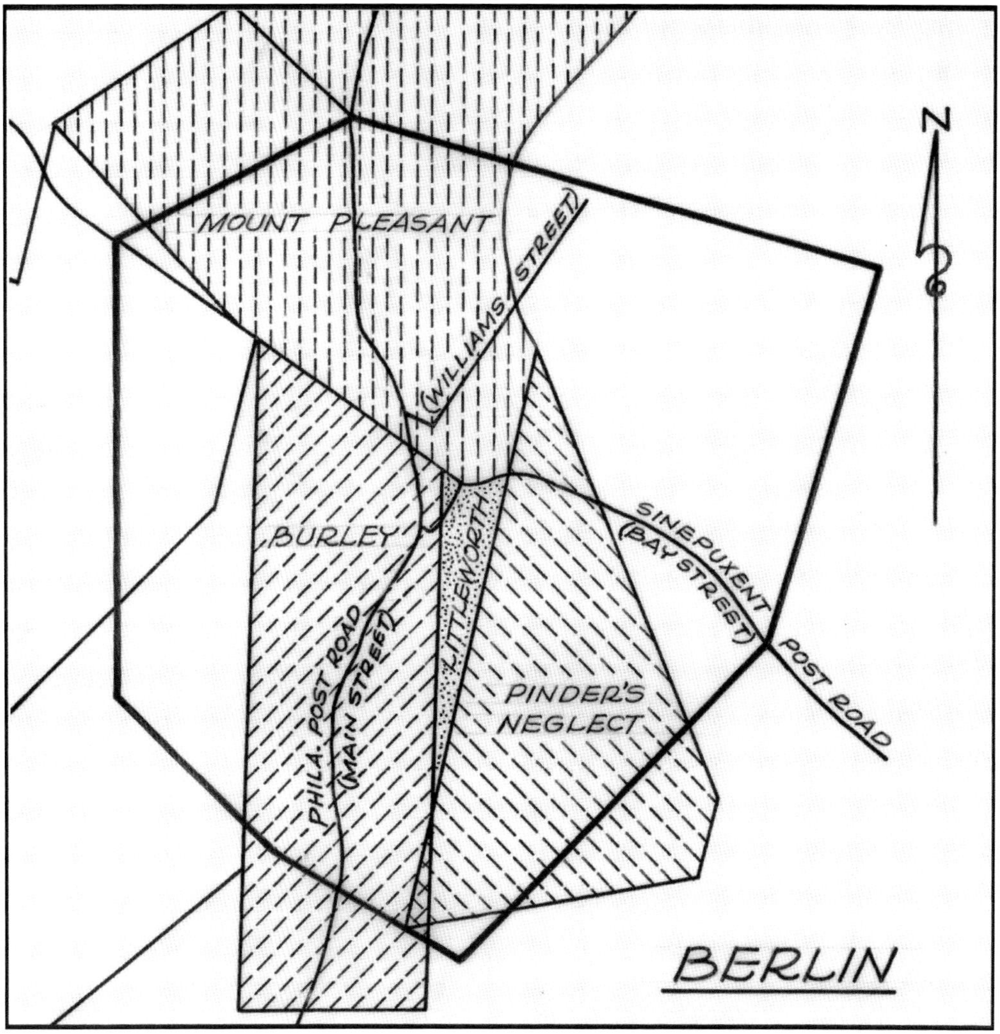


Prior to the establishment of Worcester County, several land grants were made. Four fell within the boundaries of present-day Berlin—Burley, 300 acres patented to William Tomkins on July 12, 1683, sold the next year to Col. William Stevens; Pinder's Neglect, Littleworth, and Mount Pleasant (later Engleside) were patented by John Emmoll on May 10, 1685. Several early homes were built on the Burley tract: Robin's Nest (1805), Elizabeth White House (early to mid-19th century), perhaps the Robert Pitts House (*c.* 1830), Kenwood (1833), Burley Cottage (1834), Powell House (1834), Burley Manor (1835), Pitts House (1839), John A. Purnell House (1840), Peter Brittingham House (*c.* 1840), Waverly (1842), Homewood (*c.* 1848), the Episcopal rectory (1893), and John Keas House (1893–1894). Only one home can be associated with Pinder's Neglect, the Soloman Carey House (1854). Littleworth (*c.* 1860) is on the Littleworth tract, and it is believed that David Pruitt House (1827), Williams-Stevenson House (*c.* 1830), and Walker House (*c.* 1840) are also on the same tract. Some early homes built on the Mount Pleasant tract were Stevenson House (1790s), Calvin B. Taylor House (1832), William Nelson House (*c.* 1835), John Dirickson House (1835), Engleside (1840), George A. Harrison House (*c.* 1840), and Orlando Harrison House (1899). No homes built in the 20th century were included in this listing. (Matthews Collection.)

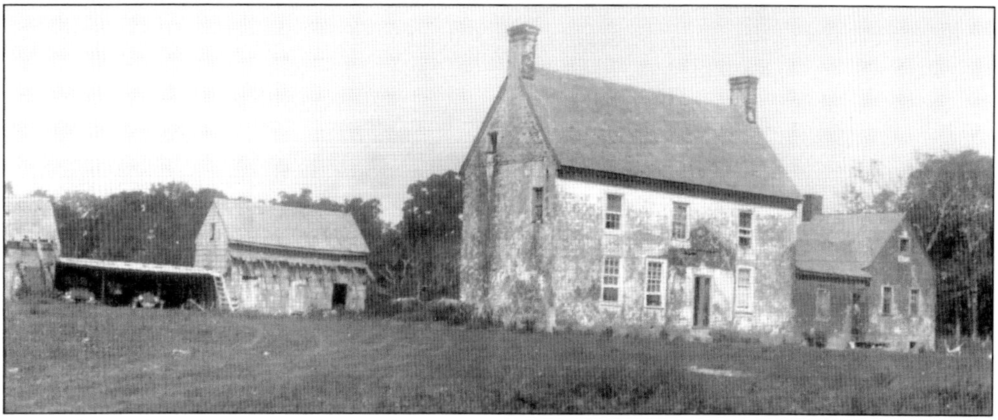

One of the oldest homes in the Berlin area is Genesar. It stands on Sinepuxent Neck near Newport Bay on land patented May 10, 1676, to Col. William Stevens. The present building was built in 1742 by Maj. John Purnell. Genesar is well known for its transitional style of architecture. It is believed to have been shelled by British ships coming from the ocean into Sinepuxent Bay through a now nonexistent inlet. (Matthews Collection.)

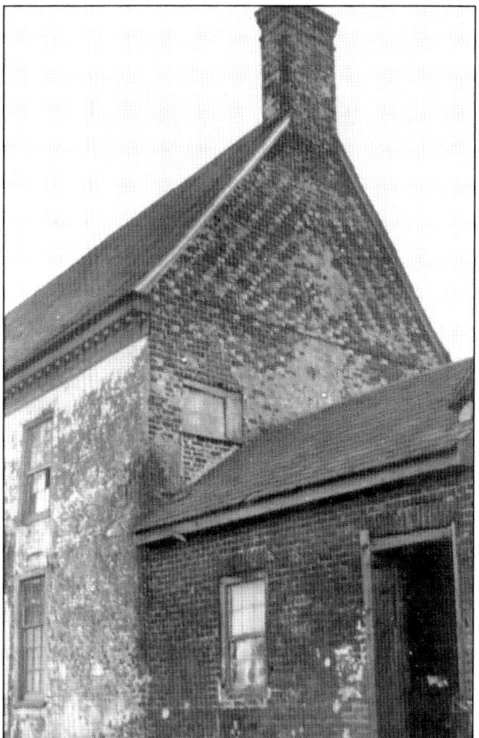

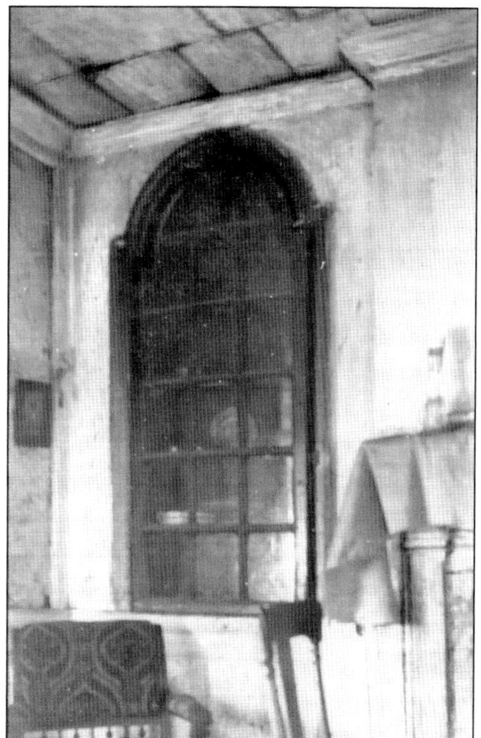

In the photograph at left, beneath the stucco presently covering Genesar, distinctive, ornate glazed brickwork decorates the front facade and the ends. This is some of "the richest glazed brick patterns in the state." The style, known as "lozenge" or "black diapering" was popular in England at the time the house was built. There are fireplaces at both ends of the house and a hyphen between the main block and the kitchen. Genesar (right), as in many early homes of Worcester County, has ceilings overlaid with wide boards. This photograph of the dining room, taken in 1928, shows this style of ceiling and the Queen Anne cupboard with scrolled shelves. (Matthews Collection.)

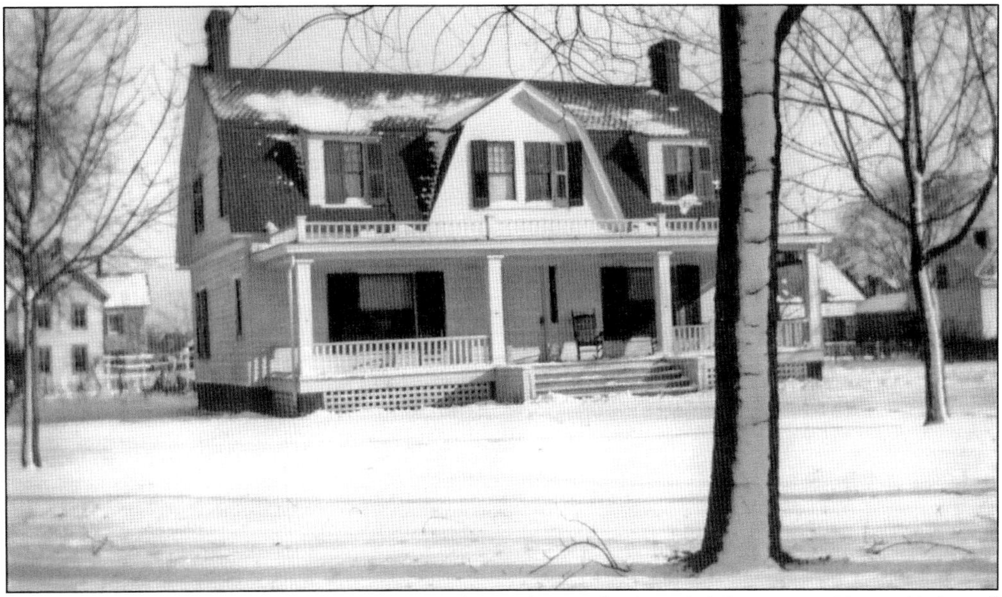

One of the oldest dwellings to survive in Berlin is the gambrel-roofed Stevenson House. Believed to have been built as early as 1790 or as late as 1798, the house has a main block, a two-story service wing, and a kitchen house, which was attached at a later date. The land was part of the Mount Pleasant tract, bequeathed to Tabitha Evans in 1770. Evans married William Stevenson. In his will, Stevenson left a half-acre for use of the Methodist Episcopal Meeting House. The Methodists named their new church the Stevenson Methodist Church.

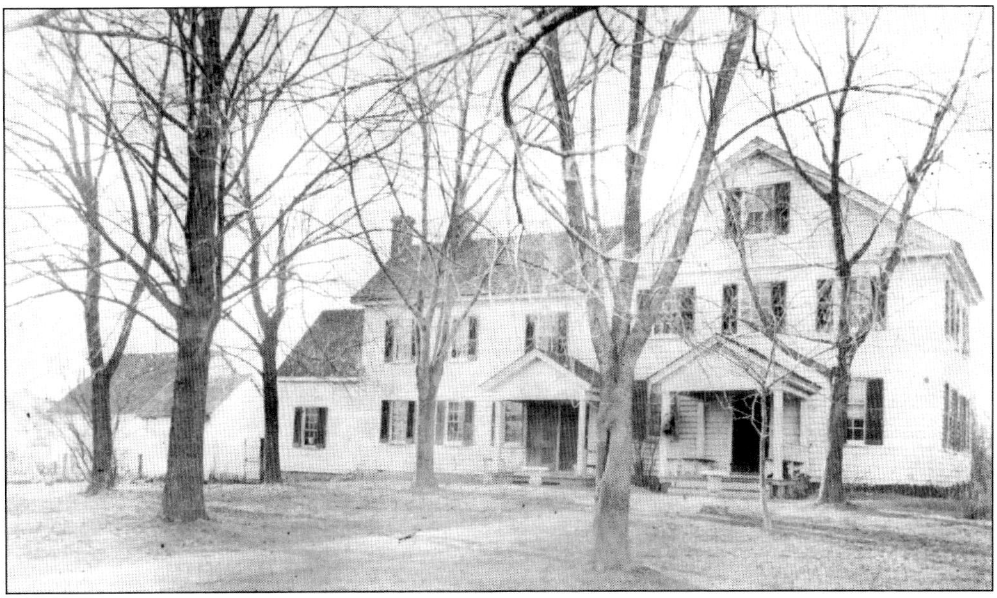

This property now known as Robin's Nest was built about 1805 by Jacob White, a local Berlin merchant. A portrait of his wife, Mary, hangs in the parlor of the Taylor Museum. The house has a temple-front and features corner fireplaces with finely carved mantels. The home was extensively restored in 1985. There has been a recent addition of four columns to the front facade. The property, at the corner of West and Broad Streets, includes an original dairy, smokehouse, granary, and privy.

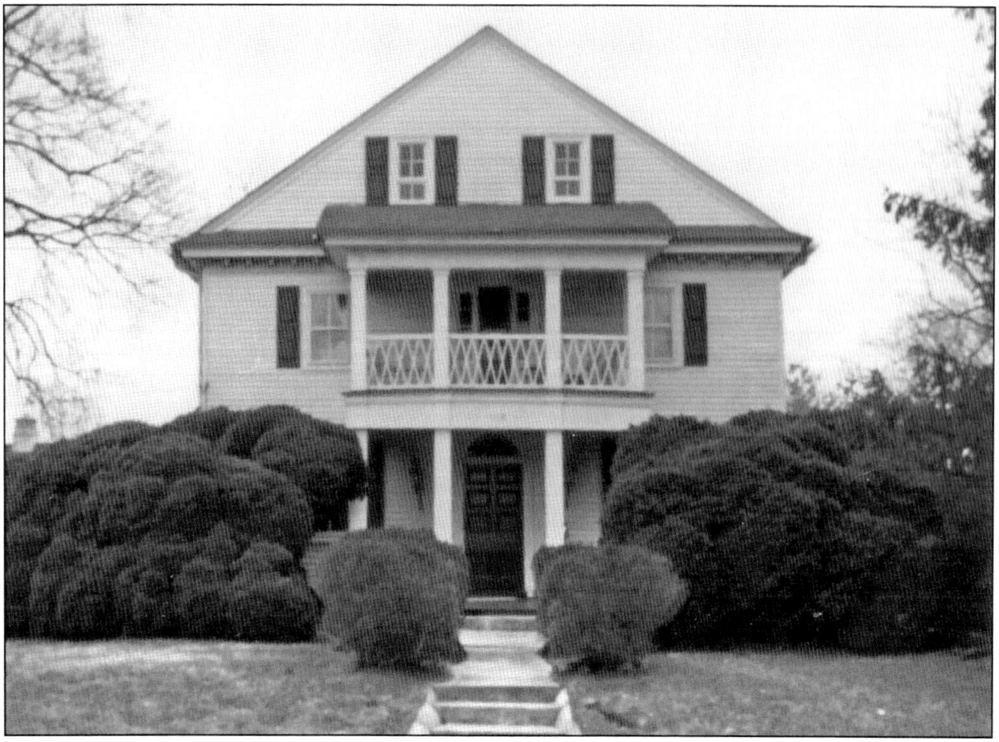

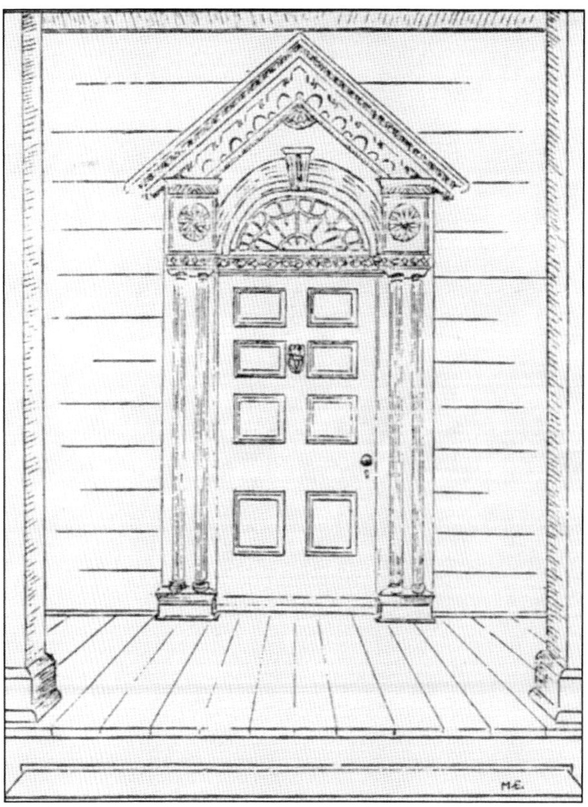

Early evidence indicates that Kenwood was built in 1833 on the Burley tract. One of the first things noticed about the house is the magnificent stand of boxwoods located in the front of the property. It is believed these boxwoods were imported from England when the house was new. Burley Manor and Burley Cottage also have exceptional boxwoods. Kenwood has one of the best examples of an Adams doorway and a double gallery.

This drawing is a detail of Kenwood's Adams doorway with its delicate fanlight. (Annual Pilgrimage, St. Paul's Episcopal Church Junior Guild, Berlin, Maryland, May 21–22, 1954.)

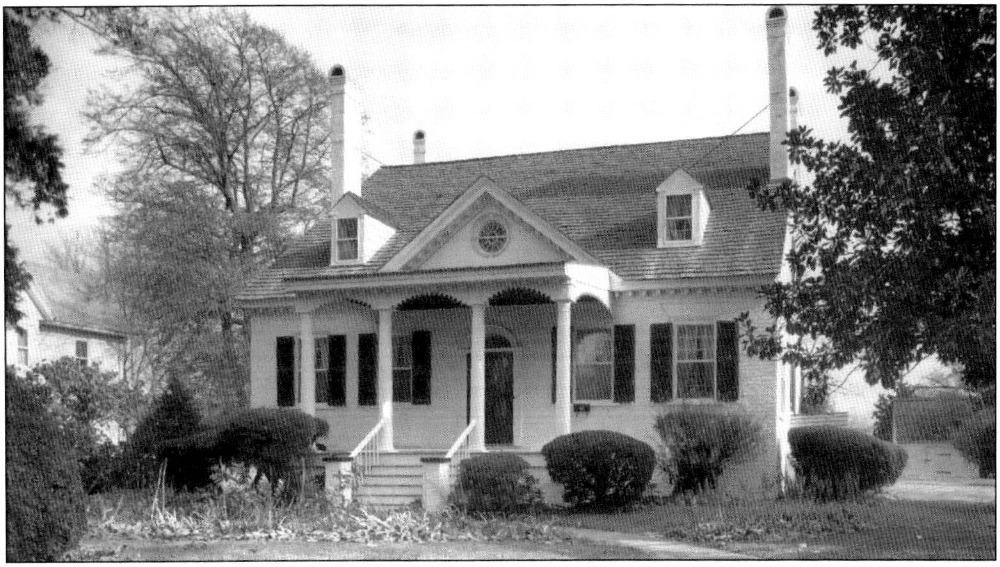

Burley Cottage is one of the early-19th-century homes in Berlin that was built on the Philadelphia Post Road; others of note include Engleside, William Nelson House, Stevenson House, Kenwood, Burley Cottage, Burley Manor, Waverly, and Merry Sherwood. Burley Cottage is a unique town house built for John Selby Purnell in 1834. The brick masons' names, the initials of the owner, "J S P," and the date "1834" are incised in brick on the south side of the home. Four predominant chimneys tower over the cottage. A rose window is prominent in the front gable. Originally the kitchen was in the cellar. Burley Cottage has many original items, including hand-carved woodwork, locks and keys, and, until recently, French wallpaper in the parlor. The original smokehouse at Burley Cottage, with its original hardware, below, is one of few left in the area.

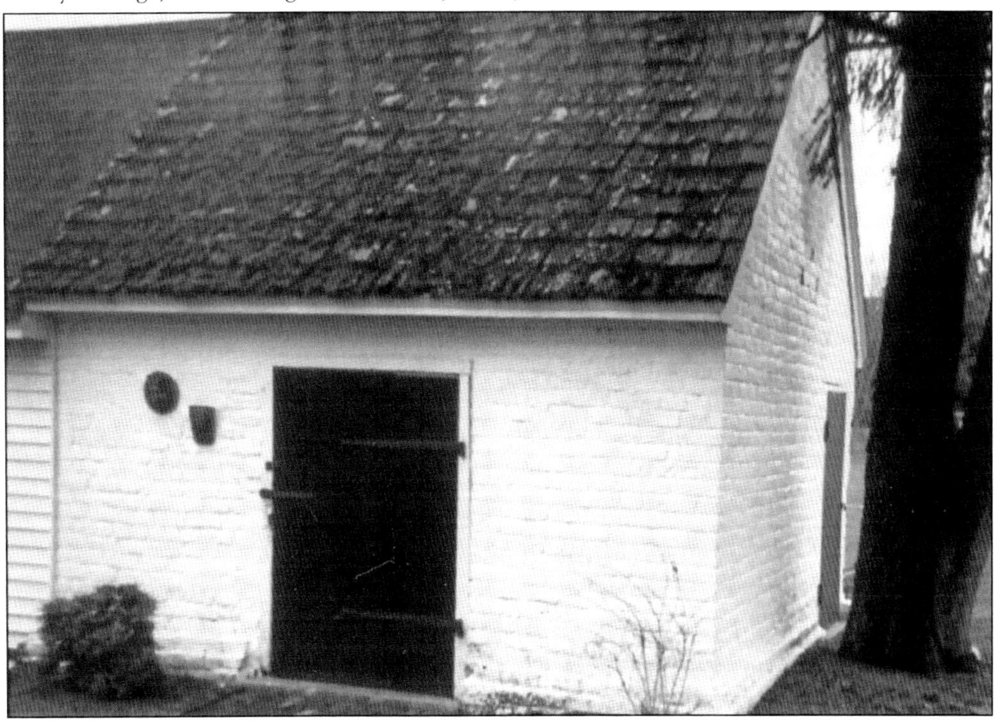

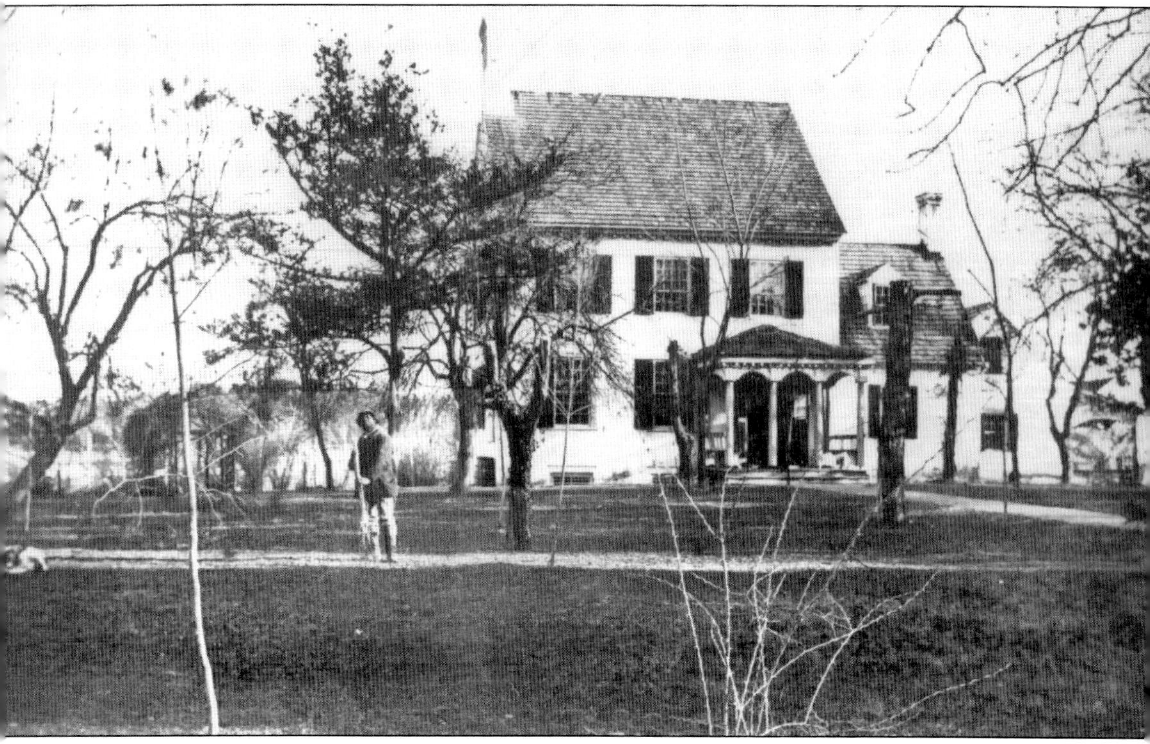

Burley Manor was built between 1832 and 1835 by John Polk Mitchell, a builder from Alabama. It consisted of a two-story block containing a side hall and double parlors, very much in the Federal style. The house was actually an addition to an earlier house, which consisted of two blocks. In 1832, Edward Hammond, great-great-great-grandson of Edward Hammond, who emigrated to Queponco (an area west of Newark, Maryland, 10 miles south of Berlin) from Virginia in the 17th century, died, leaving his widow, Elizabeth Victor Hammond, and four small children. The widow Hammond purchased the house, and the Hammonds have lived there ever since. The house is a typical Federal house, covered, probably in the 1860s, with stucco, scored in the style of Ashlar Masonry. The house has been changed very little since its building, although John T. Hammond, M.D. (1832–1902), added a window to the middle block to practice medicine through when he became too infirm to make house calls with his horse and buggy. This photograph is from the 1860s.

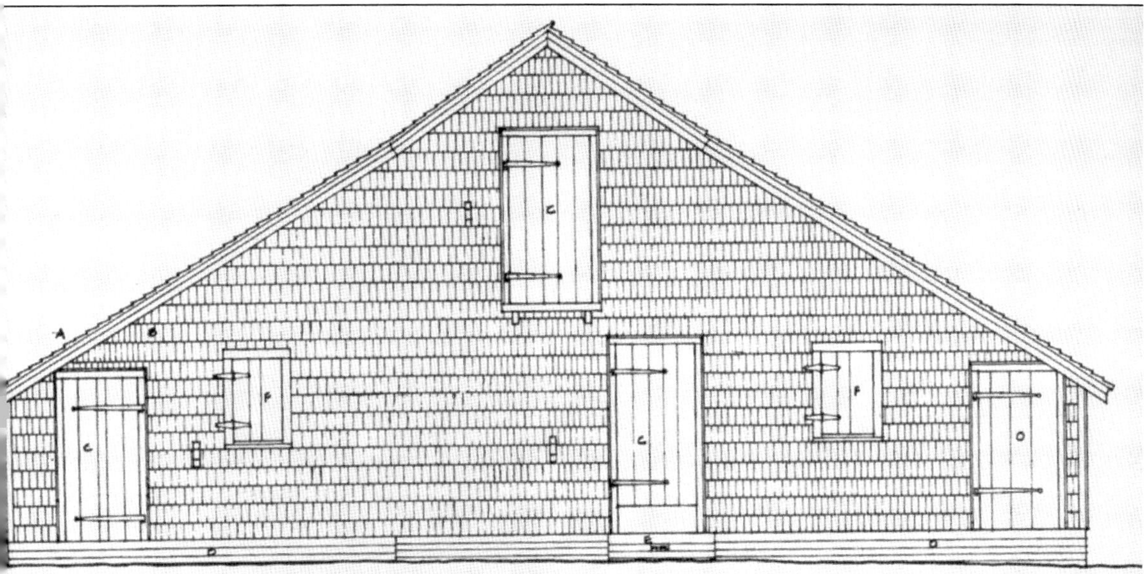

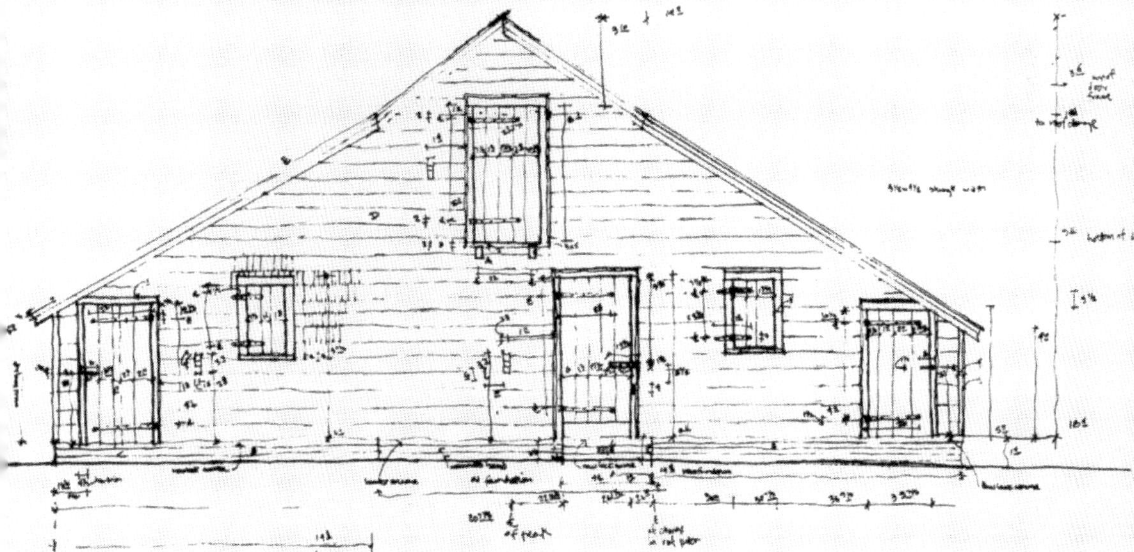


Burley Manor is in no way a manor. It was originally surveyed as a 40-acre tract. Although Elizabeth Victor Hammond owned close to 2,000 acres in Queponco, she bought what today might be called a "farmette"; she kept the 2,000 acres, too. Forty acres was believed to be the amount of land necessary to sustain a household. It included a flower garden, vegetable garden, fields to produce grain to feed the livestock and poultry, and a wood lot. The barn, actually a granary with stables, as drawn by Colonial Williamsburg architectural historians, was featured in the Williamsburg Calendar for 1988. It has a brick incised with the builder's initials, IPM 1835, for James P. Mitchell (the builder used the archaic version of *J*, which looks like an *I*). There are also seven other outbuildings (a carriage house, summer kitchen, two tool houses, a smokehouse, ash house, and privy) and the ruins of a hothouse. The well, chicken house (with its 16-foot fence to keep foxes out), and a cowshed have disappeared.

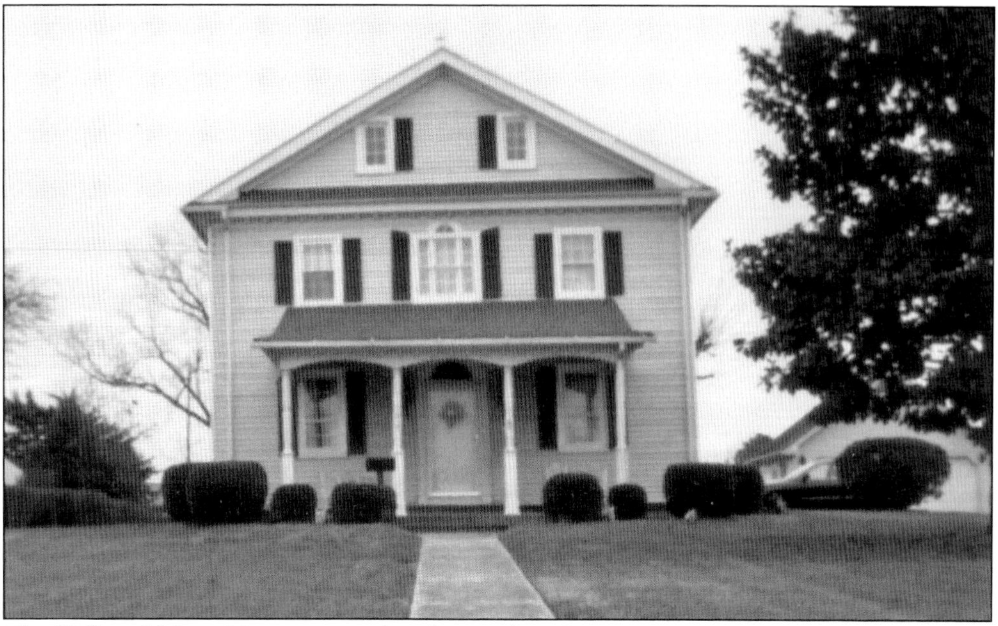

The William Nelson House, now referred to as the Thompson House, is a temple-front home. Built about 1835 on the Mount Pleasant tract, this house boasts distinctive sawtooth arches that enhance the porch. A Palladian window fills the front gable. A modillion block cornice stretches the perimeter of the gable-front roof and porch. The house is located on North Main Street along the Philadelphia Post Road.

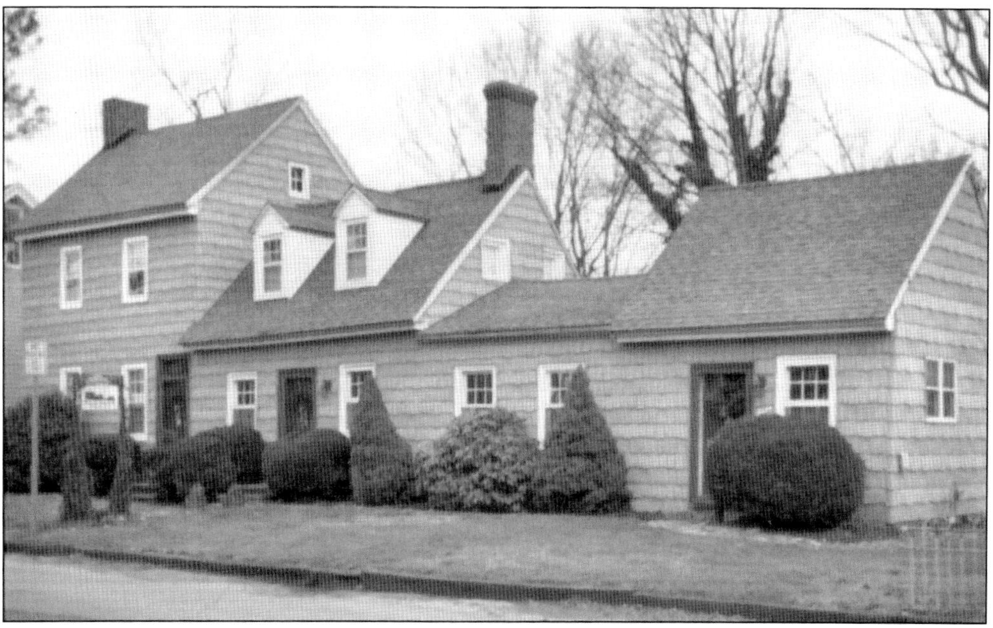

The Robert Pitts House is now called the Telescope House. Located on Vine Street, this four-part stepped dwelling was erected for one of Berlin's businessmen in the 1830s. There is a large, two-story block, a dormered section, and a single-story colonnade. The one-and-a-half-story kitchen completes the structure. It has interior Federal and Greek Revival woodwork. Houses of this stepped style are often referred to as "big house, little house, colonnade, and kitchen."

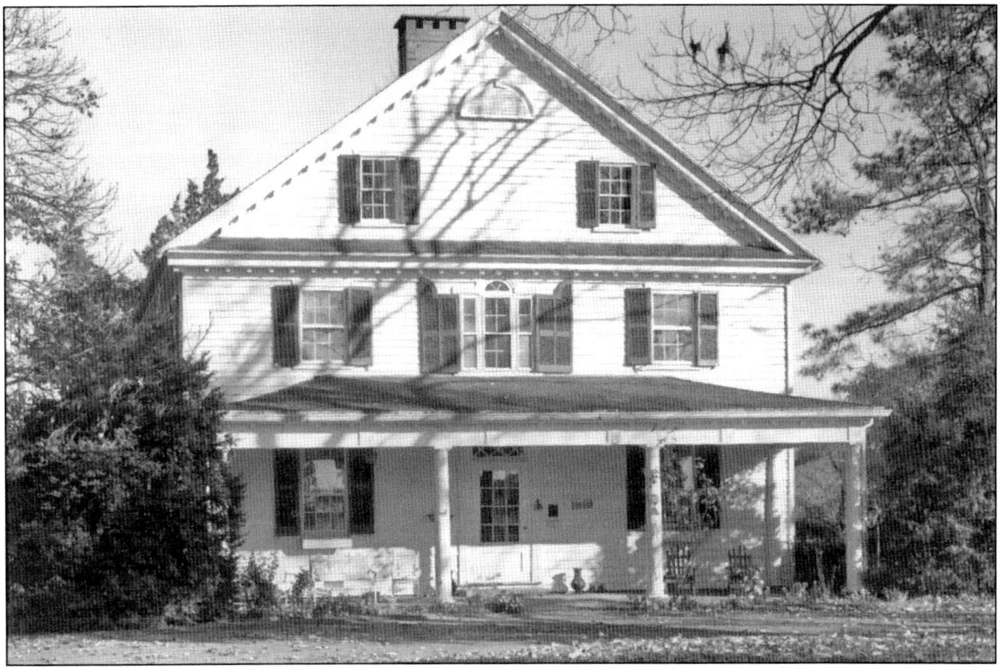

Waverly, built in 1842 on the Burley tract along the Philadelphia Post Road running through Berlin, has little changed except for a front porch added after the Civil War. Waverly is a temple-front house with a Palladian window in the second story over the entrance. The front door has the original Sheffield lock and key. The house boasts seven fireplaces, all using one chimney. Wooden pegs secure the rafters in the attic.

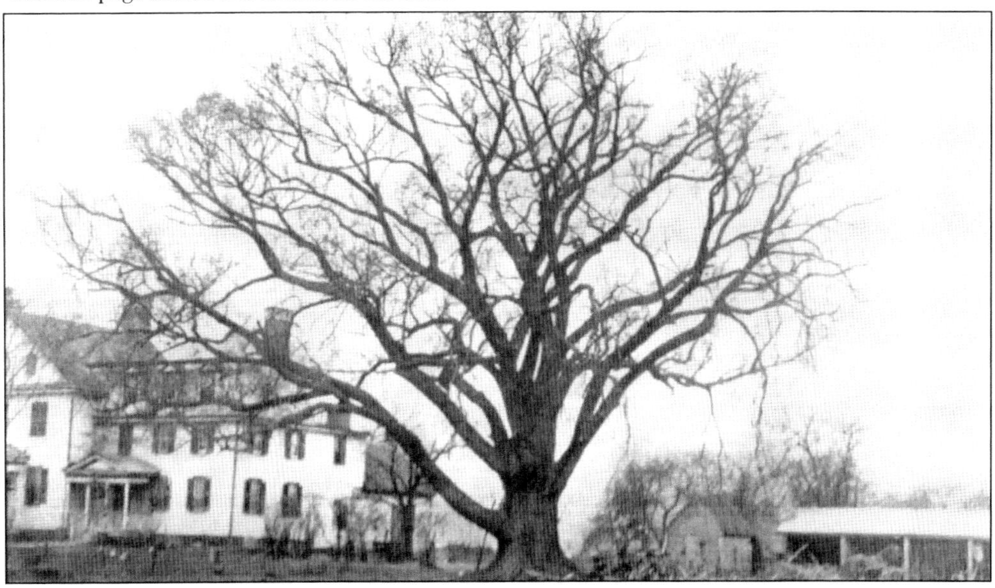

Engleside (Mount Pleasant) was built about 1840 on the Mount Pleasant tract. The twin parlors in the main block have 11.5-foot ceilings. A hand-carved banister follows the stairs to the attic, crossing the front windows on the first and second floors. Although the two blocks appear different on the exterior, the interiors closely resemble one another. At one time, Engleside was the home of the largest English elm tree in the United States.

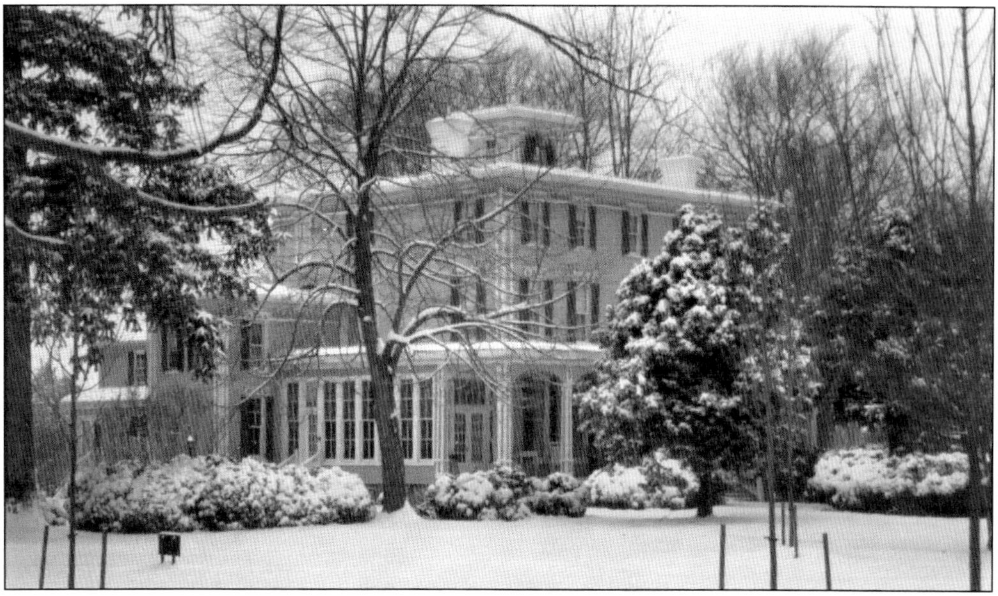

Merry Sherwood, an excellent example of the few Italianate-style houses in the area, is one of the earliest of its kind. Built in 1859, it illustrates the changing quality of houses built in the latter part of the 19th century, having a combination of handmade features and imported factory-made woodwork. The large house is a fine example of balance and symmetry, shown by the use of blind windows to ensure these qualities. Merry Sherwood appears beautiful and ethereal in this snowy fairyland. Shown below is the west end of the double parlor showing the period furniture, an oriental rug, and a marble bust. A gaslight chandelier is reflected in the pier glass mirror. (Burbage Collection.)

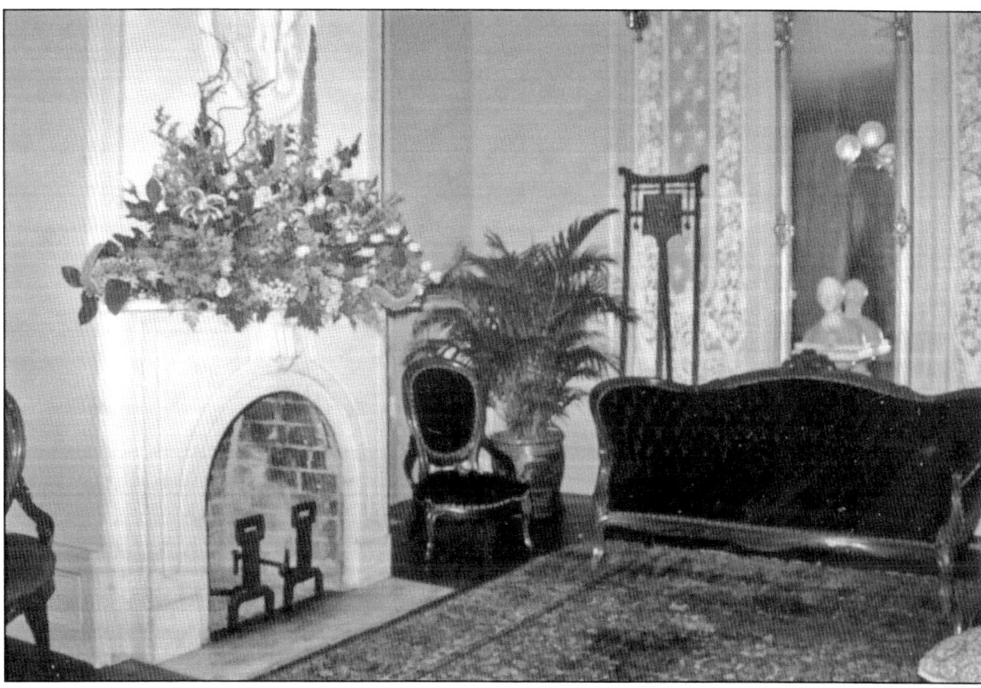

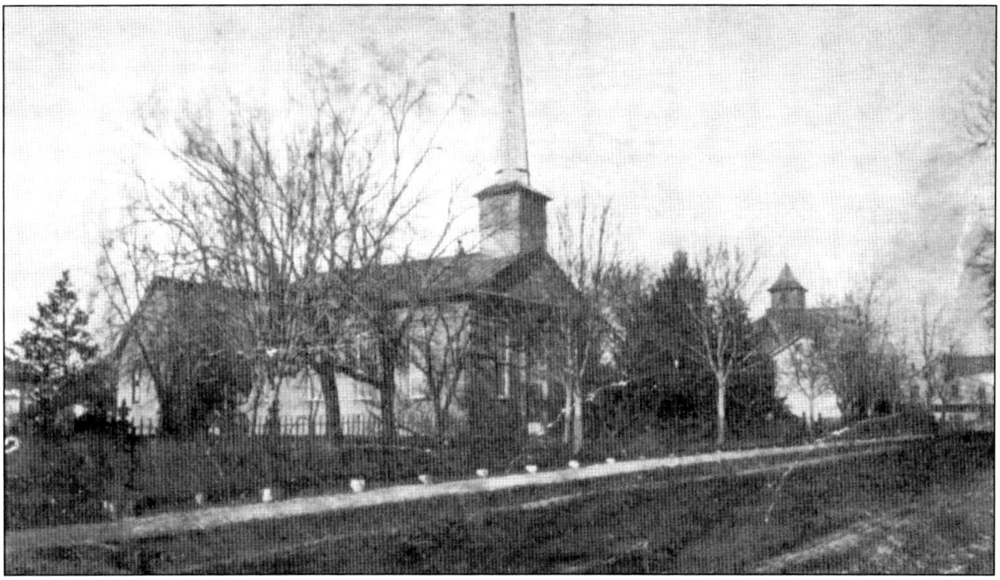

Buckingham Presbyterian Church was one of several churches founded by Rev. Francis Makemie. The congregation dates from 1683 when Makemie arrived from Ireland after being summoned by Col. William Stevens to minister to the nonconformists and the Dissenters (Presbyterians) in Somerset County. Buckingham is named for Buckingham Plantation, where it was established south of Berlin. The second and third churches were built on the site of the present Buckingham Cemetery. Paths can be seen leading from the Philadelphia Post Road to the middle of the cemetery where both churches were located. The second church was a frame building, torn down and replaced with a brick church in 1757. This church's roof collapsed during a severe snowstorm in 1857. This is a picture of the fourth Buckingham church, built in 1858 on the church's present-day location on South Main Street. It was destroyed by the 1904 fire. Buckingham School can be seen in the background. Below, the cornerstone was laid for the fifth church in June 1905. The congregation now worships there. (Matthews Collection.)

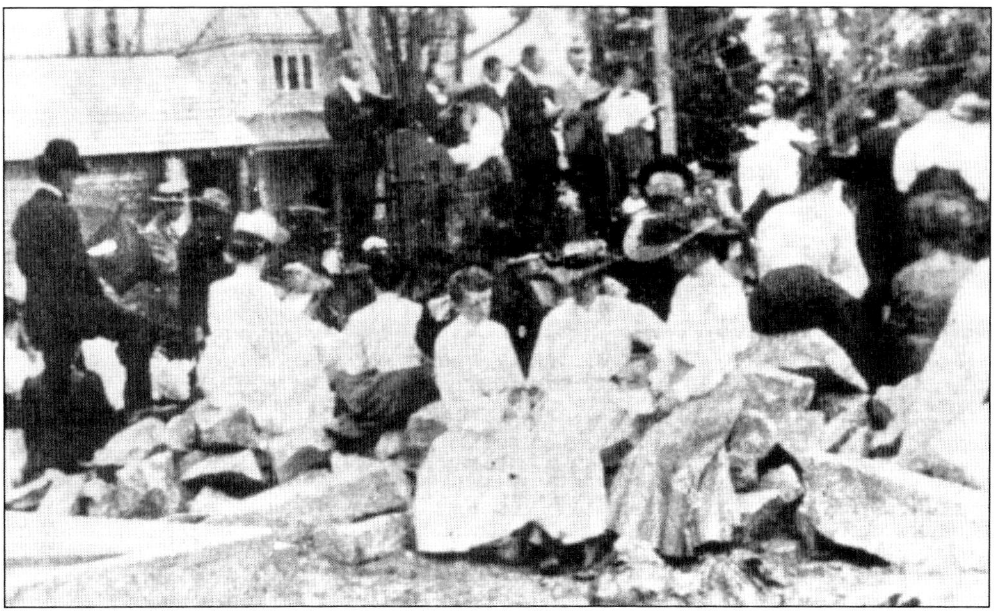

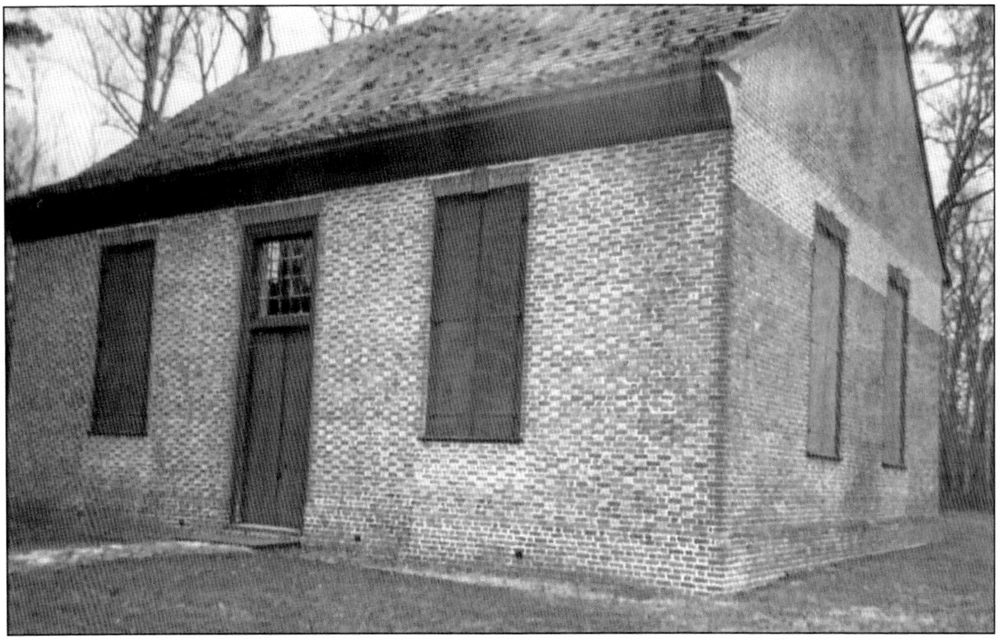

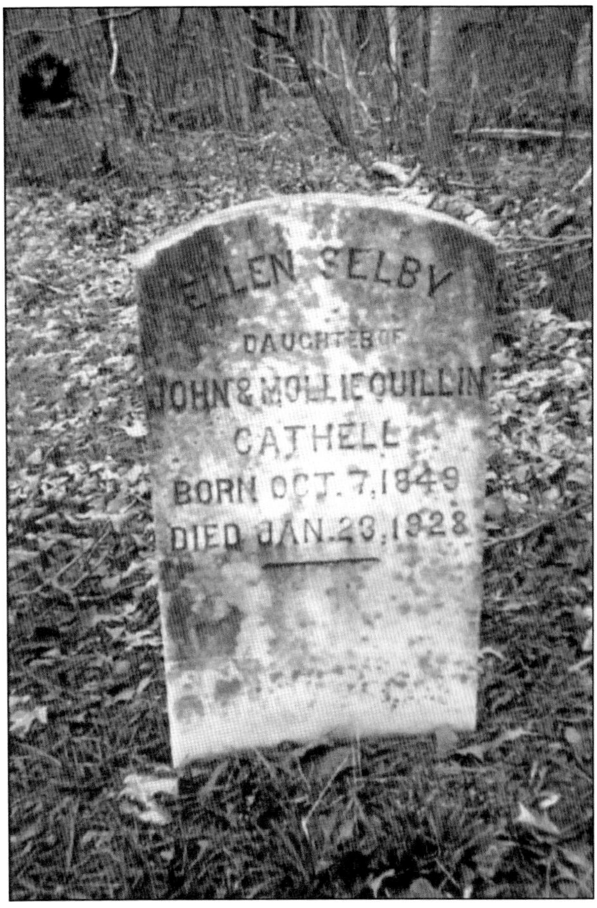


The original church register of St. Martin's in Worcester Parish provides this entry for its beginning: "Tuesday ye 6th of July, 1756, the Vestry bought two acres of land at the St Martin's Chapell of James Mumford for to build a new Church on and sd. Vestry is to give Mumford £5 for ye two acres." The church was completed in 1759 at a cost of 85,000 pounds of tobacco. The first rector was Rev. Edward Dingle followed by Rev. William MacClenahan; these two gentlemen and Rev. Samuel Tinley are buried under the floor of the transept. The original register from St. Martin's Chapel lists some of the pew holders as: Pew 0, John Henry; Pew 1, Massey and Tull; Pew 2, Collier and Powell; followed by other noted families: Hudson, Cropper, Linch, Mumford, Harrisson, and Taylor. St. Martin's has been recently restored. A historical marker is located in the area of Route 113 and Route 589. Shown on the left is one of the tombstones on the grounds.

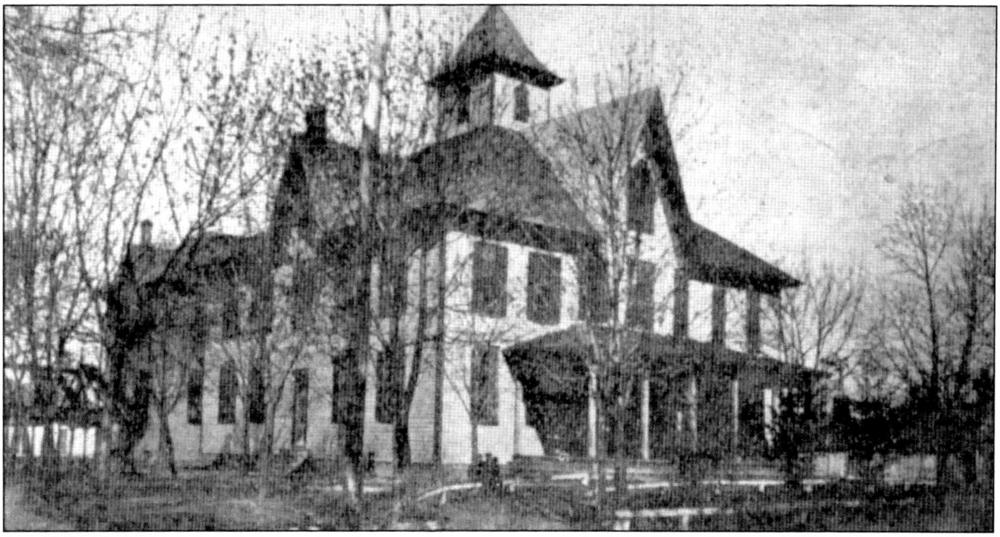

Rev. Charles Tennant of the Buckingham Presbyterian Church established Buckingham Academy in 1765. Located on the Buckingham Plantation, it was the first school in the Berlin area. In 1817, the land was sold, and the academy moved into Berlin, becoming the New Buckingham Academy. The Berlin Female Seminary was established shortly thereafter. In 1885, this two-story yellow building was built combining the academy and the seminary, becoming Berlin's first public school. The school was two stories and had interior stairways going up each side. As punishment, students remember going up the right stairs, across the upper hall, down the left stairs, across the lower hall, and starting the circle again. They referred to it as the "roller coaster." (Mabel Rogers Collection.)

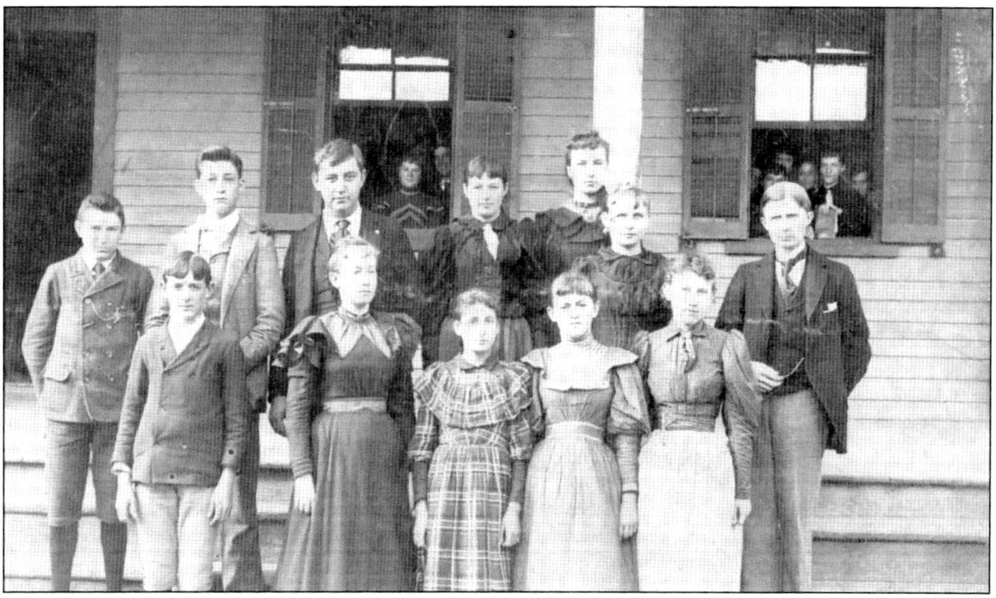

In this early-1890s photograph of Buckingham School, student Harry Selby Purnell is pictured on the far left. In World War I, his grandfather, Colonel Purnell, M.D., would serve as commander of Fort McHenry, where ironically enough Harry's father, Wilmer Purnell, had been held as a Confederate prisoner. The teacher on the far right is King Wilson of Snow Hill, believed to be the same King Wilson who was later governor and U.S. senator.

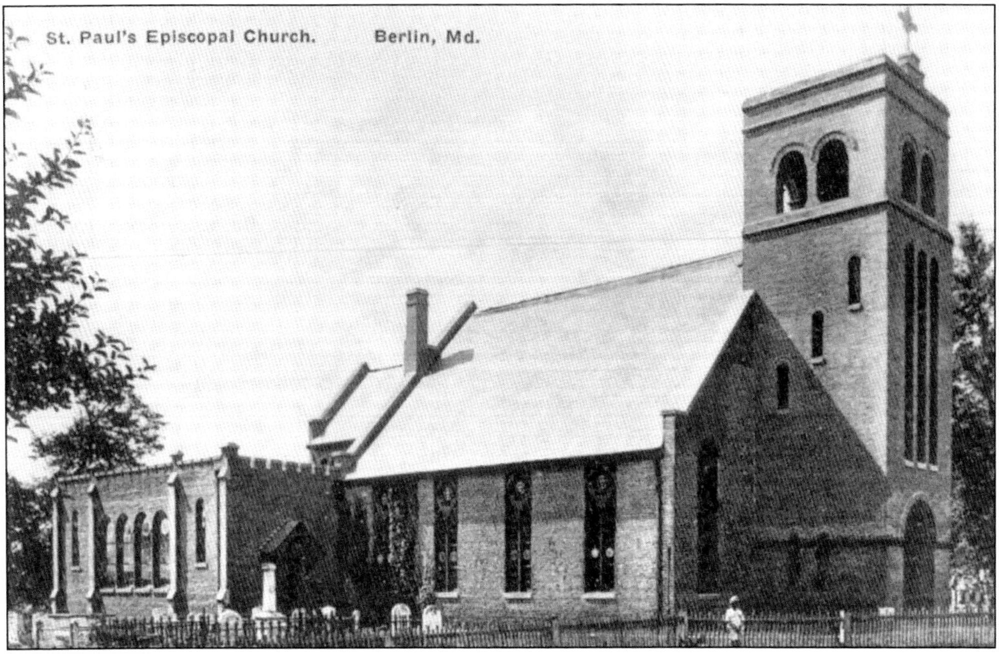


Worcester Parish is the Episcopal parish in the upper county, located north of All Hallows Parish in Snow Hill and originally extending into what was at first Maryland, then (after 1755) Pennsylvania, now Delaware. Originally it consisted of St. Martin's Church and a chapel-at-ease in what is now Dagsboro, Delaware. By 1825, the town of Berlin was becoming a population center, and St. Paul's was built behind Burley Inn on a new street now known as Church Street. It was a simple, large-scale, Colonial-style church. In the fire of 1904, the interior was gutted by fire, but the exterior walls were saved and the church rebuilt. In 1913, a tower was added. Around 1950, the charming red bricks were painted white to seal the walls. The choir photograph below is from about 1895 and shows Confederate veteran Dude Davidson (with eye patch).

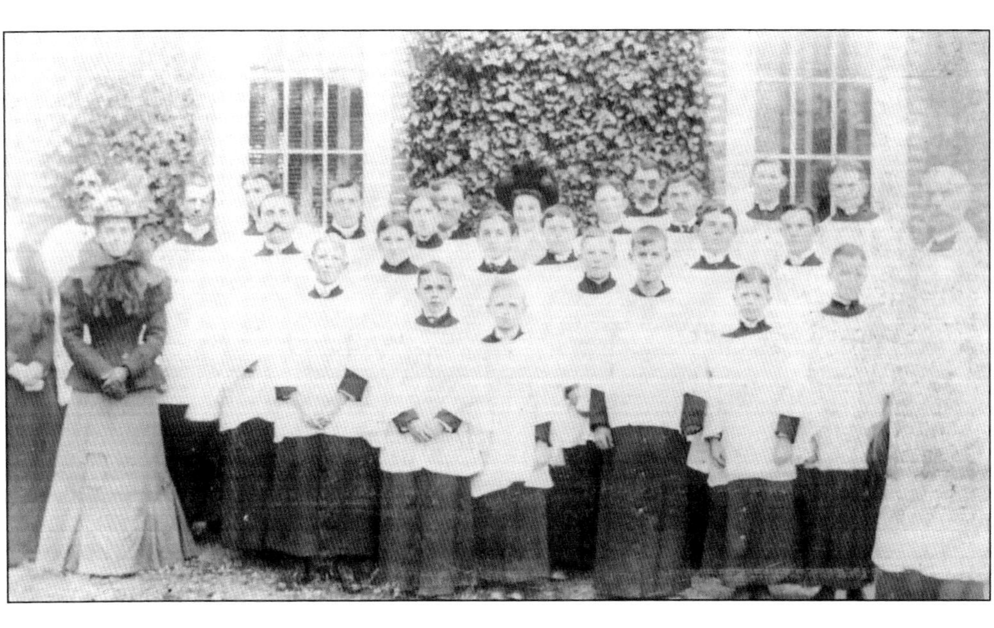

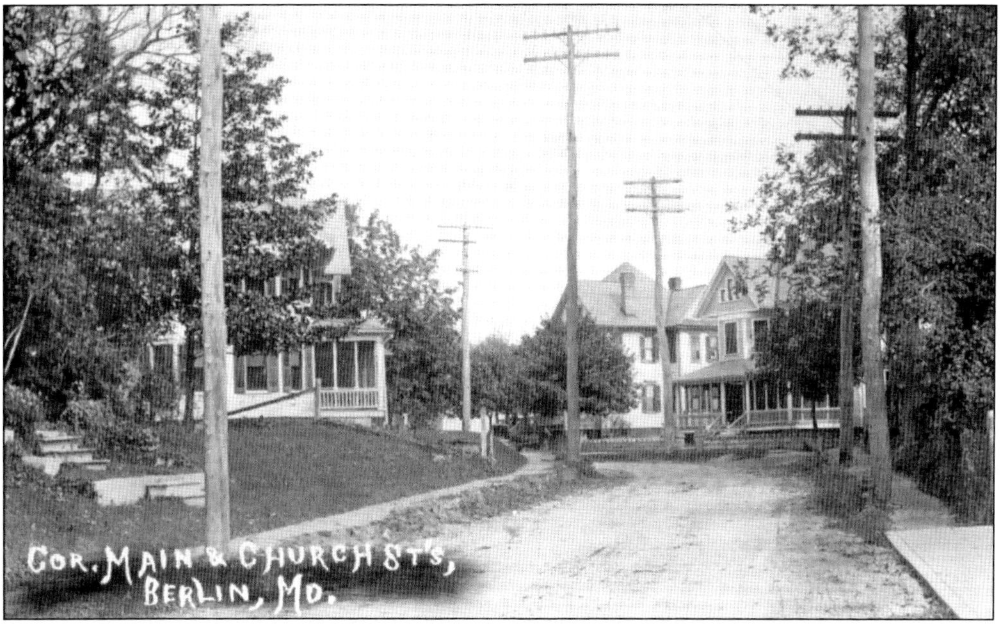

The intersection of Main and Church Streets shows three Berlin homes built after the 1904 fire. This is proven by the fact that the house on the right is not shown in pictures of the fifth Buckingham Presbyterian Church before the fire. Also, the two homes on the right have walls built of the same Holmsburg granite used in the then recently completed fifth church. (Mabel Rogers Collection.)

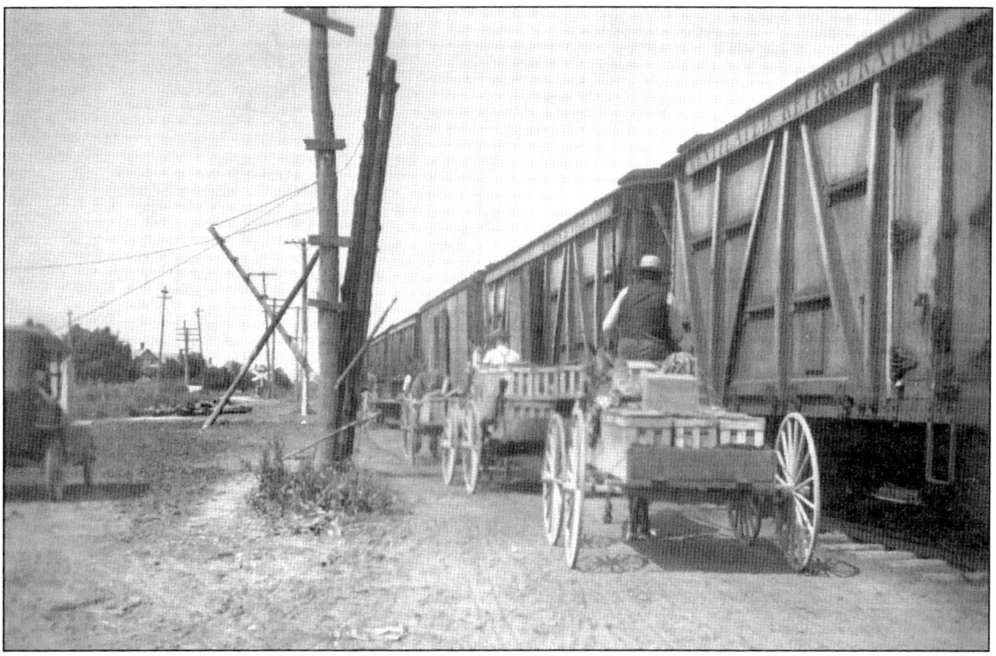
In this photograph, a wagon delivers peaches from J. G. Harrison Nurseries, forerunner of Harrison's Nurseries. Harrison's was a recently established business at the end of the 19th century, having started as peach growers in 1884, shortly adding the trees whereon the peaches were grown, and escalating into a nationwide nursery catalog business, the largest in the country.

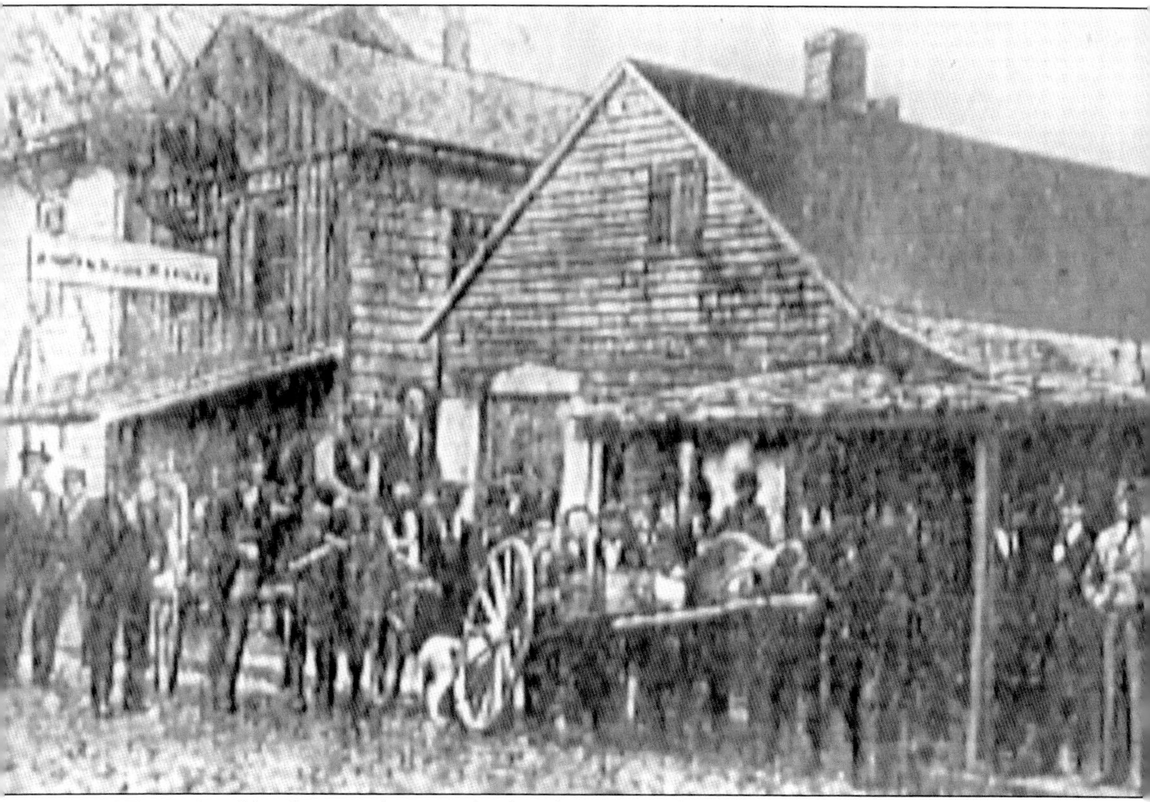

This is the oldest-known photograph of Berlin. It was taken before the first disastrous fire in 1895. The fire started behind the old wooden Atlantic Hotel. The only available water for firefighting was in the town well located on the corner of Broad and Gay Streets within a few yards of the hotel. The pumper was summoned, the leather hose lowered into the well, water was pumped, and then sprayed on the fire. When the well dried up, the pumper was abandoned. The fire then went on to burn both sides of Main Street along with the abandoned pumper, including the buildings shown in the photograph. The white building on the left was at the intersection of Main and Broad Streets. Adjoining this building was Hammond's Boot Shop; the sign reads "Boot and Shoe Makers." An 1897 map identifies those sites as a general store with a barbershop north of it. The building on the right was a saloon, later a shop where Henry Anderson sold buggies and whips. Later Bethards and Brittingham Clothing occupied the first floor with a pool hall upstairs. The location is now occupied by Rayne's Reef, j. j. Fish Studio, and Abigail's. (Matthews Collection.)

# *Two*

# Highways and Byways

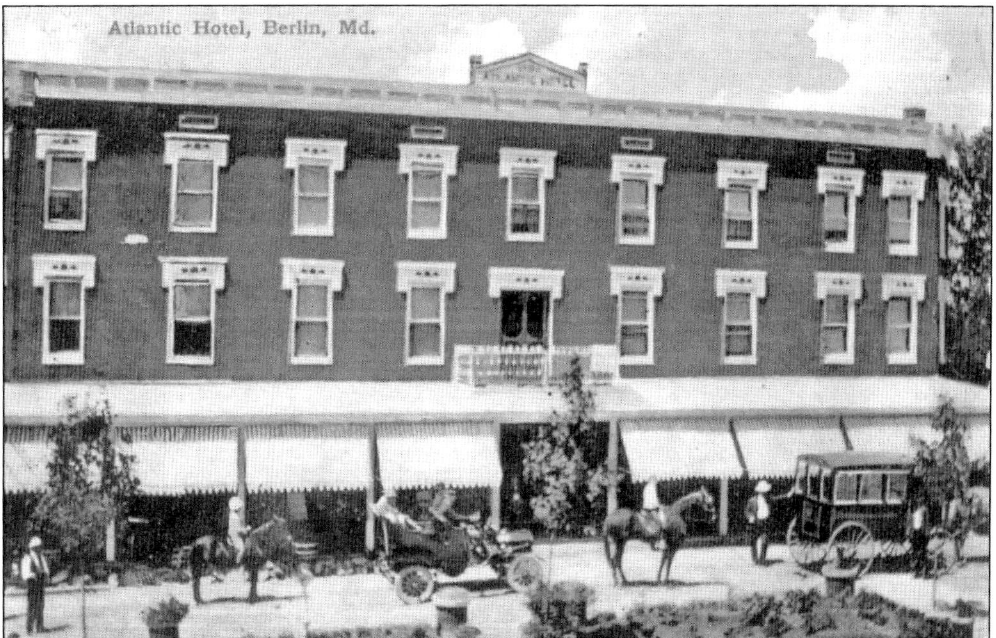


Although other towns benefited from the rivers of the Eastern Shore as conduits of trade, Berlin's location on an elevated strip of land, virtually free from water obstructions, served the town well. Its site facilitated surface transportation up, down, and across the Delmarva Peninsula. Stagecoach lines were established in Colonial America around 1756, and Stevenson's Crossroads and Burley Inn were situated on a post road connecting points along the Eastern Shore with Philadelphia. In this early-20th-century photograph, guests at the Atlantic Hotel are arriving by carriage, on horseback, and by "horseless carriage," the new-fangled invention soon to be known as the automobile. Most people, however, were dependent on livestock or their own two feet for transportation. Even children could handle an ox, mule, or horse. Soon automobiles and trucks came, as did mechanical tractors. The railroad came to Berlin in the mid-19th century and brought visitors, including salesmen called "drummers" who traveled around the county by bus taking orders from country stores. The Atlantic Hotel provided the bus and a "writing room" for compiling orders. (Ellis Wainwright Collection.)

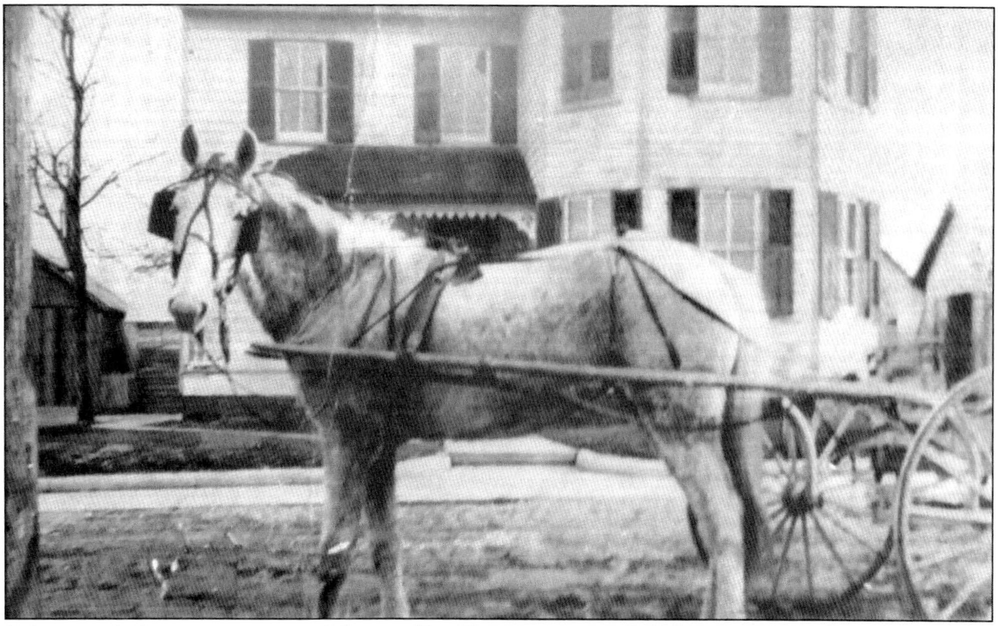

Substantial plantations, most of them self-sufficient, surrounded the town. Horses and oxen were used for hauling produce to shipping points and delivering manufactured products and supplies back from town to the plantation. This dray horse hitched to a light carriage is shown standing in front of a house south of Stevenson United Methodist Church. When this photograph was taken, the Majestic Hotel stood between the two structures.

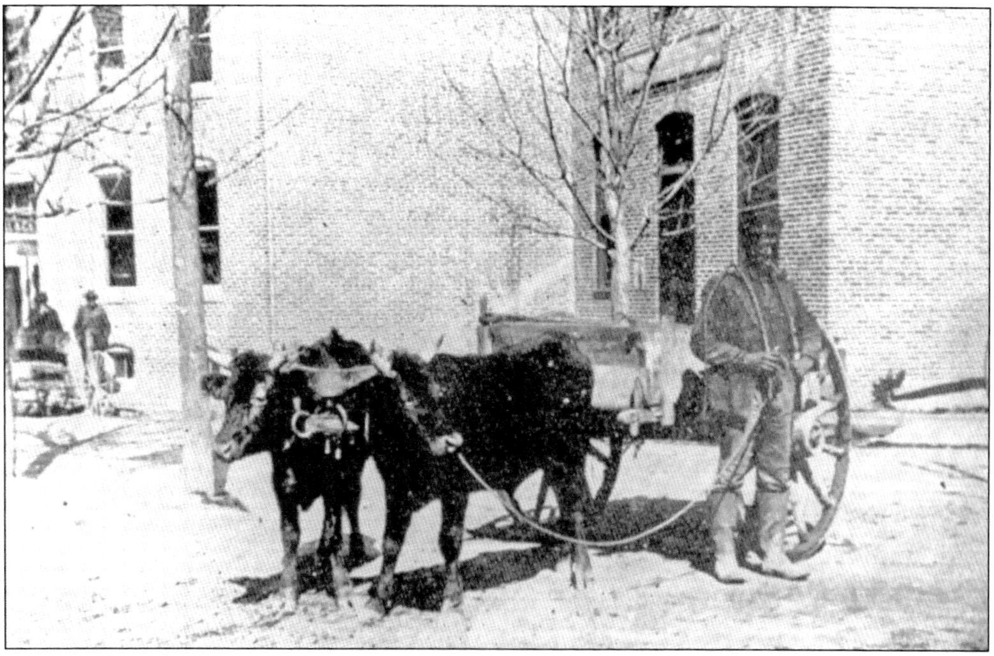

This photograph of an oxcart and driver, taken across the street from the Globe Theatre, may be of William Payne, who died in 1910. His obituary stated that he was sexton of the Episcopal church, janitor of the high school and the banks, a sailor in his youth, and "absolutely honest and much respected."

All family members were expected to share in the tasks of maintaining the plantation's operations. Thomas Victor Hammond, born in Berlin in 1863, is shown leading an oxcart in downtown Berlin.

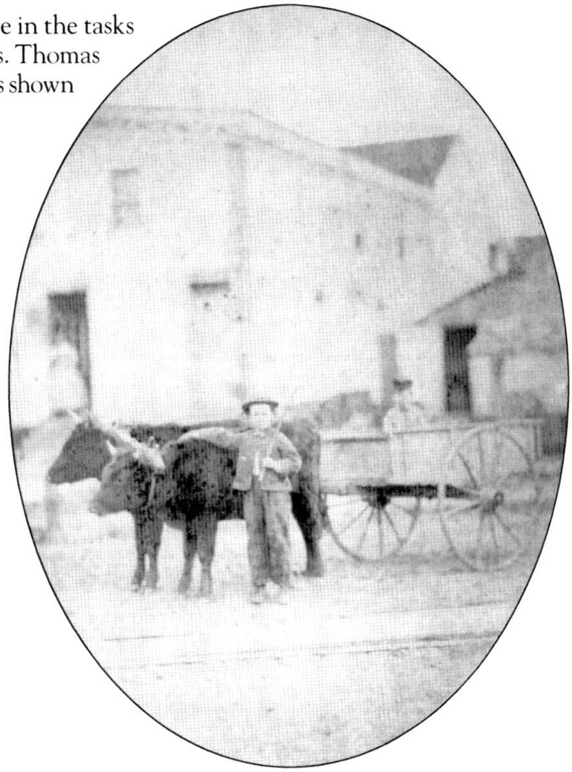

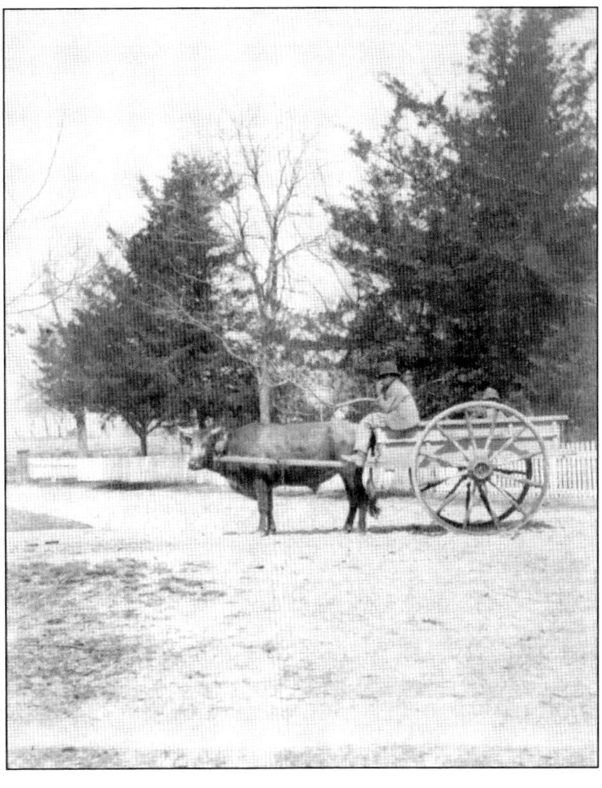

African Americans have contributed to the economic development of the Berlin area since the earliest days of European settlement. First as slaves, with relatively few being manumitted by their masters, then as freed men under the law, the presence of persons of color has been constant over the centuries. This cart driver is believed to be Charles Purnell.

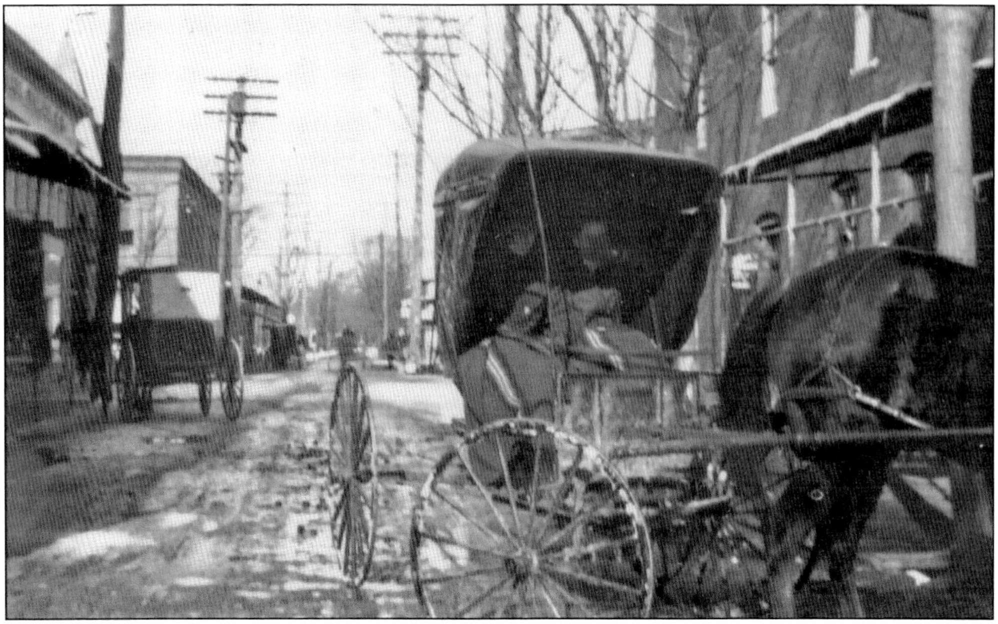

A trip into town was considered quite a treat for farm families. Most plantations would have at least one horse-drawn carriage to transport family members on errands to Berlin. A familiar sight on the streets of Berlin was a wagon filled with family members on their way to shopping, picking up the mail, or just visiting their in-town relatives and friends. (Worcester County Library Collection.)

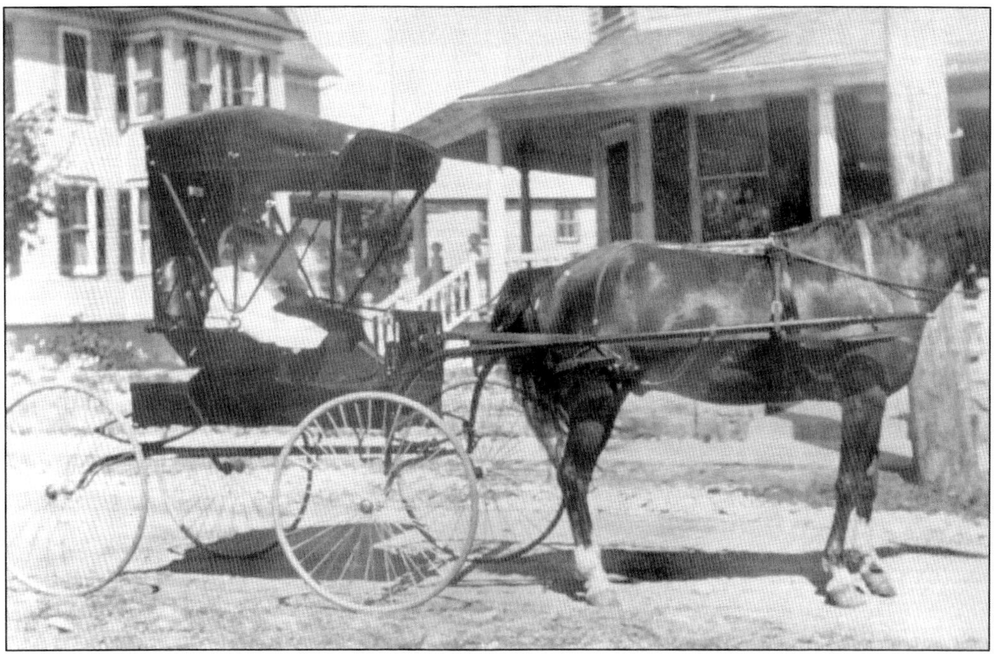

In the days before rural free delivery, mail had to be picked up and deposited at the in-town post office. This prim young lady might be running this errand as well as inspecting the latest fashions available in the town's clothing stores. This photograph was taken in front of the second Pitts house, formerly that of Nan Purnell, located at the corner of Church and Main Streets.

Two belles of Berlin prepare themselves for a ride along the country lanes of Worcester County. The woman on the right is Kate Hammond. Horseback riding, both for pleasure and as a means to get from place to place, was a necessity in the plantation economy of the pre-automobile age.

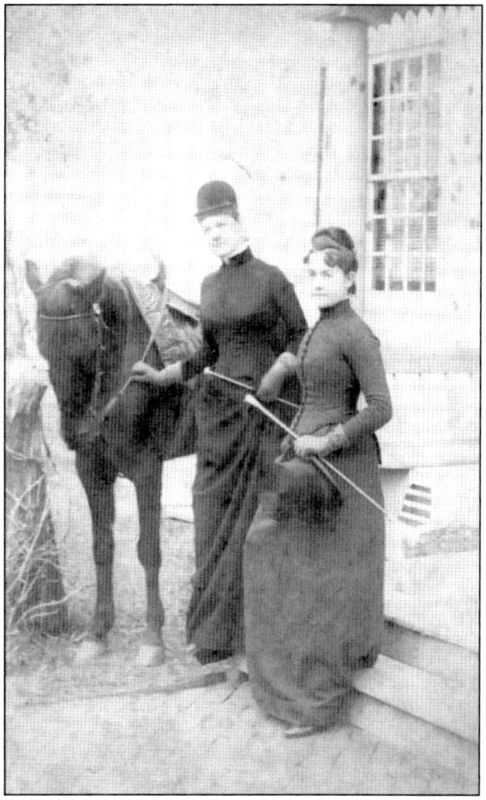

Riding had its perils for those not familiar with the roads. Many travelers would lose hours when they inadvertently strayed from the established routes. Officials had to mark the routes by establishing a system of notches carved into tree trunks adjacent to the direct roads to keep the riders on the right track. This photograph was taken in front of the Exchange and Savings Bank on Main Street and is believed to be one of Horace and Virginia Harmonson's daughters. The Harmonsons owned the Atlantic Hotel. Note the Park Hotel in the background behind the trees.

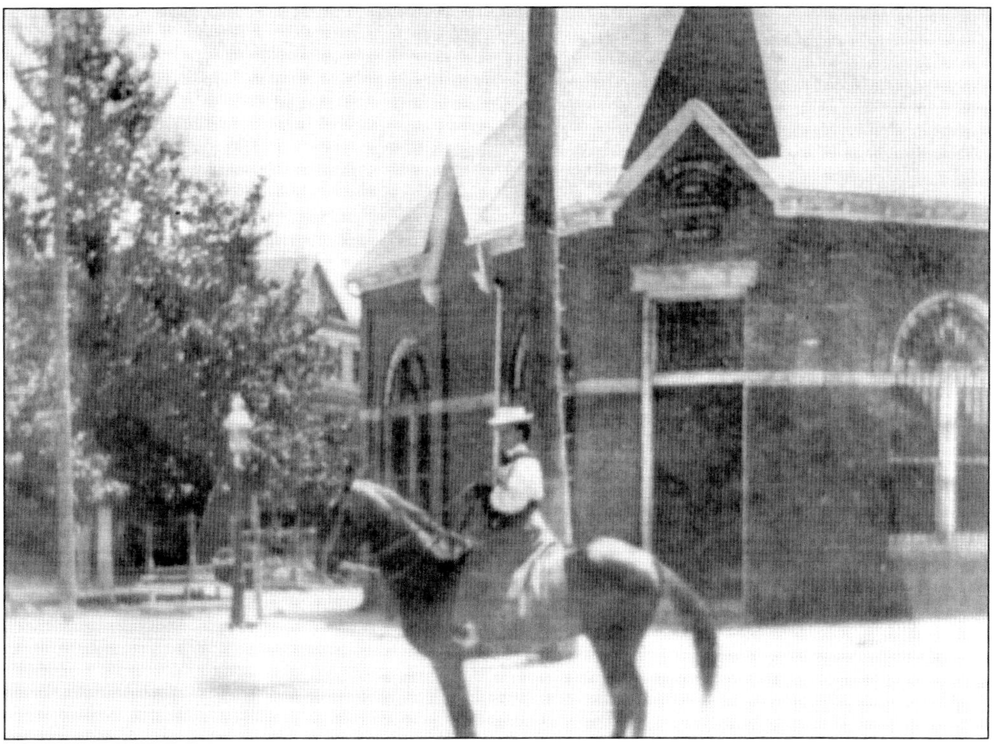

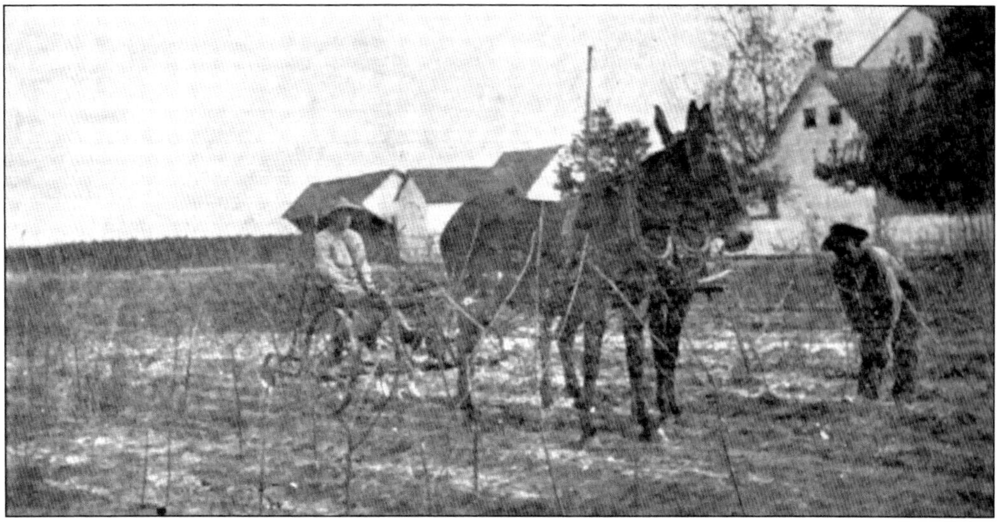

Over the centuries, the horse, a valuable and taxable asset of the plantation owner, has been the mainstay of dray animals on the plantations surrounding Berlin. One legend associated with the wild horses of Assateague is that, as the tax assessor approached, the plantation owner drove the taxable horses onto the island. When the assessment was completed, some of the livestock had wandered off and were not recovered by the owners. Their offspring may roam Assateague Island to this day. (Matthews Collection.)

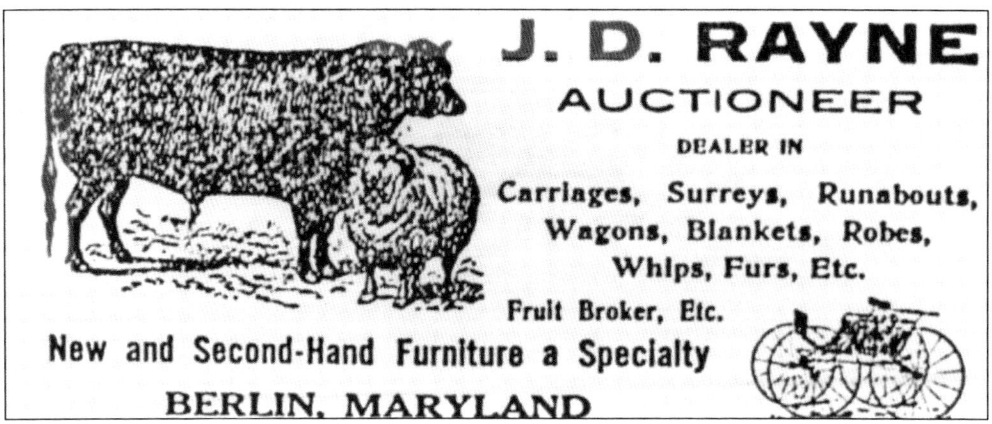


J. D. Rayne, dealer in carriages, surreys, wagons, and other transportation paraphernalia, was on Commerce Street where the new Taylor Bank offices and drive-through are today. (Matthews Collection.)

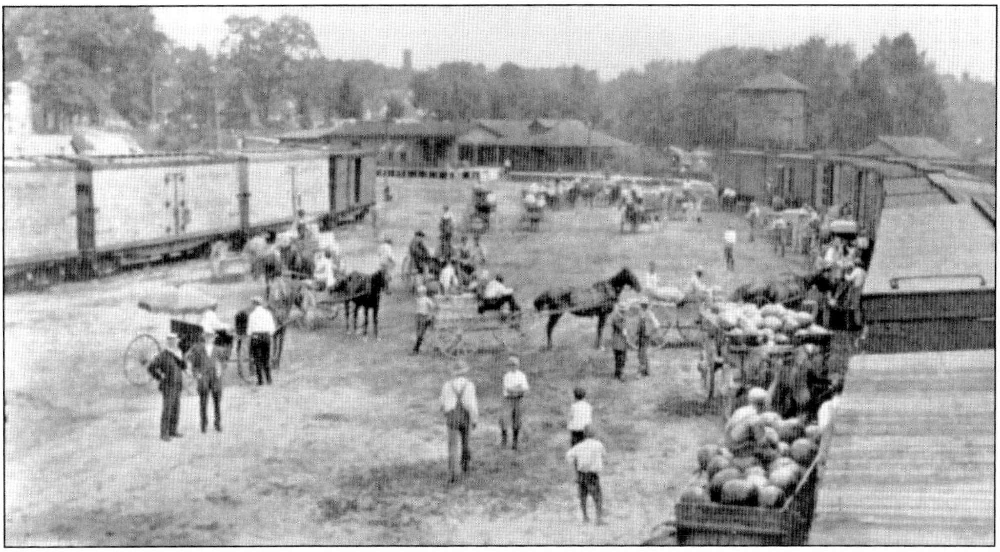

Shortly after the end of the Civil War, railroads began to crisscross Worcester County. Stretching eastward from Salisbury was the Wicomico and Pocomoke Rail Road, officially opened in May 1868. North-south lines originating in Delaware were variously named until absorbed by the Pennsylvania Railroad by 1915.

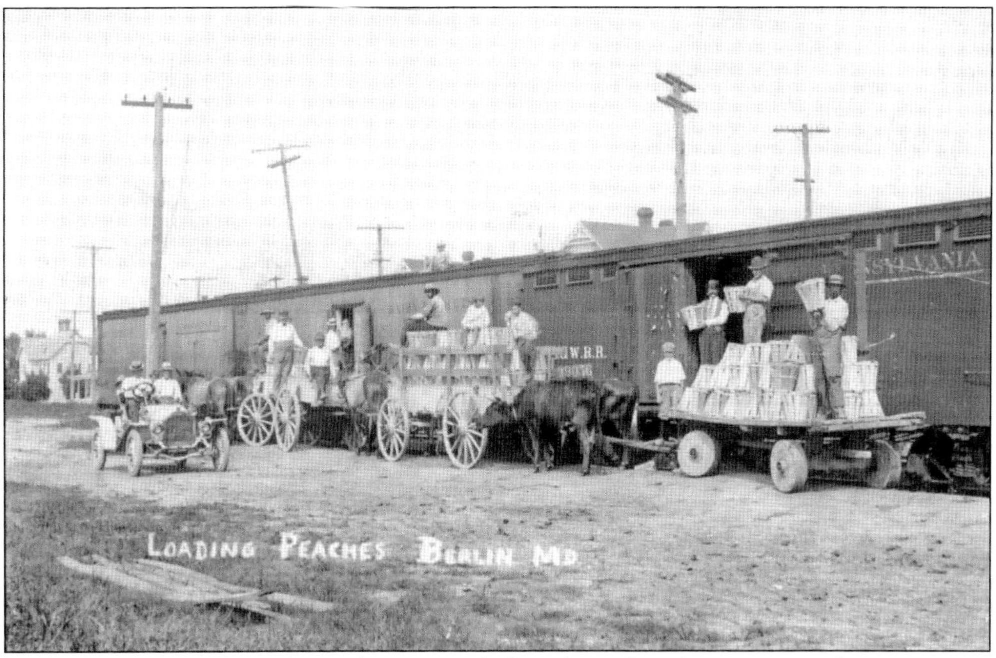


As Berlin had benefited by being the crossroad of north-south and east-west coach routes, so too it benefited by the layout of the railroads. These busy images show the interplay between the horse and the railroads as Berlin expanded its social and economic contact with surrounding areas. Here crates of Harrison's peaches are being loaded for shipment. Note the early automobile on the left. (Matthews Collection.)

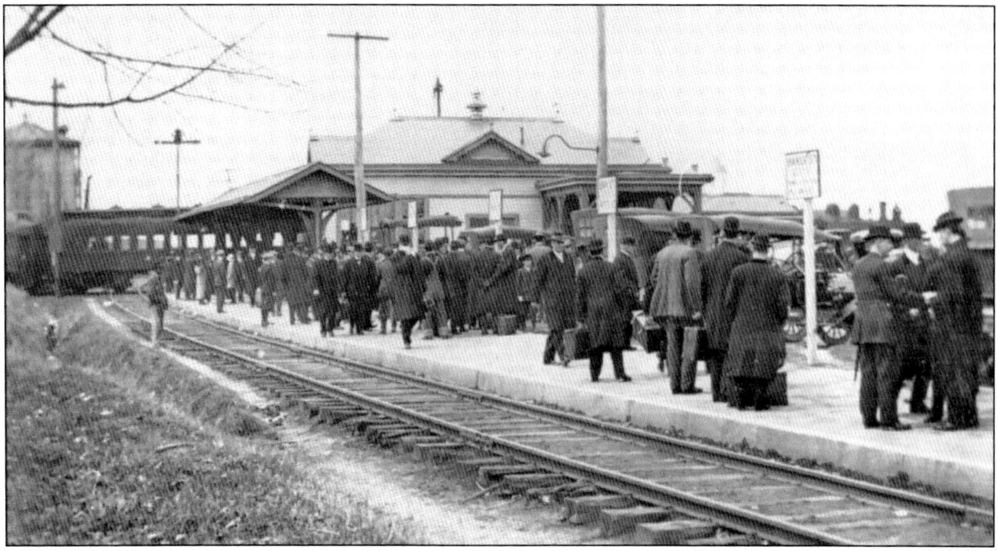

Increased rail traffic made the construction of a modern terminal a necessity for the continued growth of Berlin. Union Station, so named to indicate the joining of the two rail lines, was erected around 1905. This view shows the substantial passenger traffic flowing through town. The men carrying suitcases are probably drummers, salesmen drumming up business, their luggage filled with samples of their stock in trade.

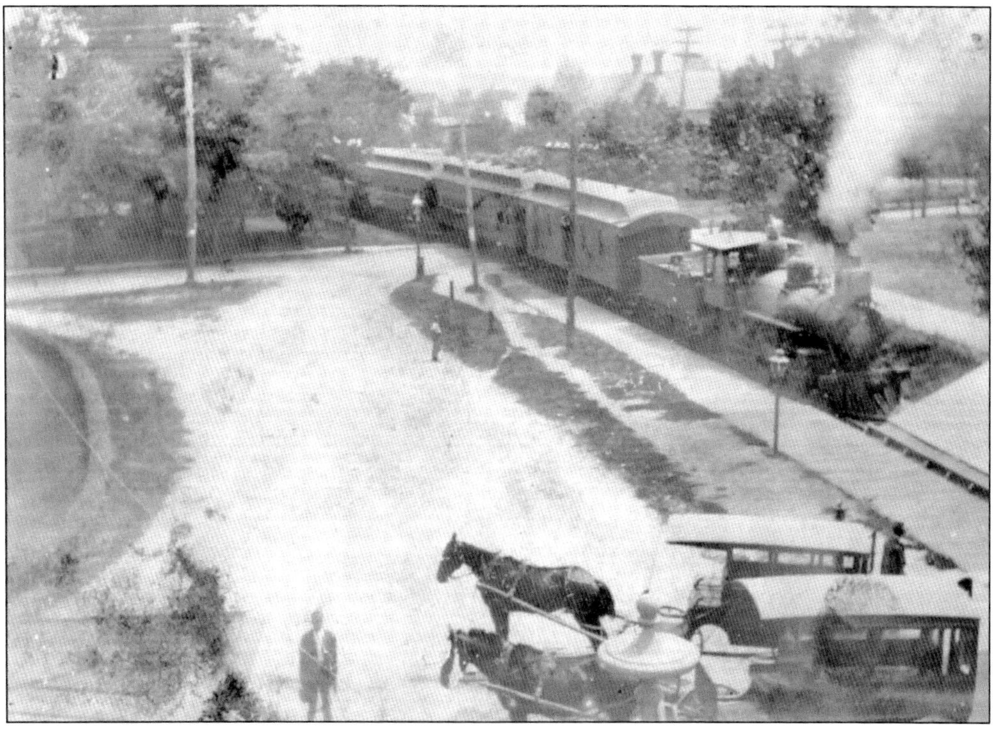

The train approaching Union Station might contain vacationers on their way to Ocean City to the east, which had been opened to land traffic by extension of the east-west line by 1876. To the west was Salisbury and Love Point from where travelers could take a steamer to Baltimore. (Mabel Rogers Collection.)

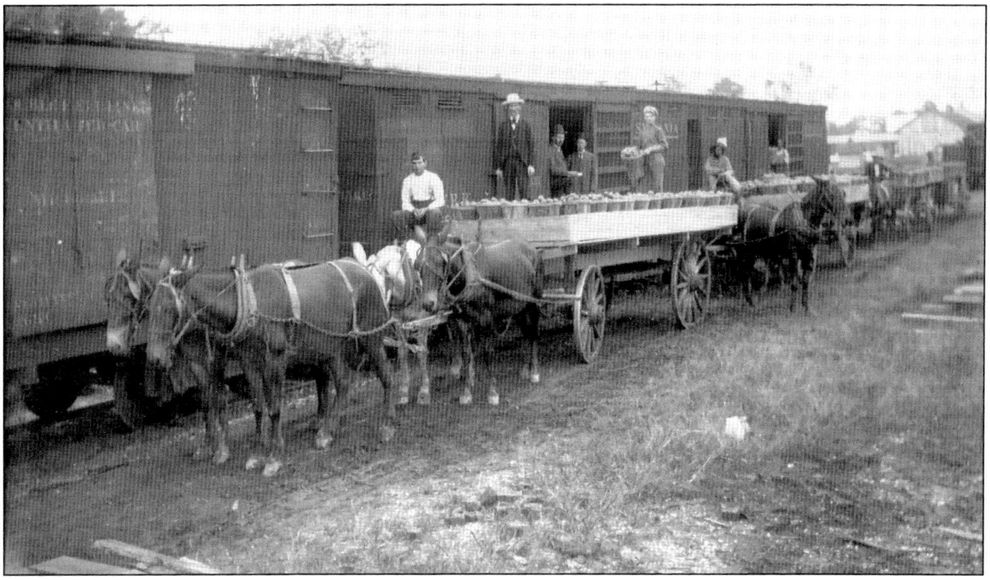

The north-south line, at one time named the Breakwater and Frankford and Worcester Rail Road (later shortened to Worcester Rail Road), provided transportation of locally grown produce to city markets. Shown are wagons of produce waiting to be loaded onto railroad boxcars.

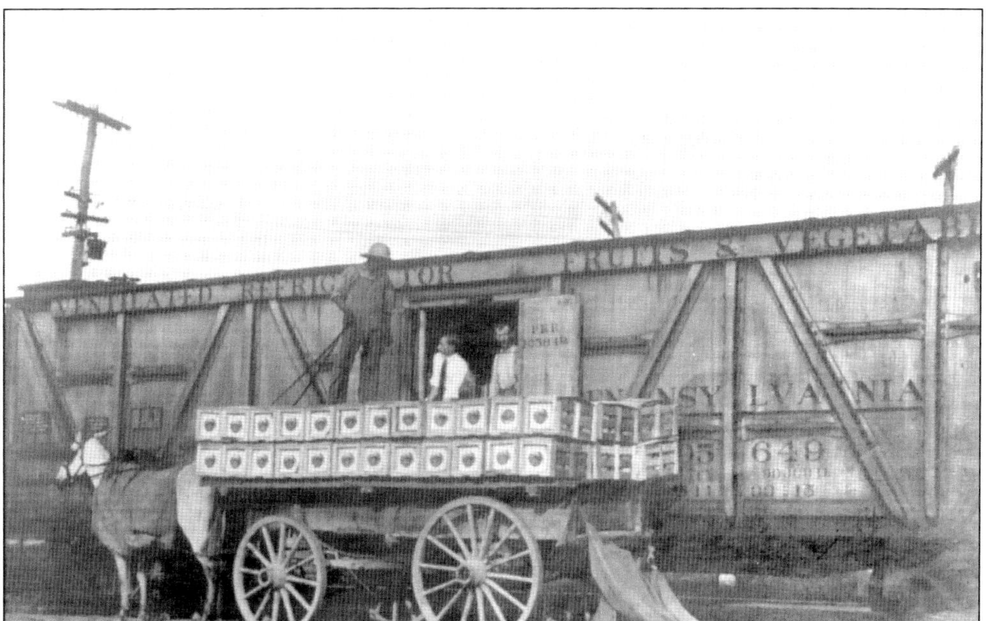

A major industry in Berlin, with facilities adjacent to Union Station, was the complex founded by Joseph G. Harrison, who developed one of the largest tree and vegetable nurseries on the peninsula. Crates of Harrison produce stand before the door of a "ventilated refrigerator" boxcar.

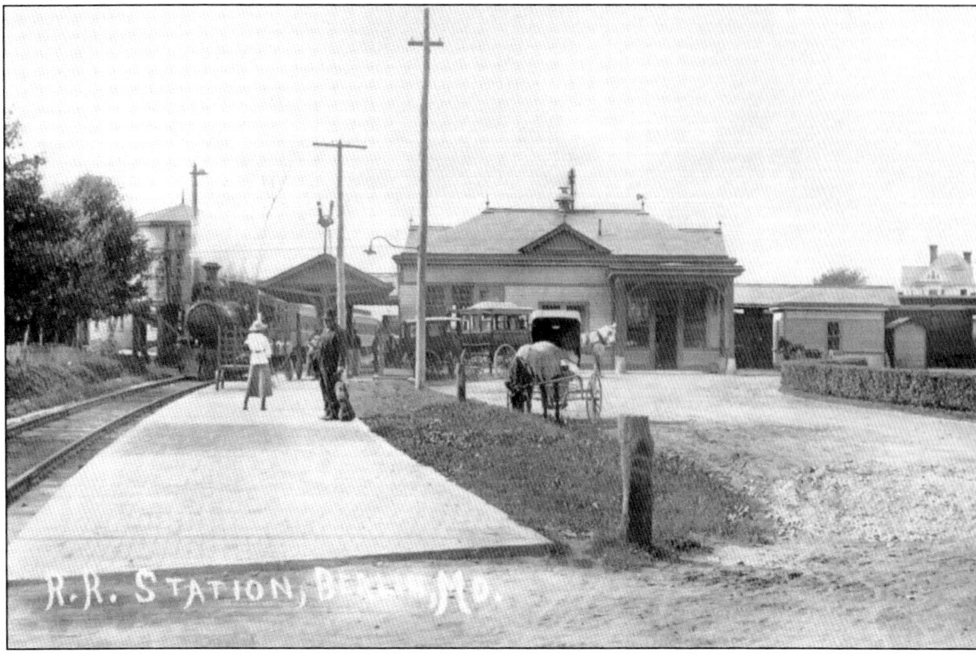


This relatively tranquil image of the usually bustling Union Station shows but a few passengers on the platform, including a sportily attired lady. Note the presence of an early automobile between the horse-drawn vehicles. (Ellis Wainwright Collection.)

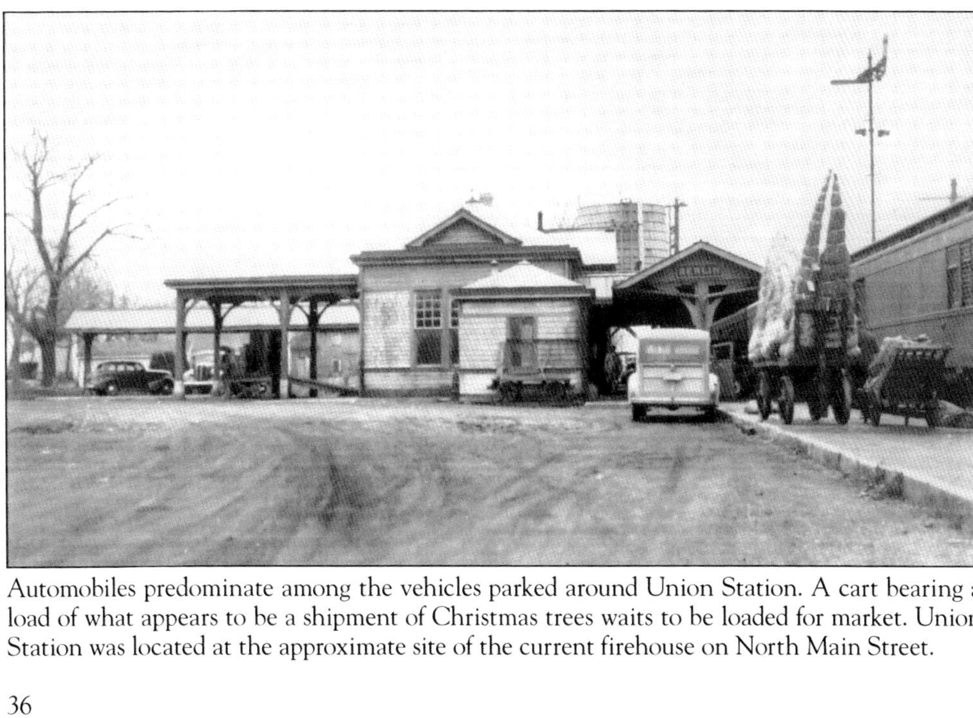


Automobiles predominate among the vehicles parked around Union Station. A cart bearing a load of what appears to be a shipment of Christmas trees waits to be loaded for market. Union Station was located at the approximate site of the current firehouse on North Main Street.

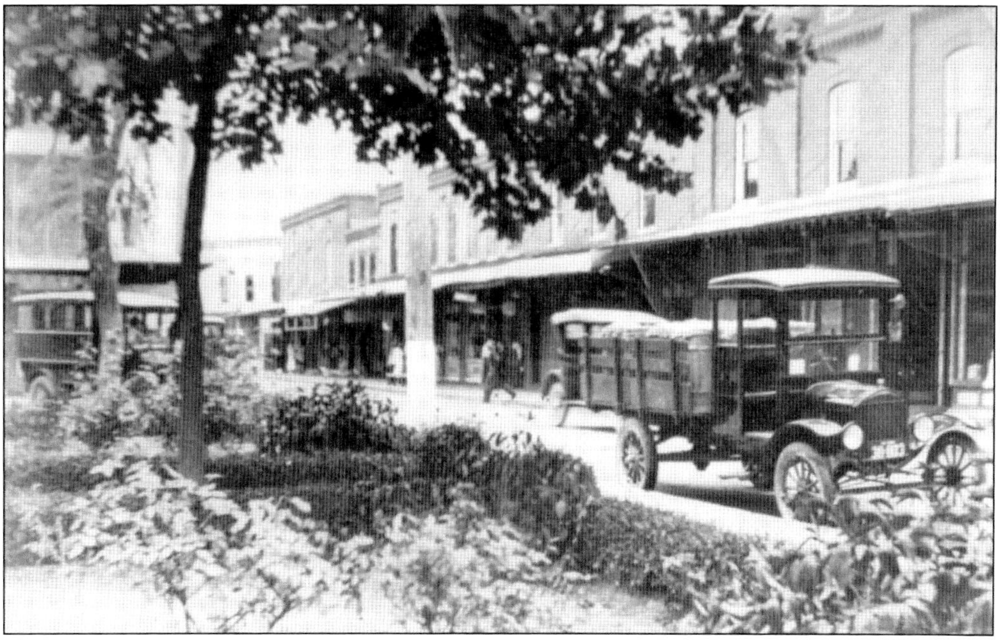

With the improvement of the internal combustion engine, trucks were made capable of hauling larger, heavier loads. Shown above is a 1920s flatbed parked in front of the Atlantic Hotel to make an in-town delivery. Note the bus for transporting drummers on the left.

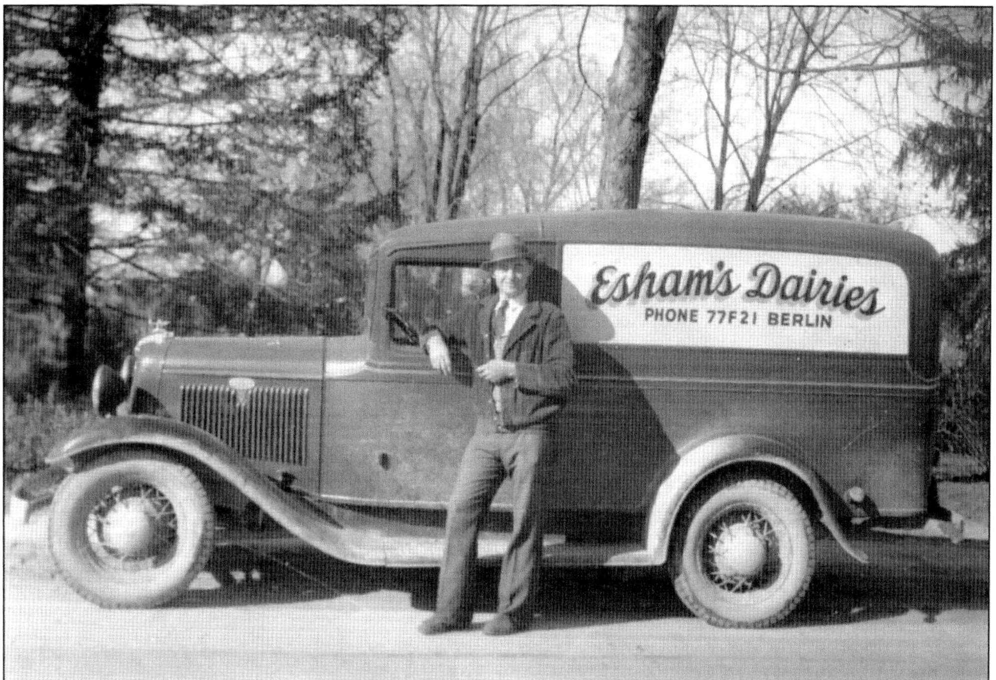


This Esham's Dairies truck was used to deliver milk in the 1930s. During World War II, when gas rationing was in effect, the company reverted to its horse and carts from an earlier time, as shown on page 56.

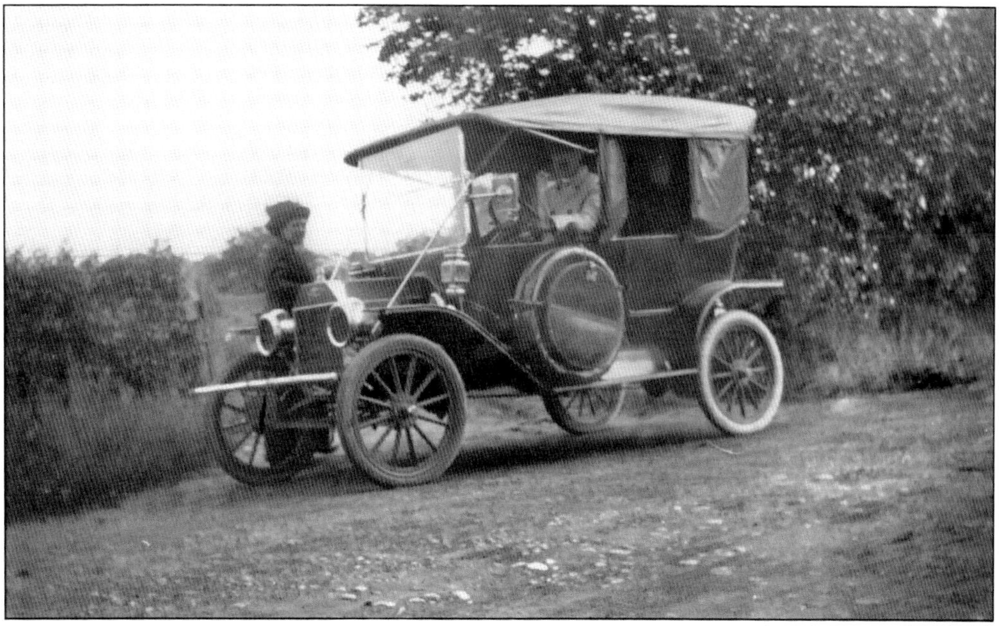

In the first decade of the 20th century, the appearance of the automobile exploded across America, including Berlin. Prior to the introduction of the Model T by Henry Ford in 1909, the automobile was in general the plaything of the rich. Ford's mass-production techniques and standardization of parts allowed reduced prices so that the average man could afford the simple, boxy, functional car, painted in any color "so long as it was black."

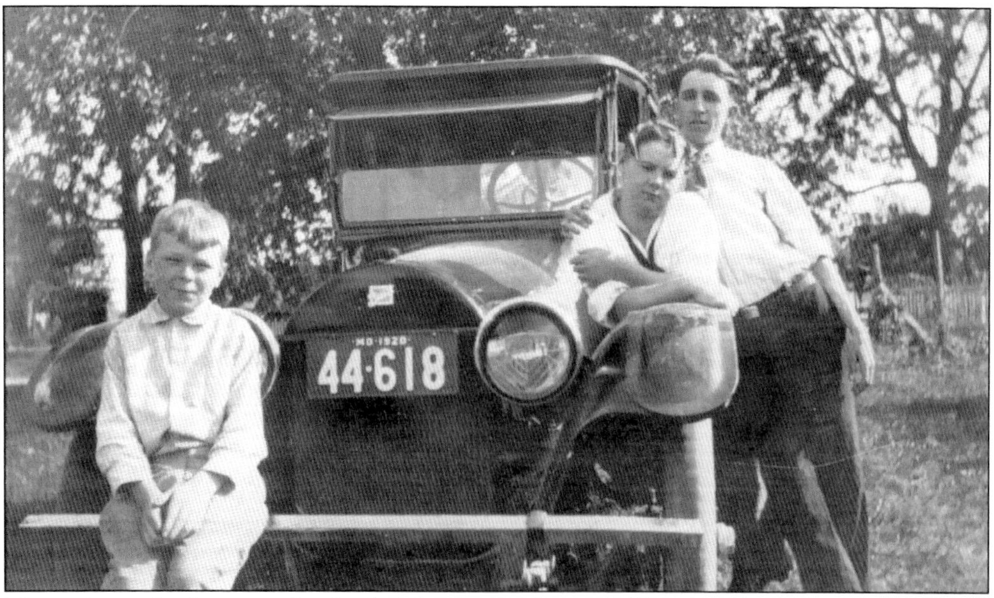


The early cars had a major drawback. They had to be started by strenuously cranking a handle to ignite the motor. An electric self-starter was first featured on the 1912 Cadillac. Its availability allowed women and older people to drive. The photograph's original caption reads, "Ken [Jarvis] Srs. old Buick car, Kendall [Jarvis] Jr., Ruth Powell Wood, & Woodie."

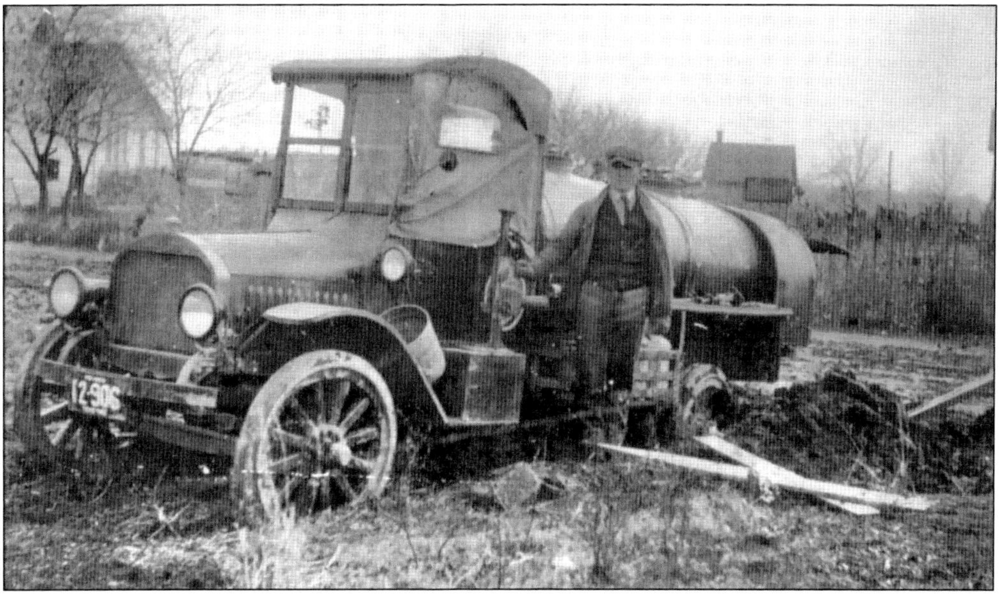

The automobile exploded onto the scene when America's roads were hardly more passable than those that carried the stagecoach lines. This view shows a common sight—a vehicle stuck in the mud. Note the wooden spokes and solid tire wheels on this 1920s oil truck. Ironically, in many cases, the motorist had to rely upon a local farmer to assist him in pulling out his car by use of a team of horses. Gradually the roads were paved with crushed oyster and clamshells, gravel and stones, macadam, asphalt, and finally concrete.

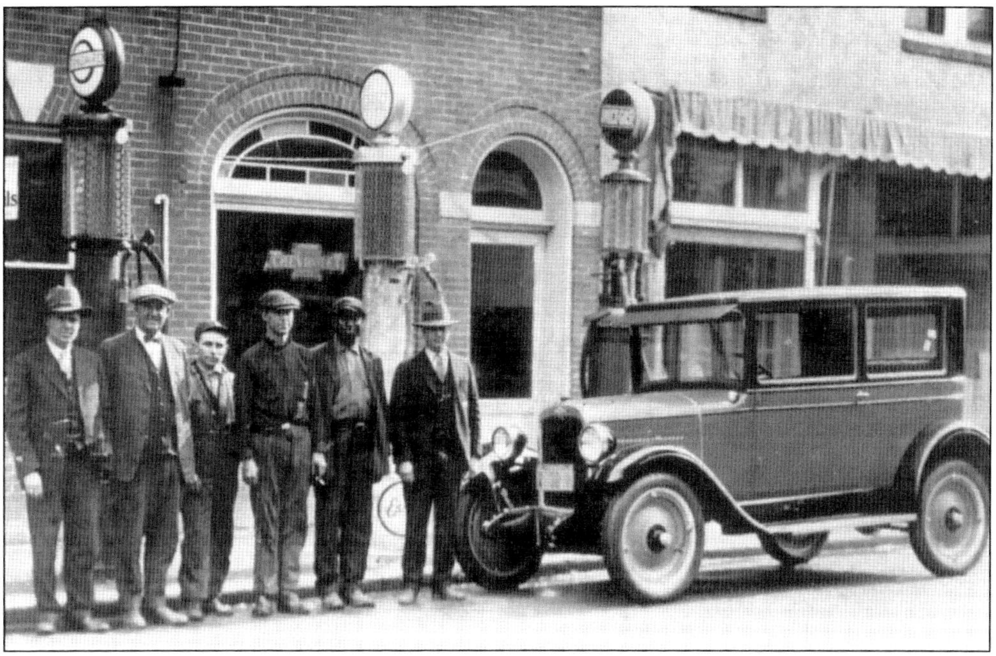

The appearance of the car spurred the establishment of many businesses created to support the automotive industry. Arrayed before the location of the Berlin Motor Company facility on Main Street are the staff and a late-1920s Chevrolet car. Note the gas pumps at curbside. (Matthews Collection.)

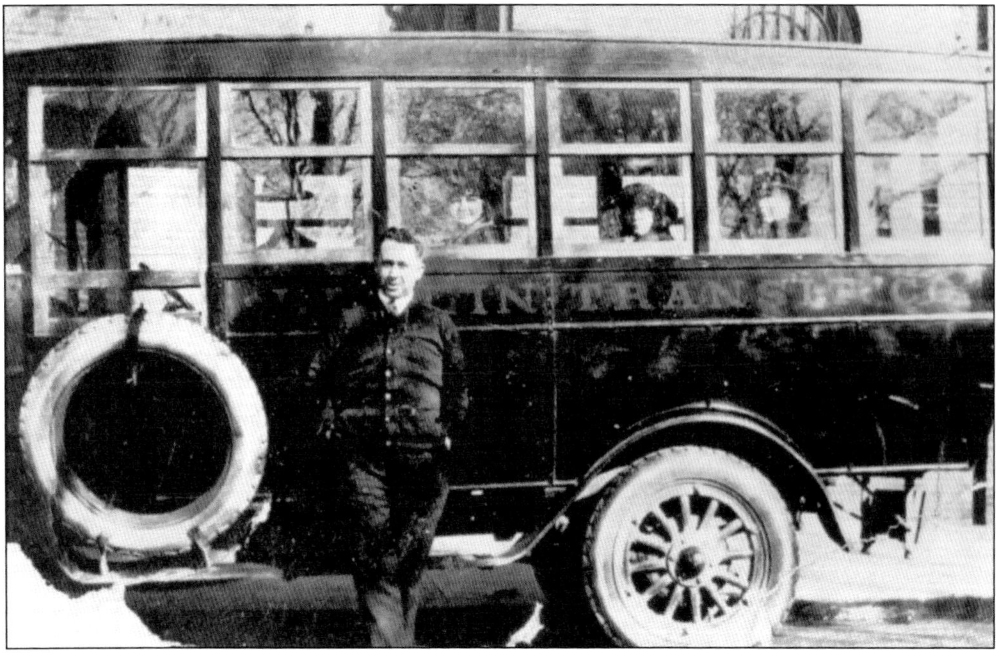

In the 1920s, Frank Baker stands beside his Berlin Transit Company bus in front of the now Mercantile-Peninsula Bank. He picked up passengers at the Atlantic Hotel in Berlin and carried them to the Atlantic Hotel in Ocean City. Local people, as well as tourists, used his services. (Matthews Collection.)

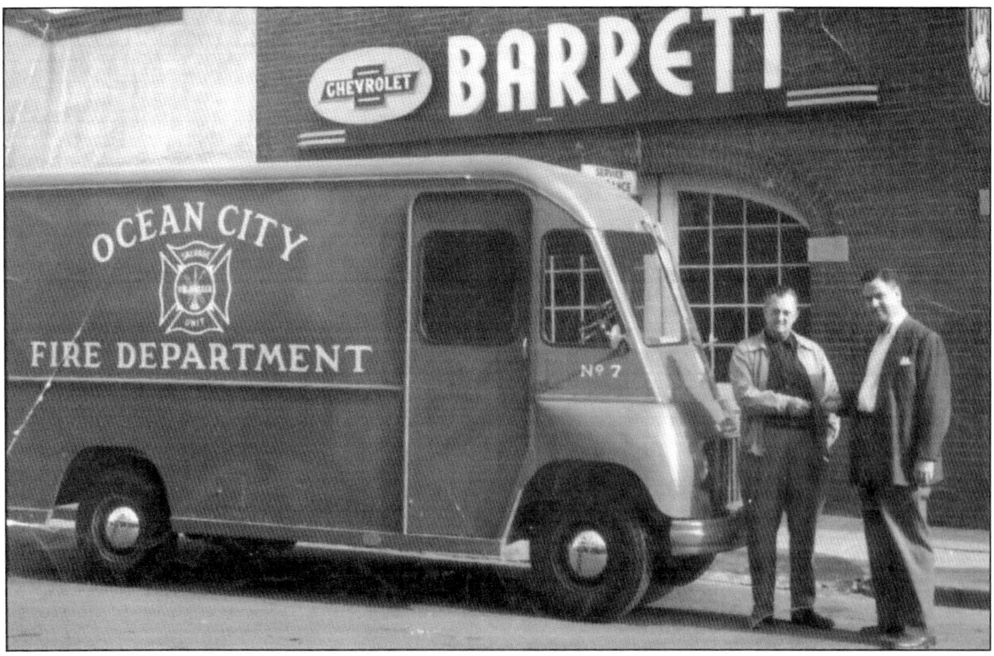


Gilbert Barrett established Barrett Chevrolet in 1951 at this downtown location, now Town Center Antiques II. He is pictured on the right. Barrett's business later expanded, and the company built and moved into a larger facility on Old Ocean City Boulevard, its present location. (Nancy Barrett Collection.)

# *Three*

# "Watch Berlin Grow!"

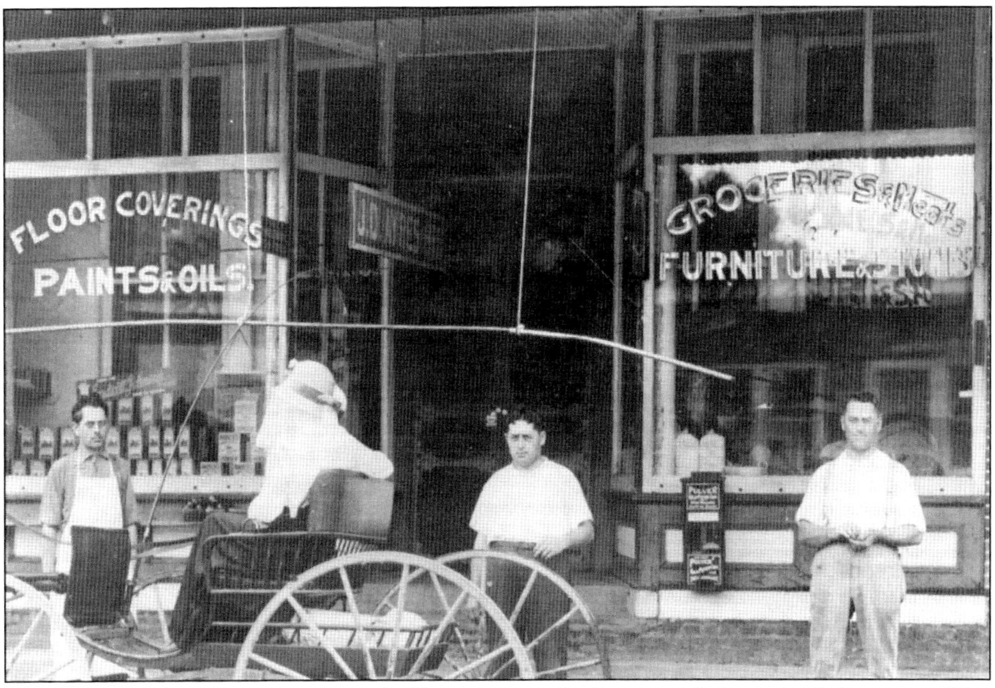


The Ayres Brothers Store was typical of businesses in Berlin around the early 20th century. The store was on South Main Street where Tea by the Sea and Ameriprise Financial are located in 2007. This shows the Ayres brothers and a cousin standing in front. The Ayres Sisters Millinery Shop was next door. Berlin adopted "Watch Berlin Grow!" as its slogan in 1910. The Ayres Brothers Store was a part of that growth.

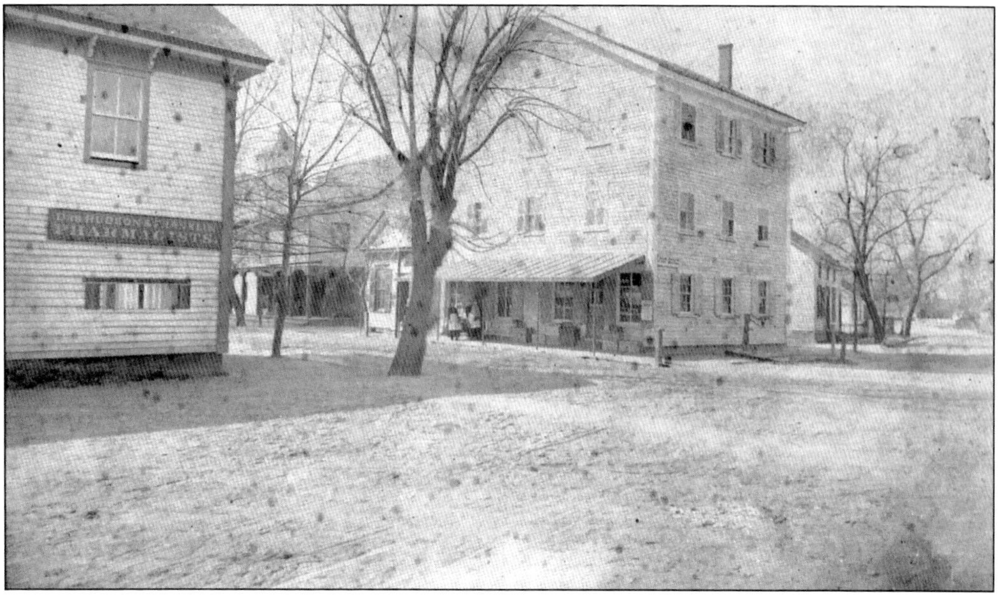

Fueled by a strong southwest wind, Berlin's second devastating fire on November 12, 1901, burned the Armory, Ayres Brothers Store, and the John Ayres home, jumped the Park Hotel only to ignite its barns and stables, then went on to burn the Southern Methodist Church and other homes. The Armory site, center, is now occupied by the Odd Fellows Hall; Mercantile-Peninsula Bank is now on the left. The location is at the convergence of Main, Jefferson, William, and Bay Streets. (Mabel Rogers Collection.)

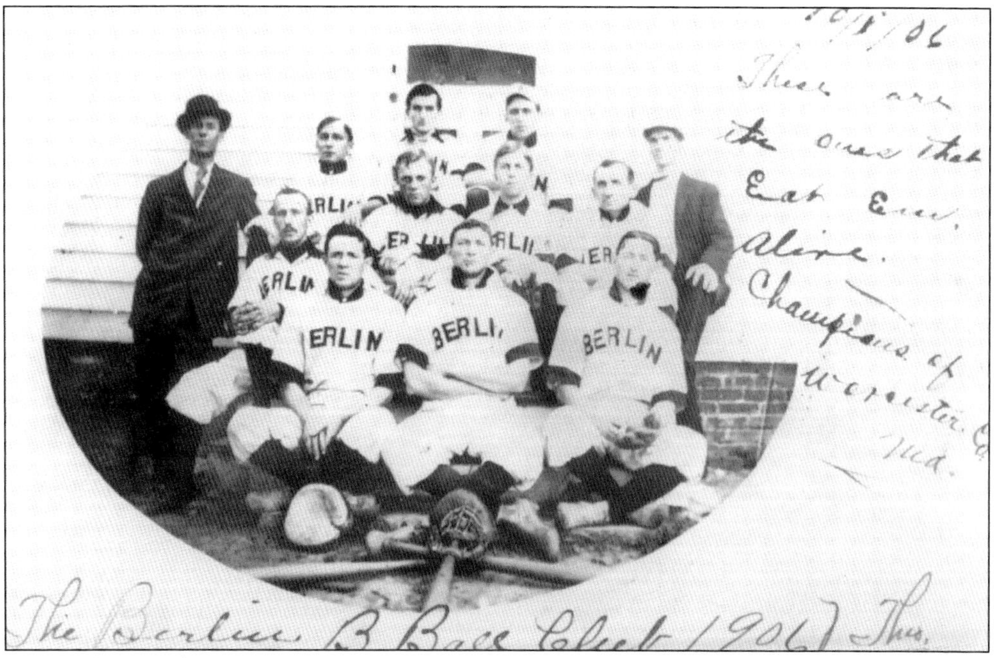


Buckingham High School's strong competitive spirit produced many championship ball teams through the early and mid-1900s, including the group of Buckingham graduates calling themselves the Berlin Base Ball Club, Worcester Champions in 1906. The one player identified is Clarence Tingle, pictured on the right in the second row.

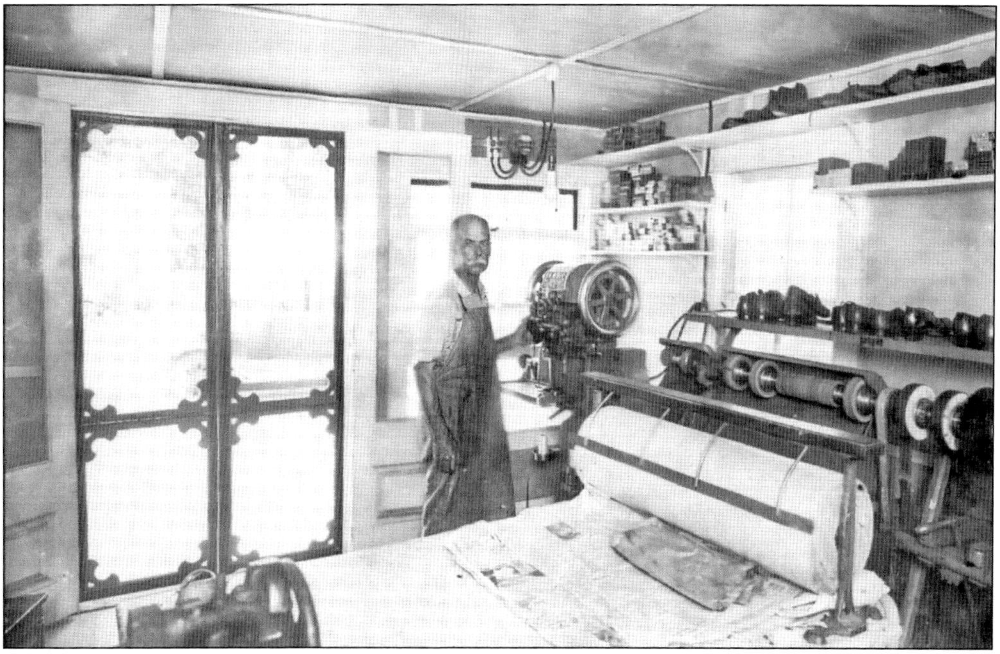

The shoes lined up on the wall give ample evidence of Eugene Powell's business, located on Commerce Street. As seen below, the seven beautiful young ladies with their cinched waists, frilly shirtwaists, and carefully coiffed hair are the epitome of females in the early 1900s. The young lady standing at left is Mattie Powell, later owner of the Jeanne Shoppe; other young ladies in the photograph are her sisters, Emily; Myra; Mabel, who married Kendall Jarvis; and Elizabeth "Bettie," who married the town mailman, Columbus Marshall. Contrary to the popular saying, it appears that the cobbler's children do have new shoes.

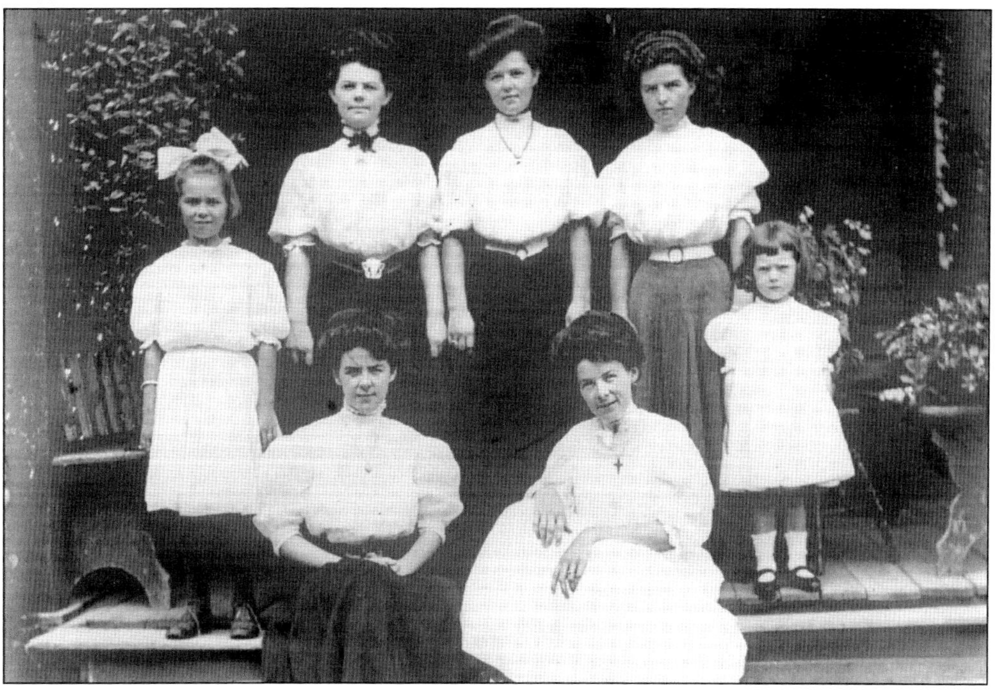

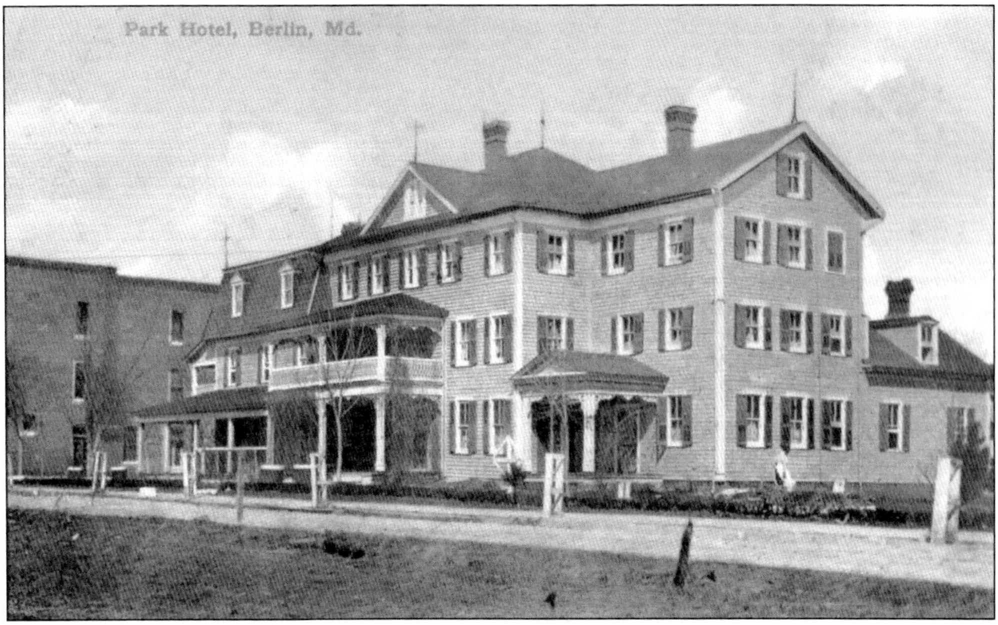


The Park Hotel was a large hotel located on Bay Street near where the mayor's and council offices are now situated. With a still-unknown cause, it burned in 1913, but it could have started from a stove or fireplace or a match from smoking. The ashes had to be sifted because Mrs. Thomas Savage, the proprietor's wife, lost her diamonds in the fire. Guards were placed around the hotel until the sifting could be accomplished. The diamonds were not discovered. (Ellis Wainwright Collection.)

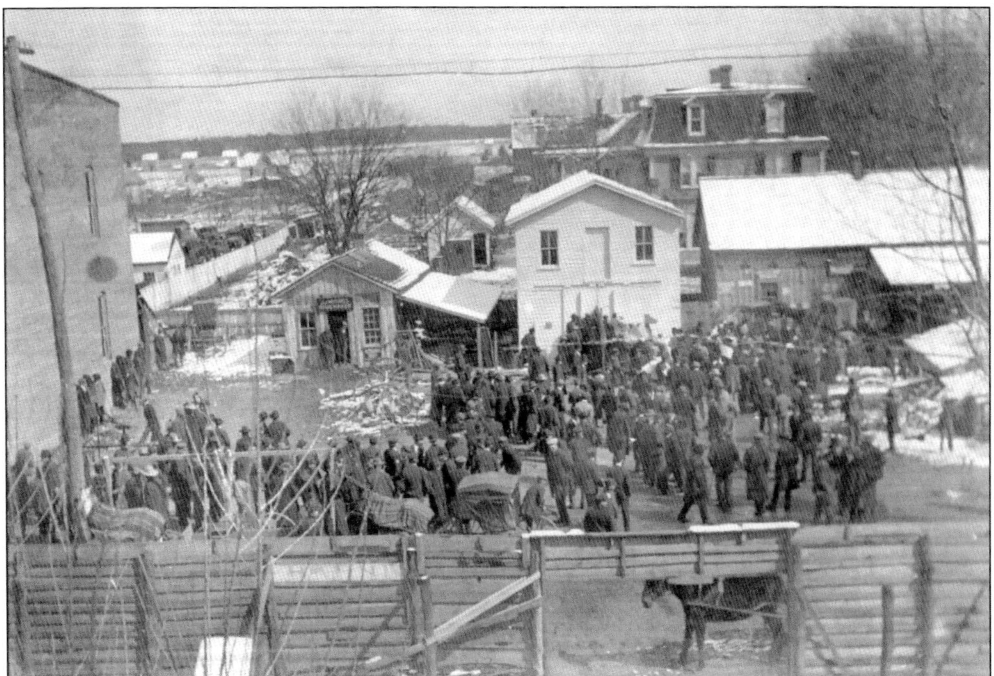

This stockyard was in the middle of Berlin, in the parking lot near the junction of Pitts and William Streets. (Ellis Wainwright Collection.)

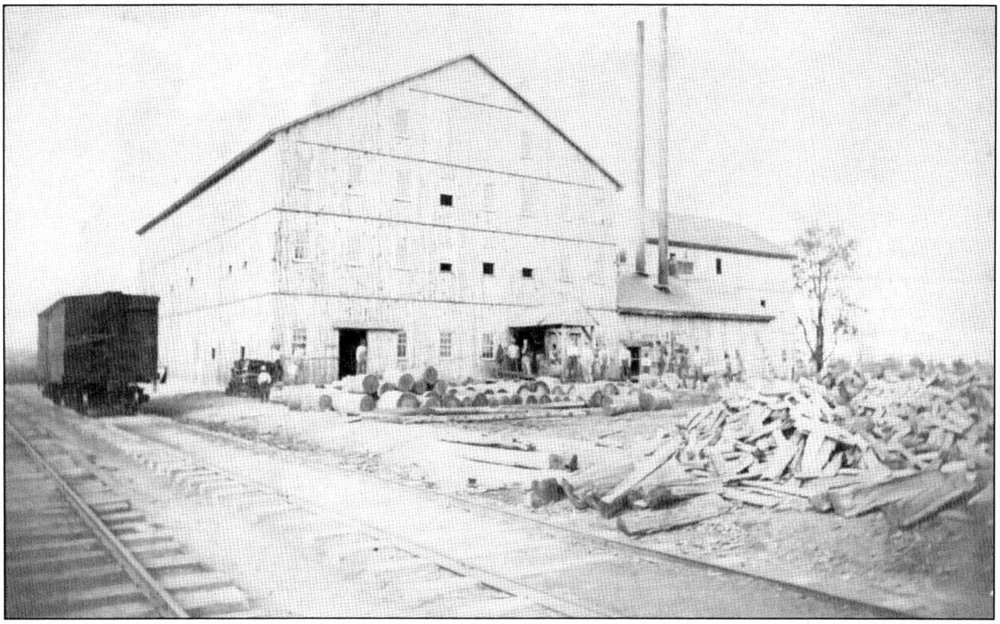

"The fire started at the Veneer Works, a great big place, one of the largest veneer works on the Shore. Those sheets of veneer caught in the wind just like airplanes. Two churches were burning at once." This is a quote from William Pitts, surveyor and local historian about the Berlin Fire of October 1, 1904. The Veneer Works made fruit baskets and crates for transporting local produce. It was located at the west end of West Street; thus, the sheets mentioned above flew about three-quarters of a mile into the town. (Mabel Rogers Collection.)

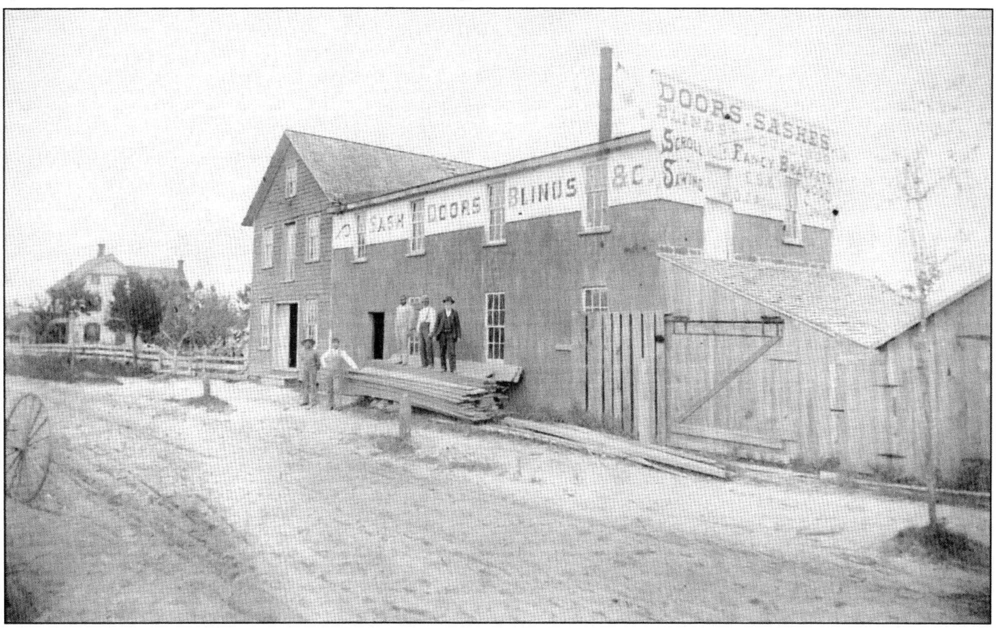


The Adkins Company is one of Berlin's most enduring businesses. It has been a part of the town since 1908. Although it has suffered many fires because of the nature of the business, this lumber and hardware supply company is a growing venture, with three branches in the Berlin area. (Mabel Rogers Collection.)

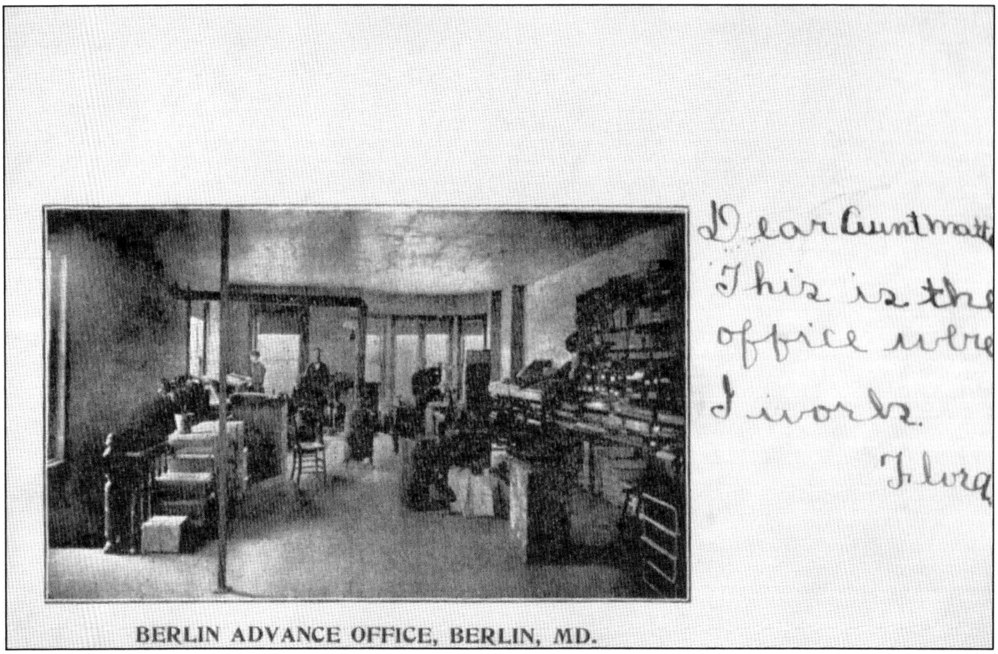


The *Berlin Advance*, above, operated in Berlin from 1904 to 1921 on the upper floor of the recently restored Renaissance Building over what is now Berlin Florist and Stewart's Antiques. The owners, Jesse and Alice Tucker, produced not only newspapers, but other types of printing, such as postcards of Berlin, like the one above, and this one below showing the *City of Paris* on a cart with its builder, J. F. Selby. (Ellis Wainwright Collection.)

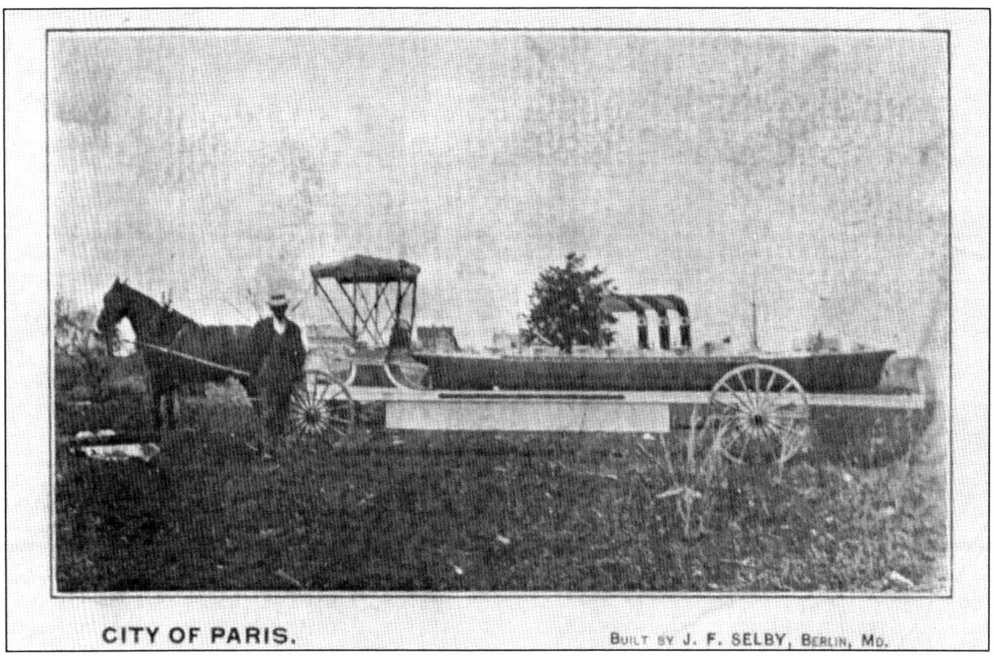

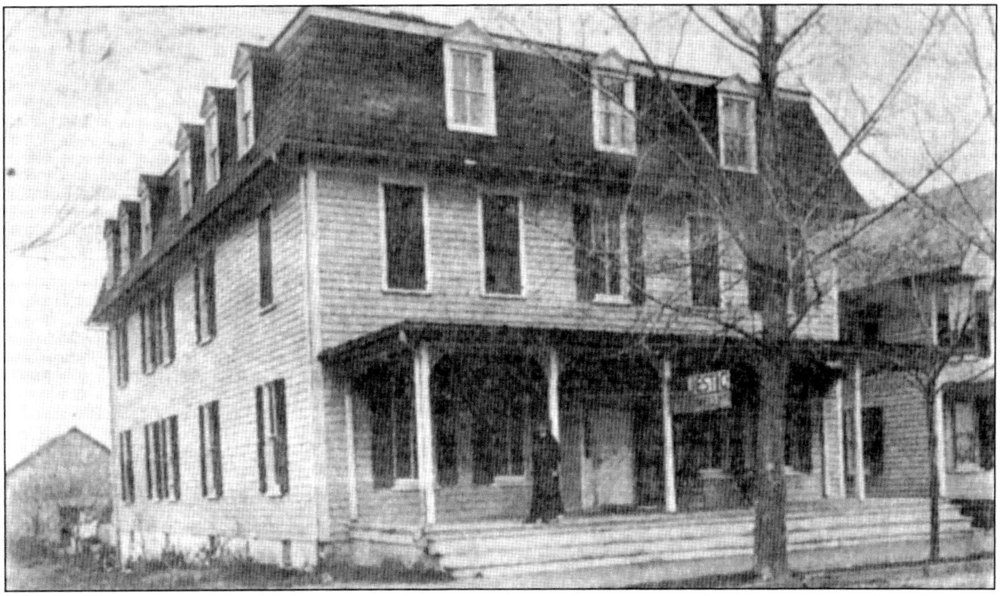

One of Berlin's hotels, the Majestic, was located on North Main Street, across Purnell Alley from the Stevenson United Methodist Church. Being at the crossroads of the Baltimore, Chesapeake, and Atlantic and the Pennsylvania line railroads, Berlin had many hotels. This smaller hotel was managed by many people, including R. Powell and Jerry Connelly; the last manager was Mary Hastings. There were livery stables associated with it. Before it was demolished, it was a television repair shop. (Mabel Rogers Collection.)

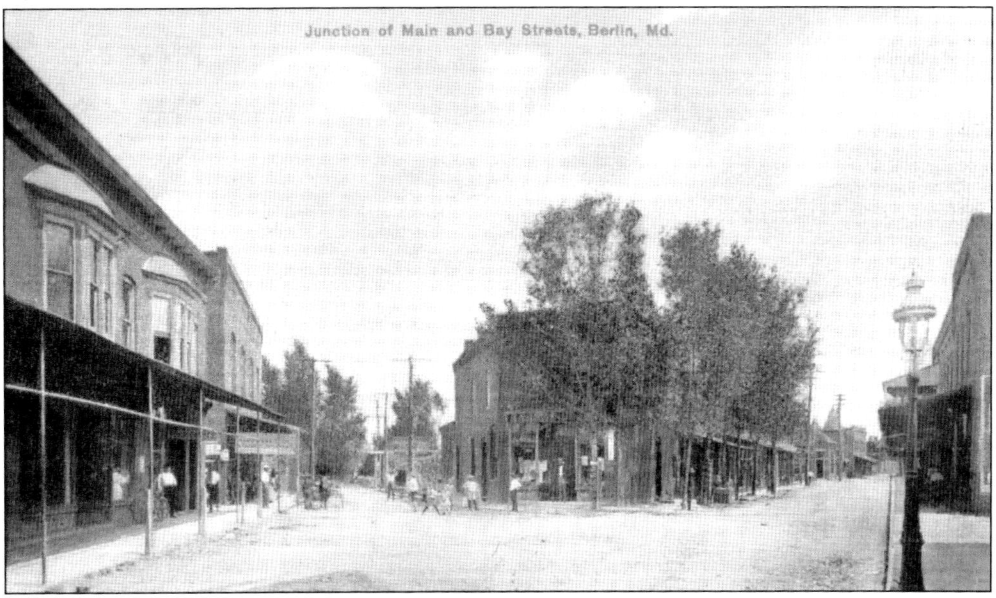


Main Street at the corner of Pitts Street shows unpaved streets and a street lamp similar to the ones of today. The buildings on the left, now the Renaissance Plaza, have housed many shops and stores: U.S. Post Office, E. S. Furbush Dry Goods, grocery stores, and variety stores. The bay windows on the left were the offices of the *Berlin Advance*. Another social meeting place was located on the point at the center of the photograph, later becoming the Kozy Korner. Main Street Gift Gallery now occupies the site. (Mabel Rogers Collection.)

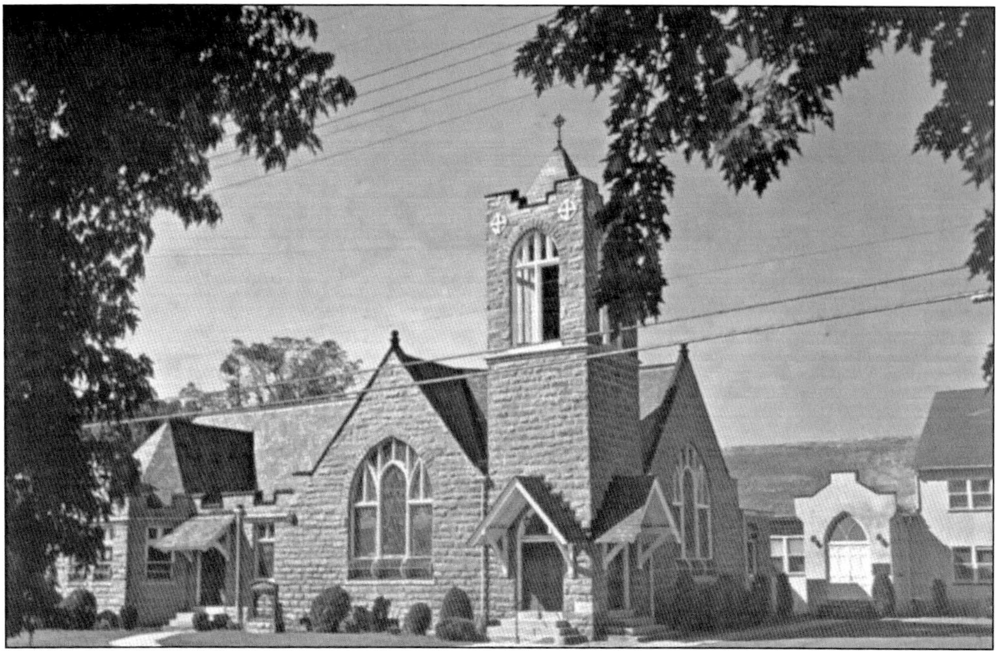

Buckingham Presbyterian Church, as it stands today, is on South Main Street. The previous house of worship was burned in the October 1, 1904, fire to be replaced by this beautiful Holmesburg granite structure. In 2006, the congregation celebrated this building's 100-year anniversary with a year of historic events.

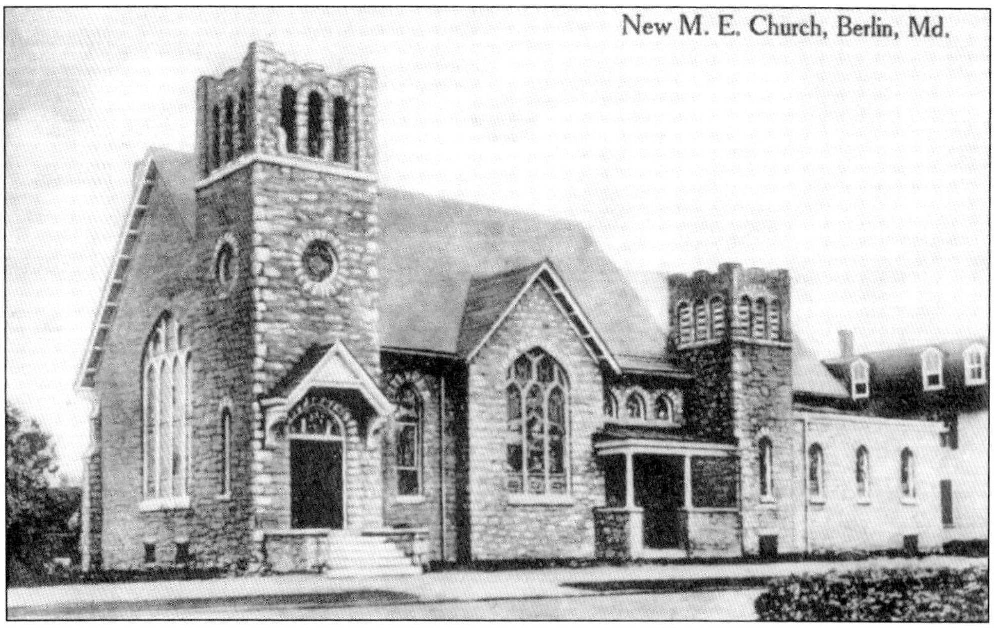


The Methodists first worshipped at Cedar Chapel, erected in 1835, near the Buckingham Cemetery. In 1847, a wooden structure was built on the land now occupied by the present church. It was named Stevenson Methodist Church to honor Edward Stevenson, who donated the land. This church burned, and the new church of Port Deposit granite was built in 1912, now named Stevenson United Methodist Church.

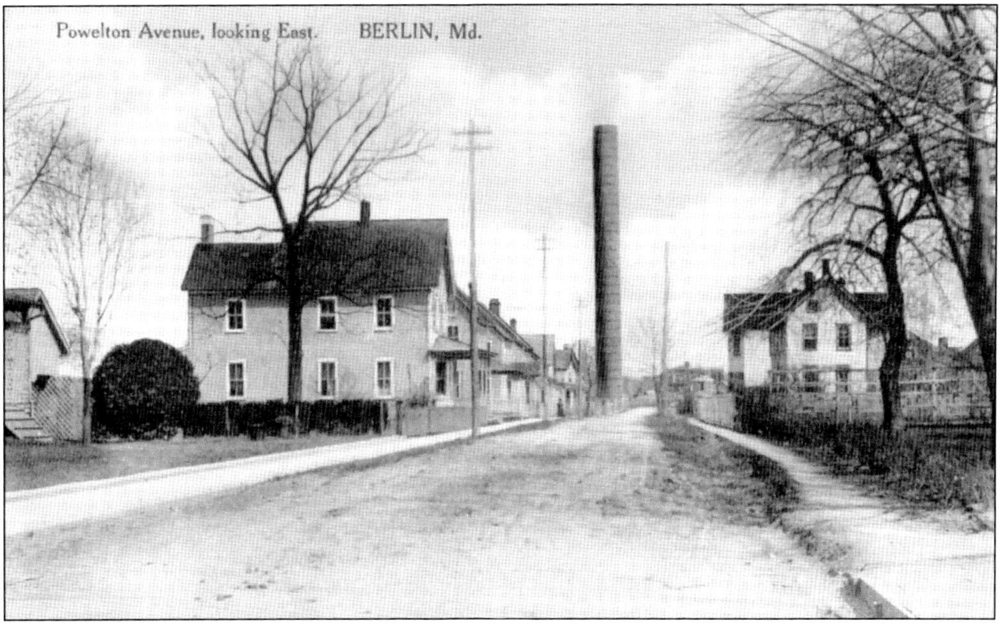


Powellton Avenue, one of the earlier streets in Berlin, ends in front of the Taylor Museum. It was the location of Berlin's first standpipe, erected in 1907 and seen in the middle of this photograph. Youngsters remember standing on the base and looking up. When the standpipe started to spin, so did they! It was dismantled in 1999. A piece of the stanchion is displayed in the gallery of the Taylor Museum. (Matthews Collection.)

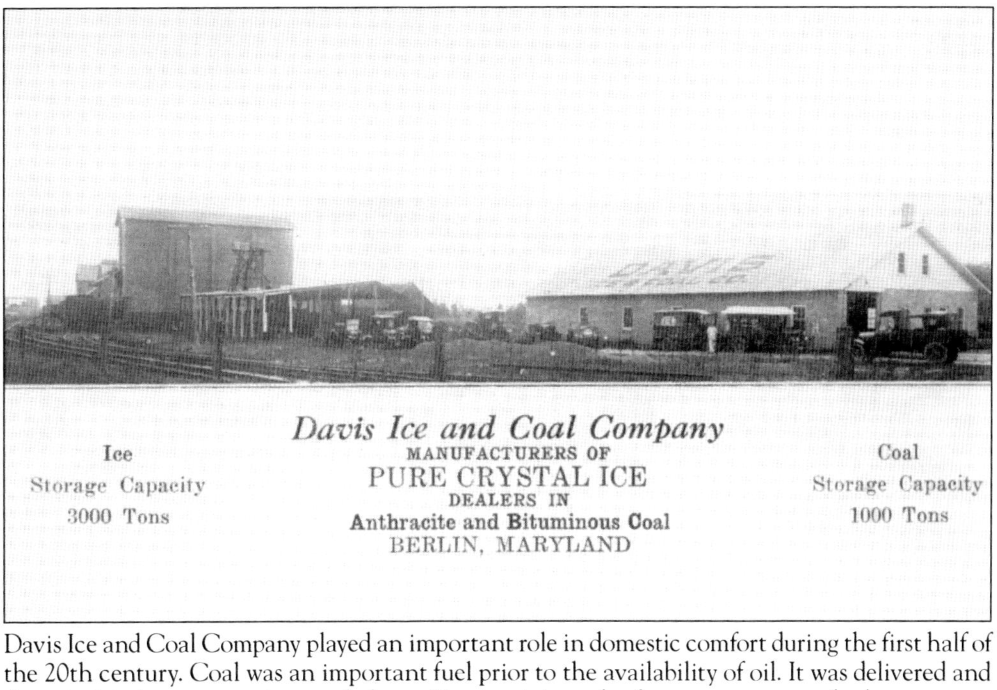


Davis Ice and Coal Company played an important role in domestic comfort during the first half of the 20th century. Coal was an important fuel prior to the availability of oil. It was delivered and deposited in basements via a coal chute. Getting it into the furnace was up to the homeowner. The ice was delivered in 30-pound blocks for use in iceboxes. Electric refrigerators were a thing of the future. Discarded ice-making forms were often used as trash incinerators.

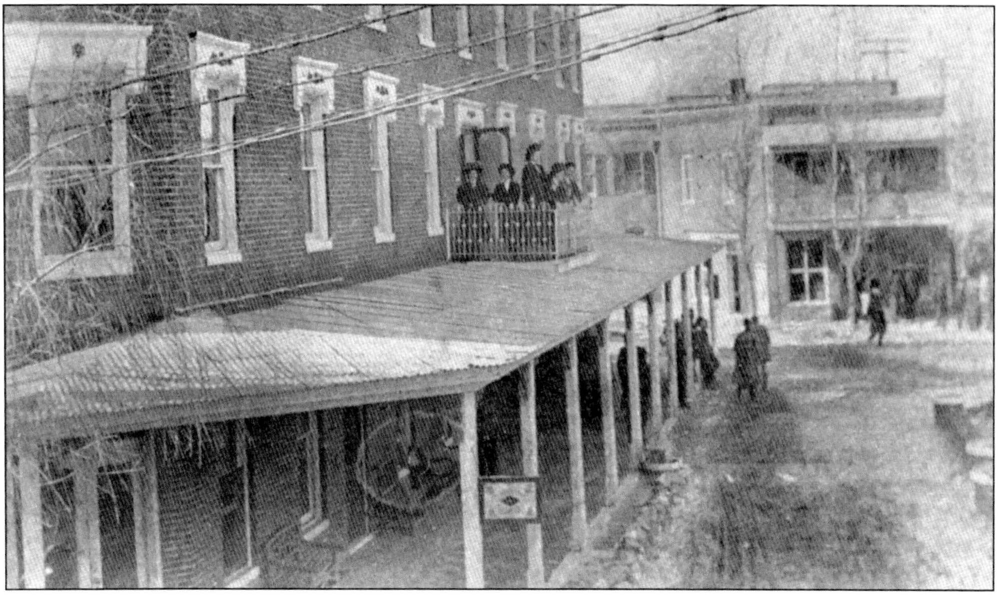

On March 2, 1908, Worcester County voted for Prohibition. This group of ladies standing on the small balcony of the Atlantic Hotel is reviewing the celebratory 1908 Temperance Day Parade on Main Street. At that time, prohibition of alcohol was by local option in Maryland counties. Public sentiment ran high. Voters were exhorted by local leaders, including Calvin B. Taylor, to vote against "evil alcohol." Taylor wrote, "continued indulgence in it tends to poverty, degradation, and crime, . . . entails on our descendants ignorance, dwarfed intellect, and moral degenerancy, . . . dissipates success, fortune, and virtue, . . . lowers the standard of civilization, and corrupts the ballot, . . . menaces liberty, . . . dulls our reason, observation and experience. All teach us that it is the greatest evil." Although demon rum was soundly defeated in the county-wide election, there were plenty of bootleggers in and around town. One local doctor said he had never written as many prescriptions in a life-long practice as he wrote for whiskey.

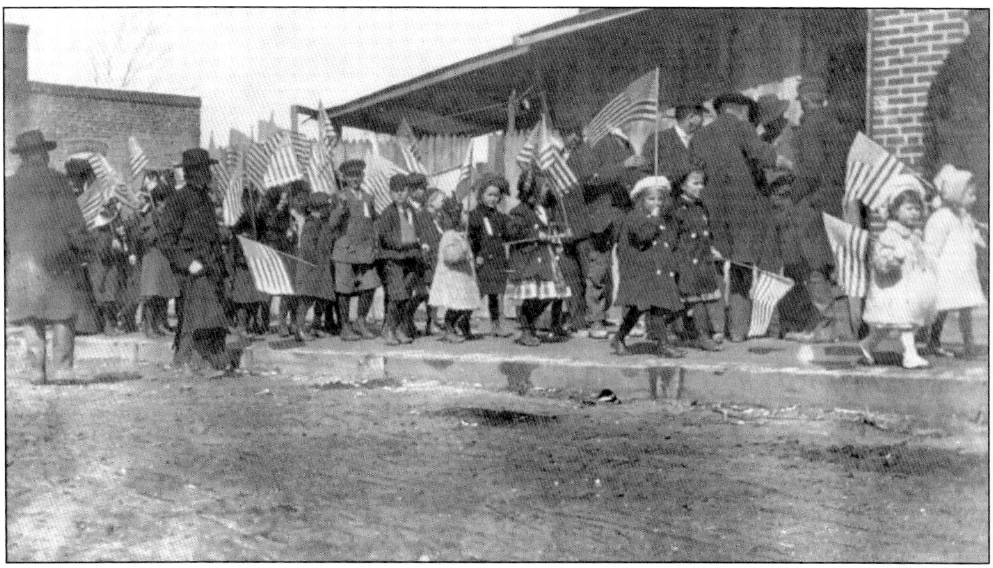

On March 14, 1908, children carrying American flags showed their approval of county Prohibition, as they marched in a temperance parade. (Ellis Wainwright Collection.)

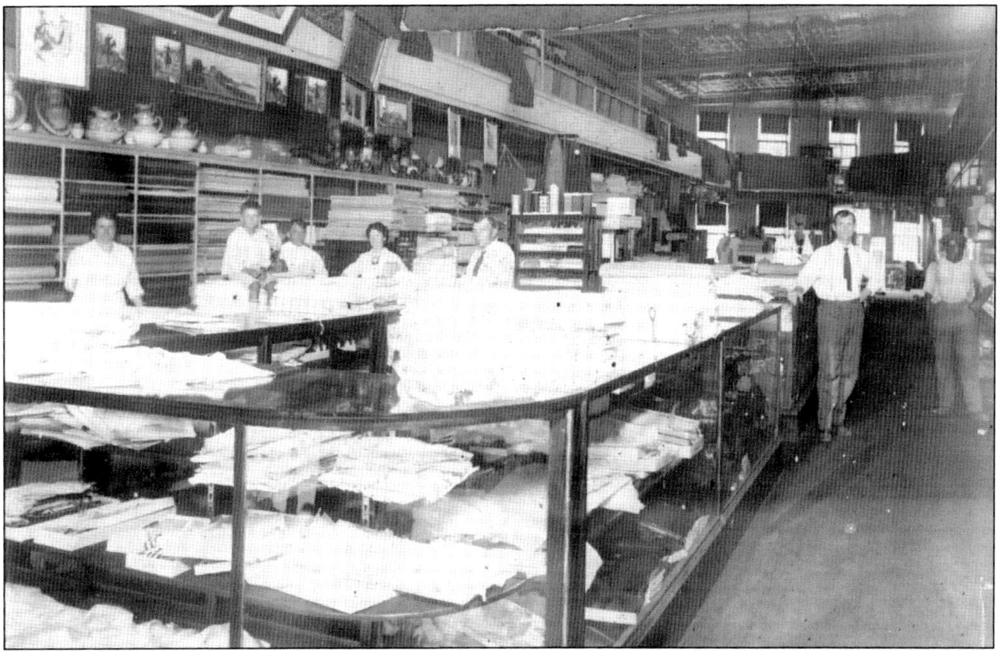

A 1920 advertisement for Burbage, Powell and Company called it the "biggest store in Worcester County . . . where you can get everything from a cambric needle to a cookstove." Women's clothing and goods were on the left side, men's items on the right. This *c.* 1915 photograph, above, shows two of the early owners, Kendall Jarvis, behind the counter, and Ernest Burbage, with his hand on the counter. Note the tin ceiling and the items for sale: wash bowls and pitchers, lamps, pictures, and textiles. It is now incorporated into the Taylor Bank offices on North Main Street. An early photograph of the exterior of Burbage, Powell and Company is shown below. (Below, Ellis Wainwright Collection.)

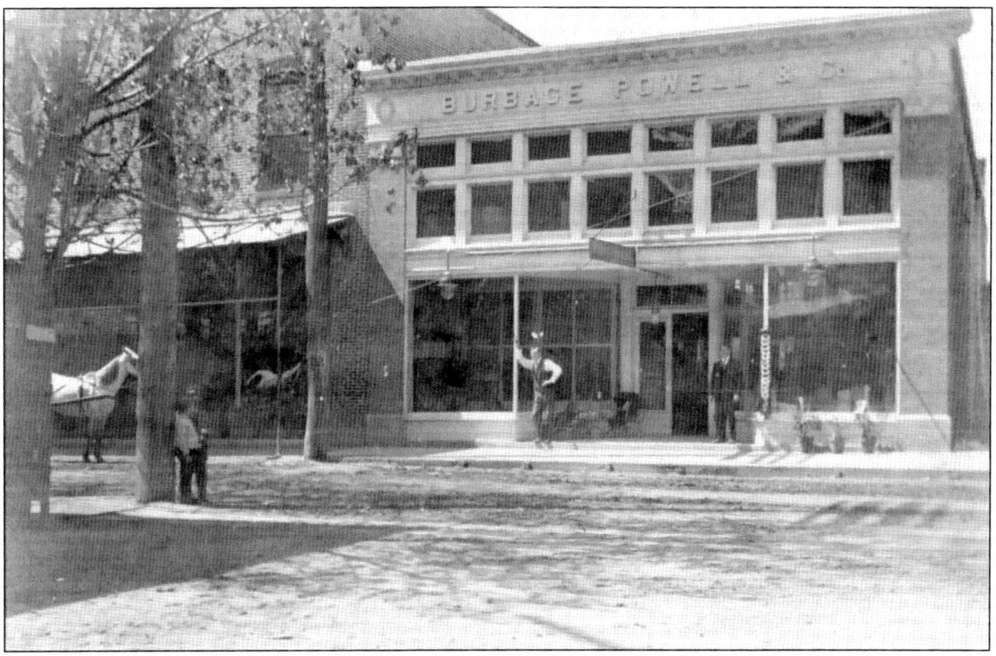

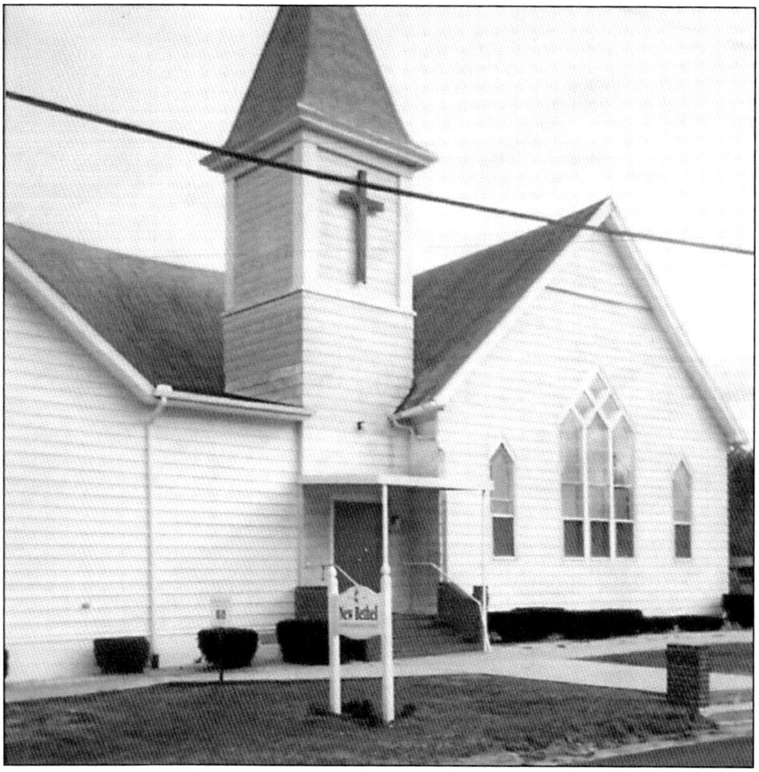


Many early African American congregations were Methodists because of that faith's strong anti-slavery stance. One of the oldest African American congregations, New Bethel Methodist Church, is located in Germantown, southeast of Berlin. Organized in 1855 by a group of free families, New Bethel Methodists were formerly members of the Stevenson Methodist Episcopal Church.

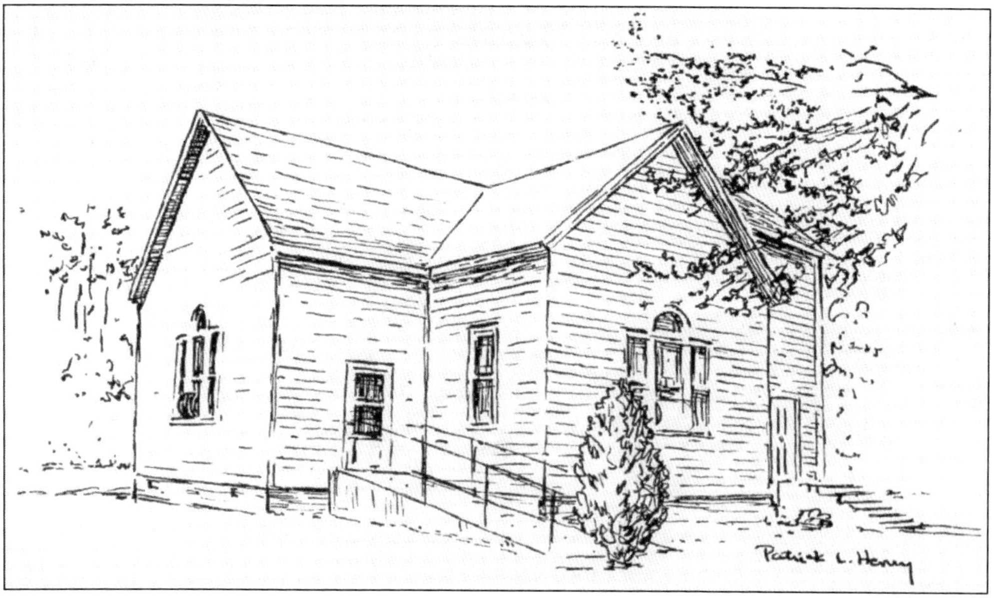


Tyree African Methodist Episcopal Church was organized on March 16, 1913, at the home of Peter Tindley by Rev. Robert Williams and a group led by George and Peter Tindley, E. B. Smack, and Isma Ayres. Meetings were held at the home of Isma Ayres until a pavilion was built in June 1913 to hold the worship service. The cornerstone for a new church building on Germantown Road was laid in October 1915. On November 15, 1915, the church was dedicated by its namesake, Bishop Evans Tyree, then bishop of the Philadelphia Conference. (Drawing by Patrick L. Henry.)

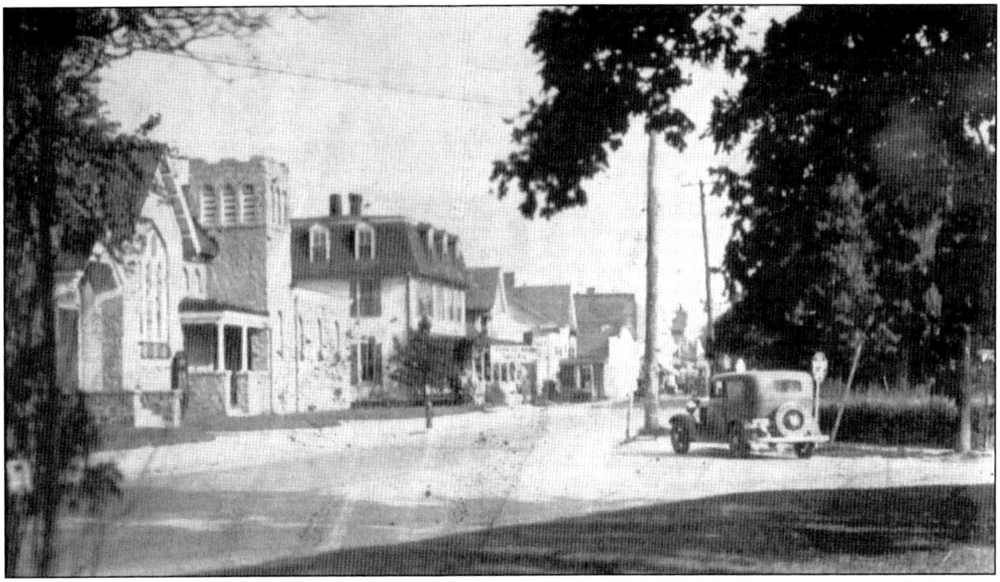

Main Street, looking south from the Taylor Museum property, shows the Stevenson Methodist Church, the Majestic Hotel, and two houses. The Majestic Hotel lot and the lots of the two houses are now parking lots. The brick building farther on now houses Town Center Antiques II. (Ellis Wainwright Collection.)

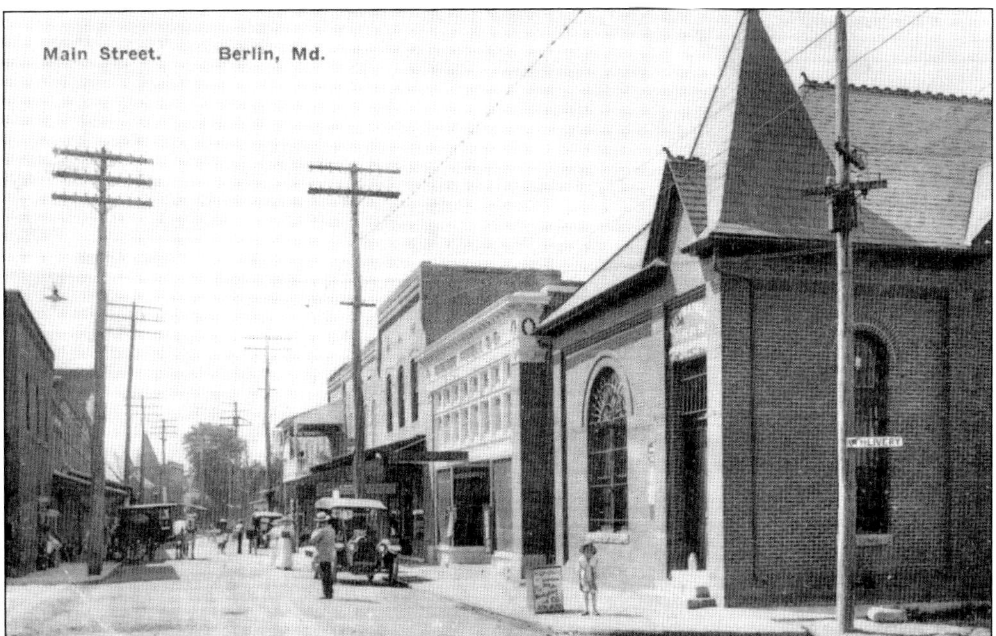


From left to right, beginning at the Calvin B. Taylor Bank, the stores on Main Street are Burbage, Powell and Company, now part of the Taylor Bank, and William's Five and Dime, now the Treasure Chest. Through the years, many business have conducted their trade in the storefronts leading south to Rayne's Reef. (Matthews Collection.)

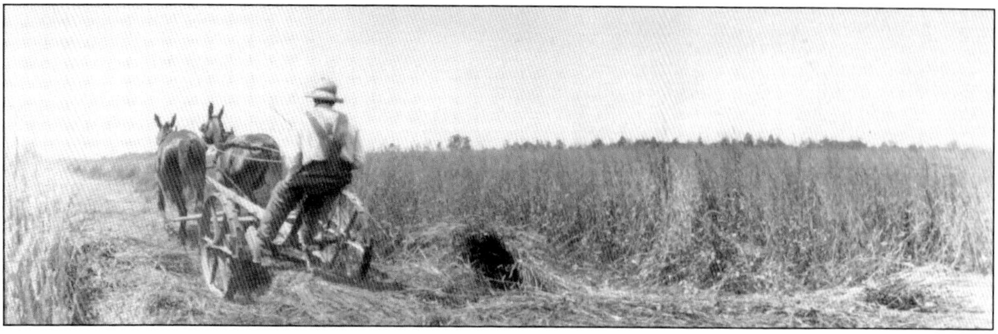

Berlin can be called an agricultural community with its farmlands, truck farms, orchards, dairies, mills, and later the chicken industry. This farmer with his mule team, above, is cutting timothy hay; the strawberry pickers, below, are standing with their pickings for the day. They were paid by the quart. The Maryland Strawberry Pickers is a *Berlin Advance* postcard. (Below, Matthews Collection.)

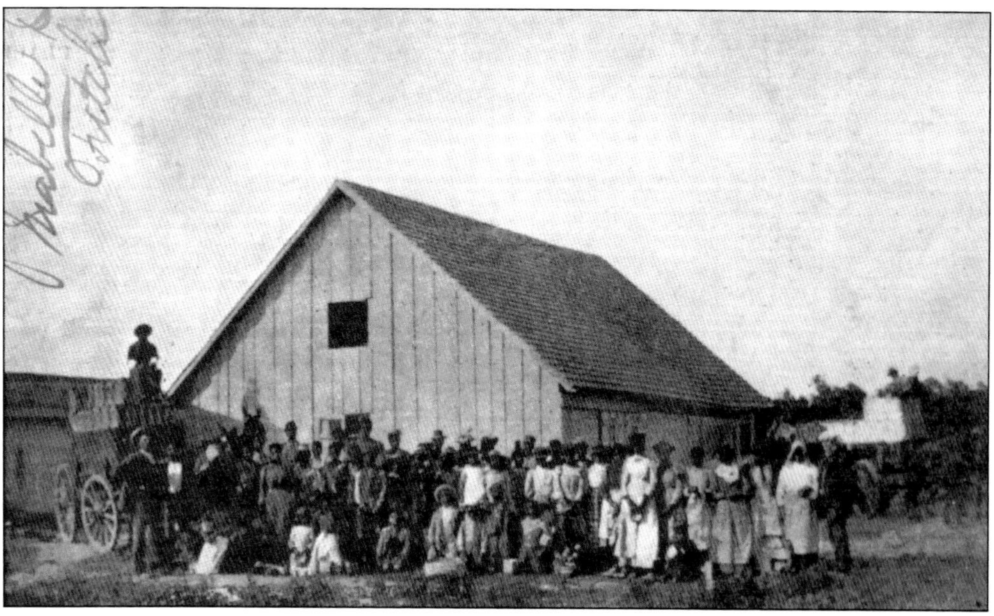

# *Four*

# "Attractive and Active"

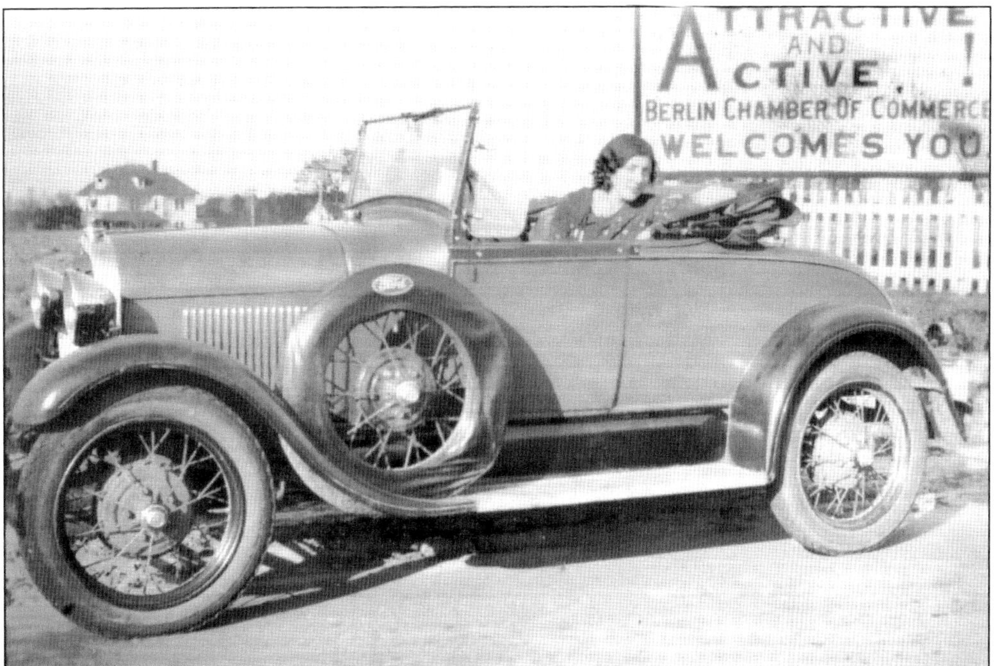


Anna Louise Brittingham Taylor shows off the town's slogan as she sits in her 1931 roadster. The Berlin Chamber of Commerce adopted the slogan "Attractive and Active" in 1924. (E. Dean Richardson Collection.)

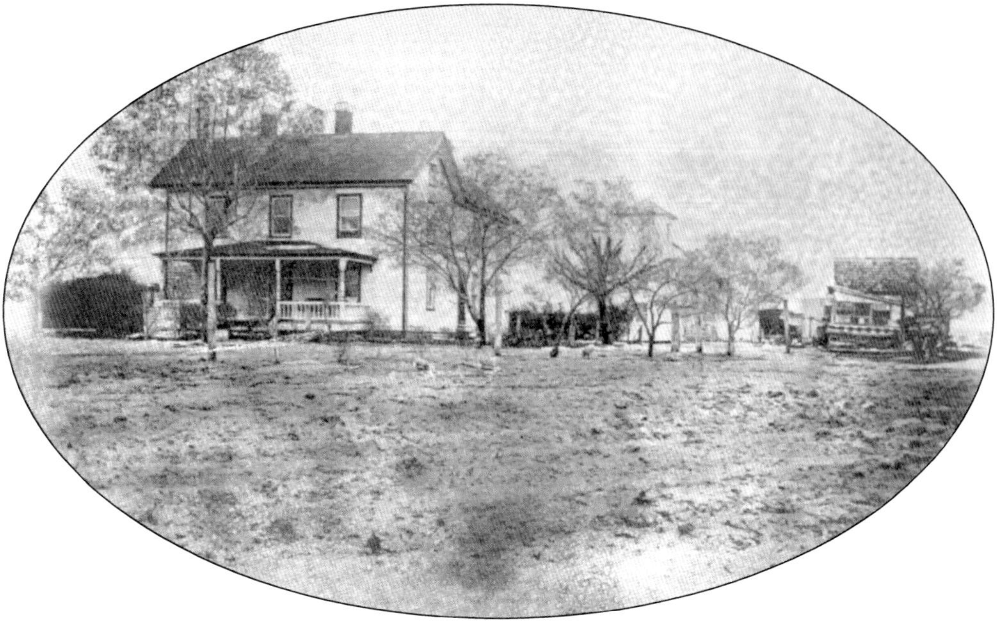

Pictured above is the Esham's Dairies farm, located on property now occupied by the Atlantic General Hospital and the Berlin Nursing Home. A mural in the lobby of the hospital depicts this farm. For many years, Esham's served the town with their milk. On freezing mornings, youngsters eagerly awaited when moms would let them go out to get the milk. The frozen cream stood up straight from the bottle, cap still on; it tasted just like ice cream.

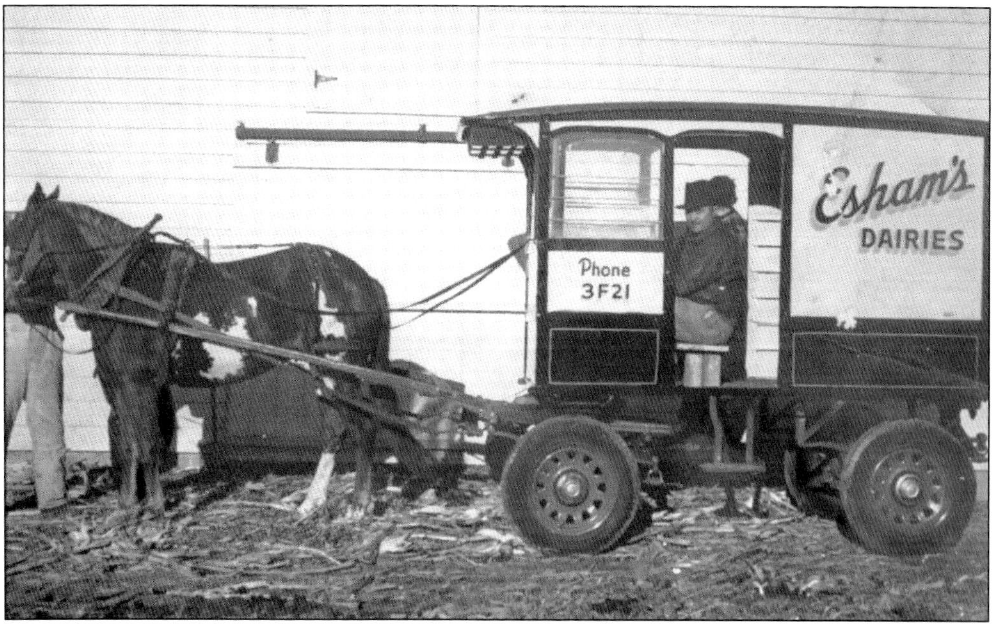


This is one of Esham's Dairies' milk wagons that delivered Berlin's milk. The wagons had mostly retired when World War II began. They were brought back into service to assist with the requirement for gas rationing. Note the four-digit telephone number on the side of the wagon; the F in the number indicates that it was on a party line, meaning the line had at least three subscribers. Most county lines were party lines.

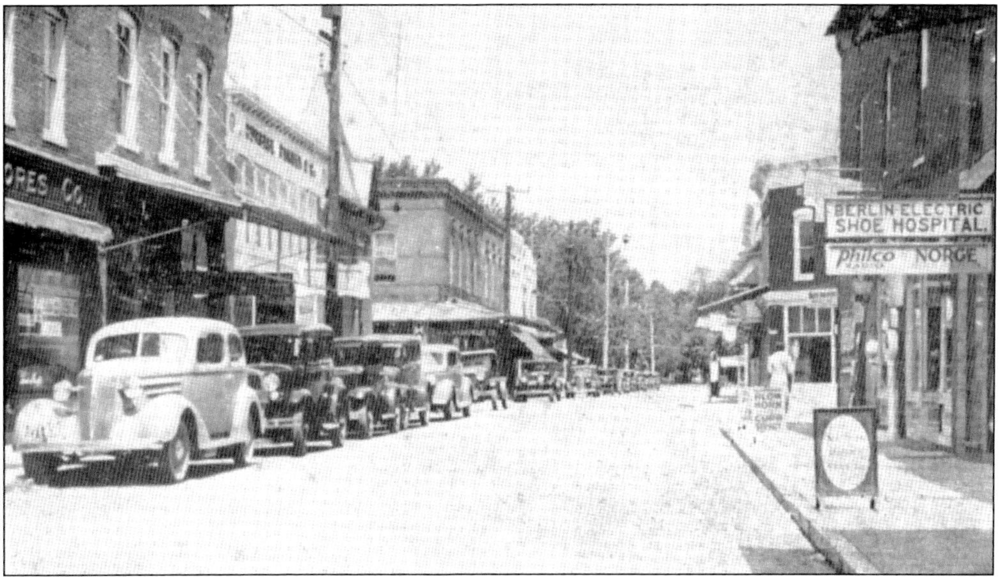


Main Street looking north shows much of the town as it looked in the late 1920s and the early 1930s. The Acme Stores Company; William's Five and Dime; Burbage, Powell and Company; Calvin B. Taylor Bank; and Purnell's Hardware Store are prominent on the left. The right side of the street shows the Berlin Electric Shoe Hospital and Esham's Soda Fountain, which suggests that customers "Blow horn for curb service." Esham's was another popular gathering place in the center of town. (Matthews Collection.)

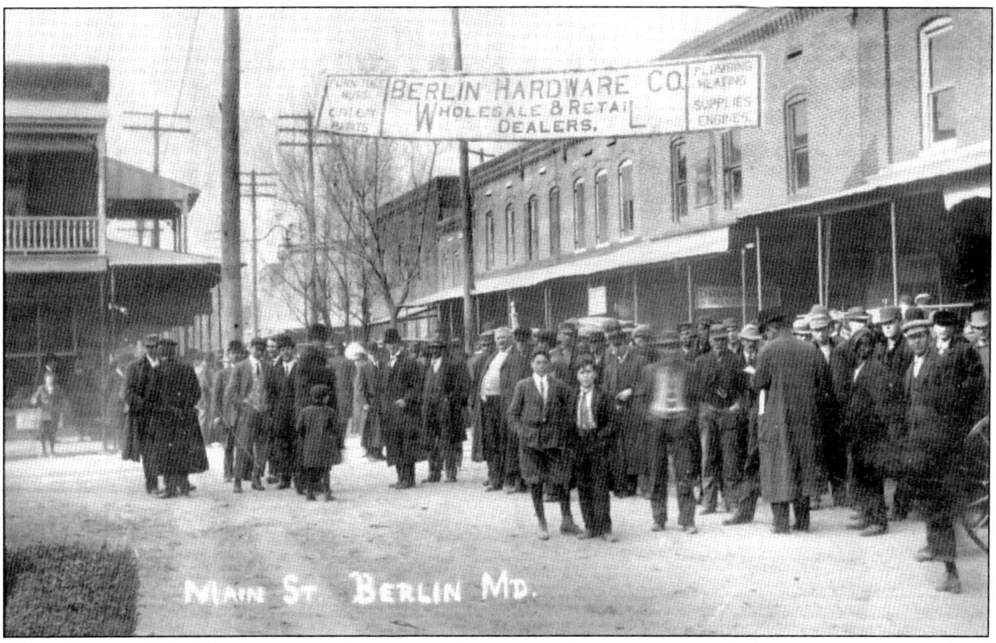


A large crowd of men stands at the corner of Main and Broad Streets. Their purpose is unclear, perhaps a small convention, or since there are no ladies present, it may have been an election. The sign overhead advertises the "Berlin Hardware Store, Wholesale Retail Dealers—Furniture, Rugs, Cutlery, Paints—Plumbing, Heating Supplies, Engines." It has been speculated that Berlin Hardware was located in that area of Main Street at that time. (Ellis Wainwright Collection.)

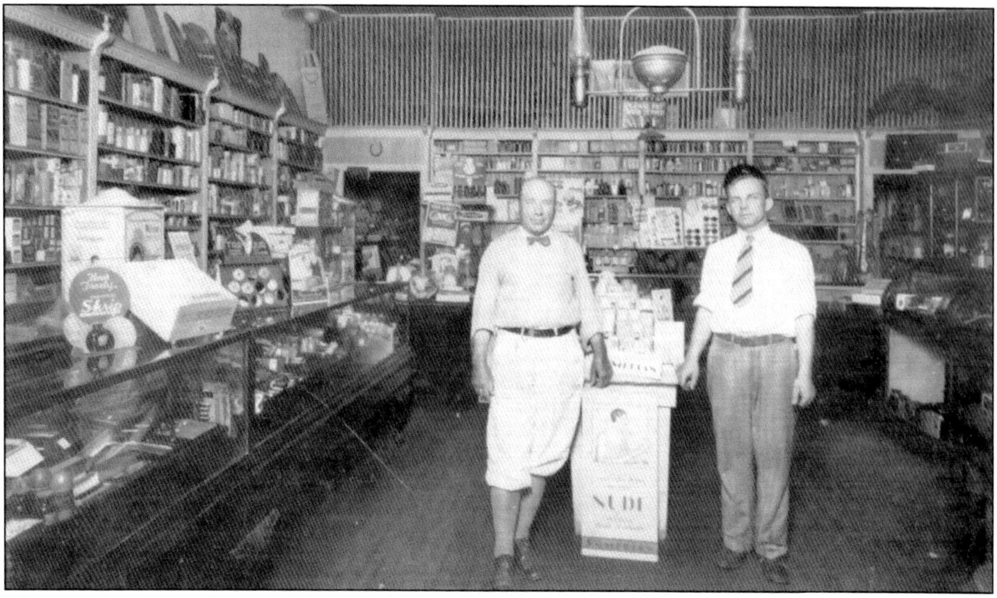

This 1926 interior photograph of Farlow's Pharmacy, then located across Main Street from the Atlantic Hotel, pictures John H. Farlow, left, who opened this drugstore in 1910. His nephew, Bill Farlow, right, ran the business after his uncle's death in 1928 until 1947. Through the ensuing years, ownership of Farlow's passed to Dr. Webster Seward, Walt Savage, Phil Lindeman, Bennett Bozman, and finally J. E. Parker, who operated the pharmacy from 1976 until its closing. (Parker Family Collection.)

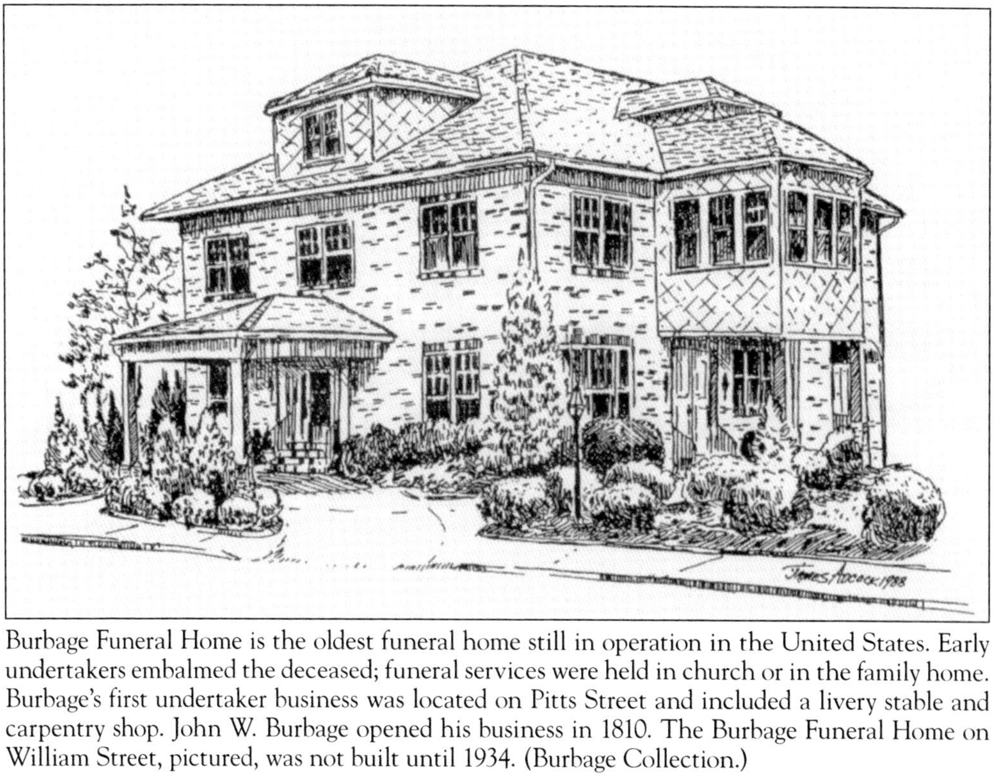

Burbage Funeral Home is the oldest funeral home still in operation in the United States. Early undertakers embalmed the deceased; funeral services were held in church or in the family home. Burbage's first undertaker business was located on Pitts Street and included a livery stable and carpentry shop. John W. Burbage opened his business in 1810. The Burbage Funeral Home on William Street, pictured, was not built until 1934. (Burbage Collection.)

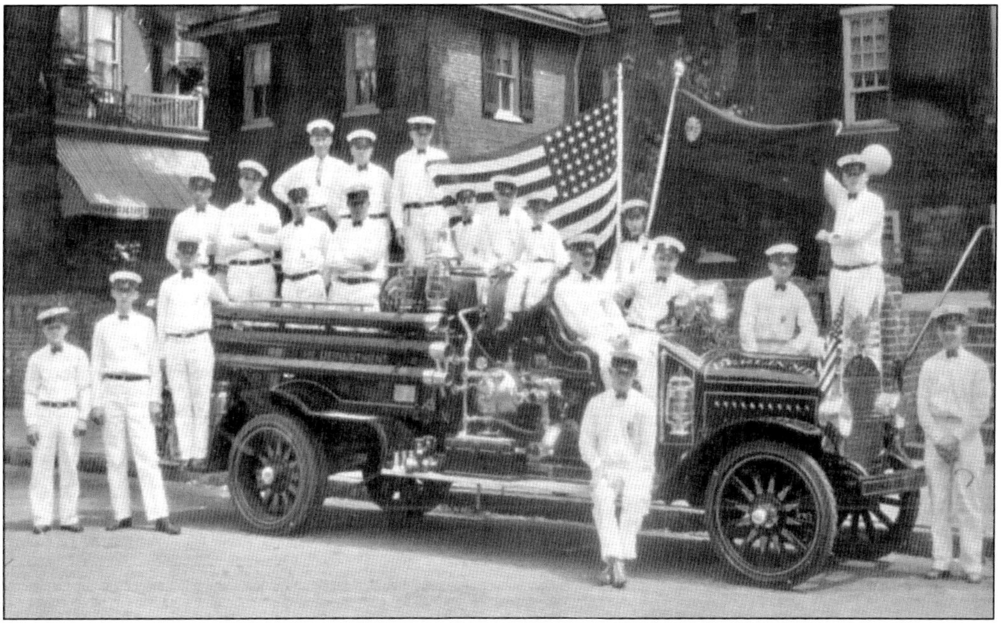

"Berlin's Ole Mack," a 1924 Mack AB-3 chemical pumper-type fire engine was purchased on December 9, 1924, with proceeds from fund-raising carnivals. This photograph of "Ole Mack" was taken in Annapolis in June 1927. Retired in 1954, the chain-driven truck has been fully restored with all its standard equipment, including wooden wheels, hard rubber tires, and the original bell, and is now used in parades and special events.

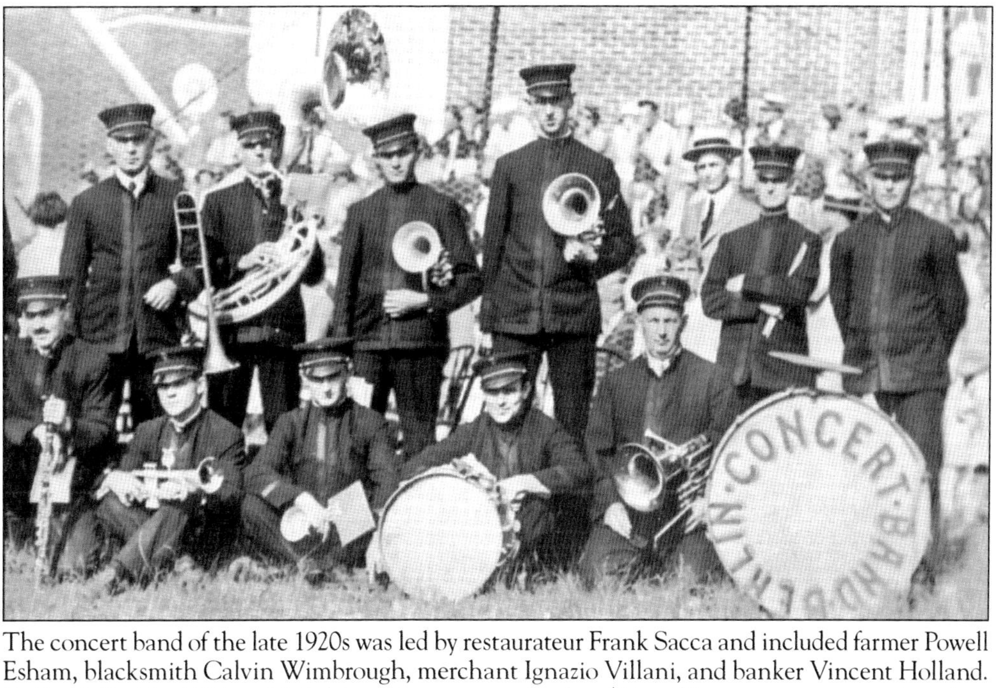


The concert band of the late 1920s was led by restaurateur Frank Sacca and included farmer Powell Esham, blacksmith Calvin Wimbrough, merchant Ignazio Villani, and banker Vincent Holland. Holland died in 2002 and left his entire estate valued at $15 million to community churches, the hospital, and charitable organizations. There was also a town African American band led by Sam Houston Showell, which performed its first concert in 1910 on Thanksgiving Day.

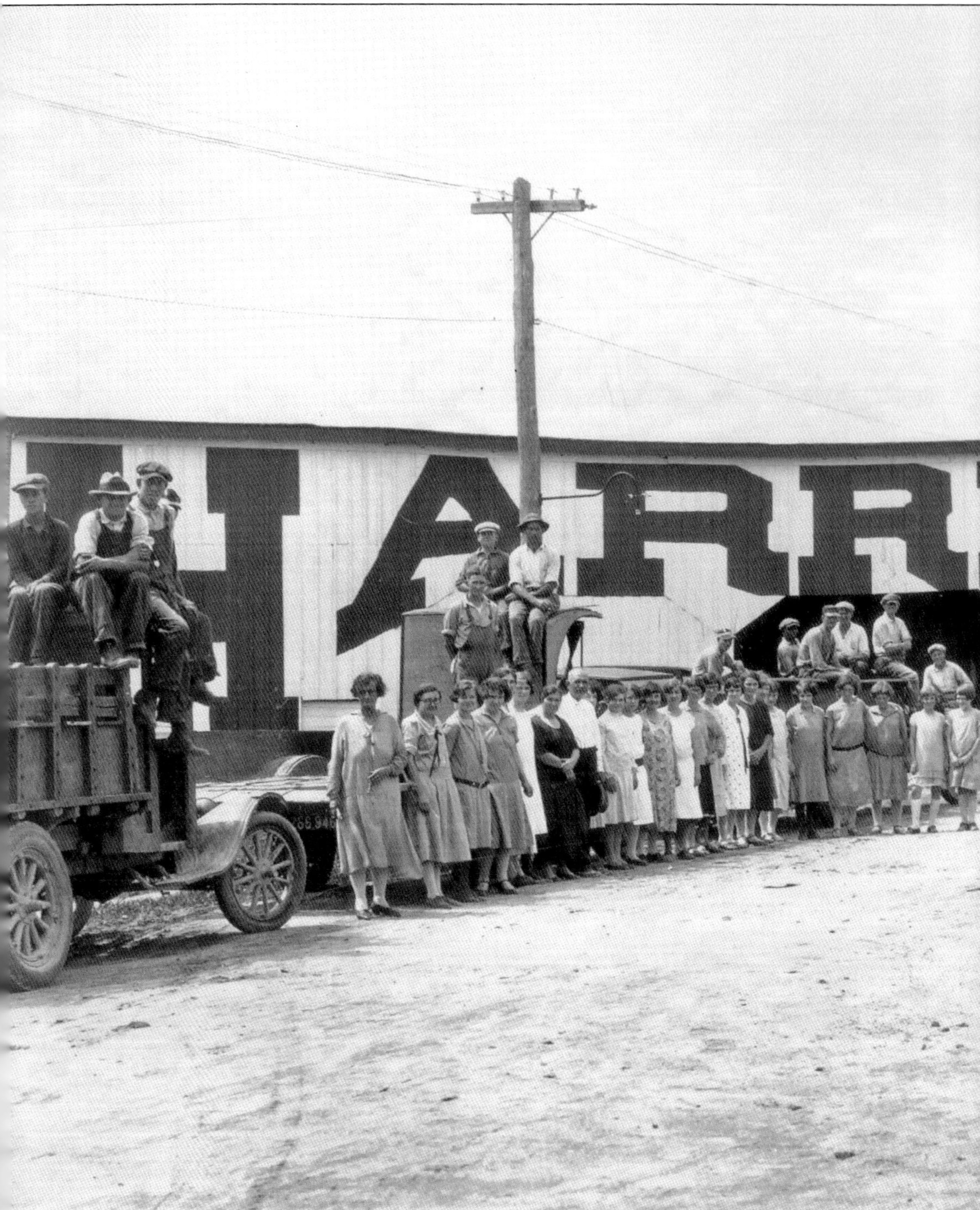


Harrison's Nurseries was started in 1884 by Joseph George Harrison on the Home Farm, now the site of Stephen Decatur High School on U.S. Route 50, east of Berlin. It began when the family decided that in addition to growing peach trees for the peaches, they would grow trees for selling, thus establishing the J. G. Harrison Nurseries. Other trees and fruits were added. In

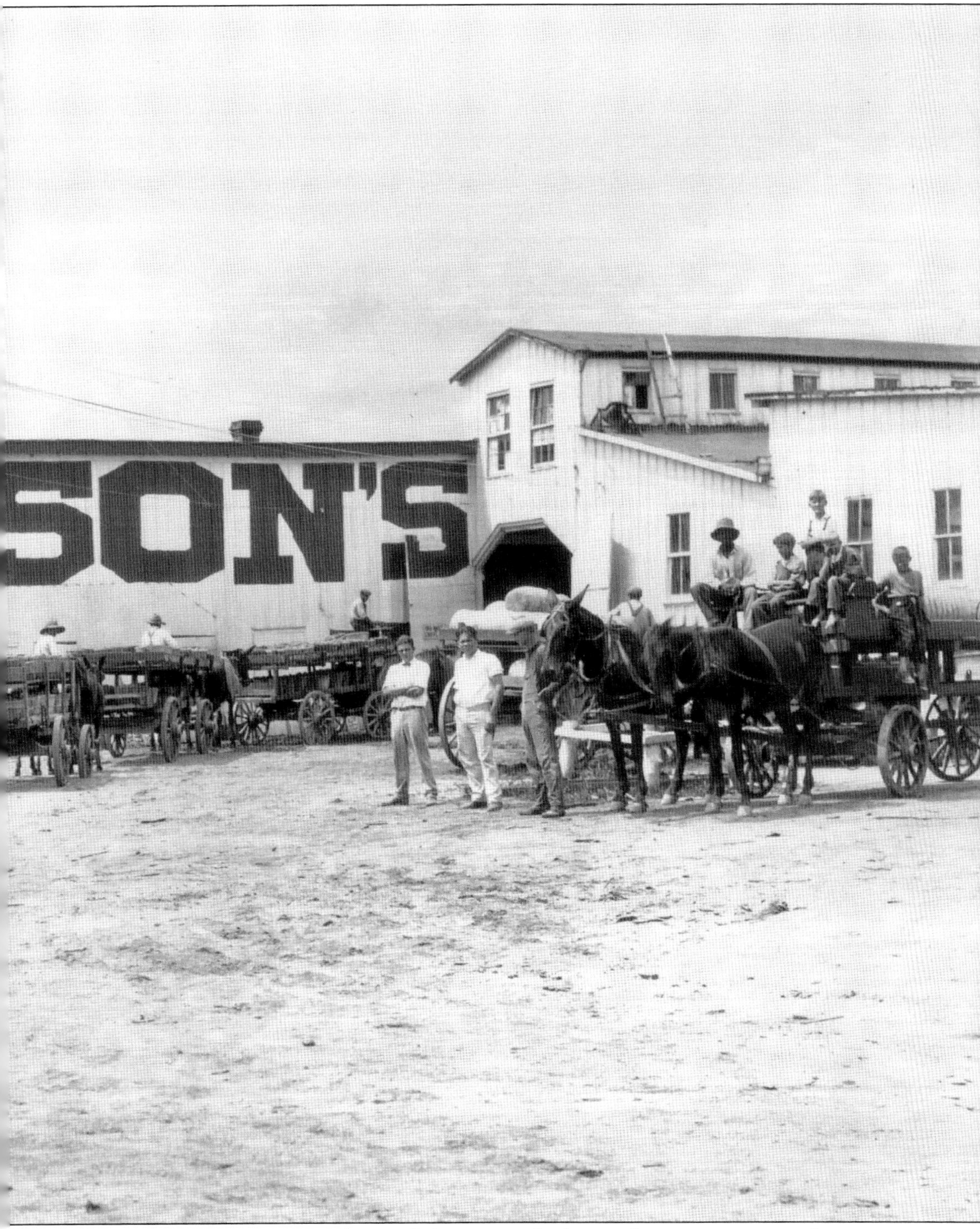


the 1920s, Harrison's Nurseries advertised that it was the largest fruit tree nursery and nursery catalog business in the United States. Although the Great August Storm of 1933 diminished the output of the business, Harrison's Nurseries operated until 1962. In this photograph, employees of Harrison's Nurseries stand in front of the long shed.

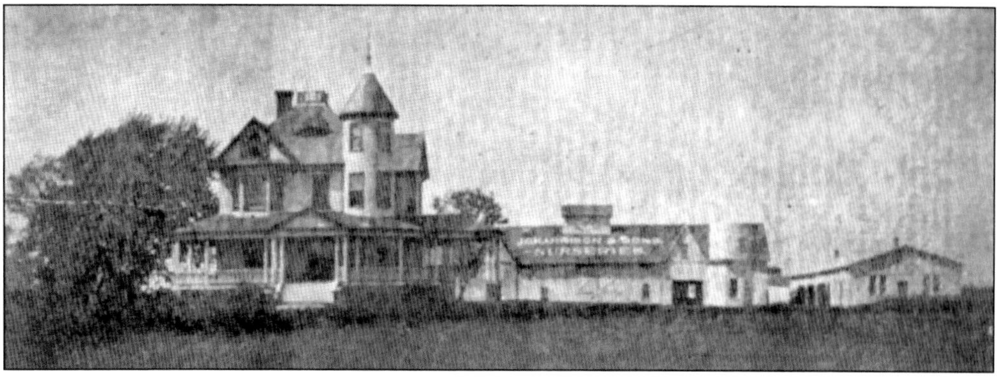

Pictured above is the Harrison home in Berlin. Shown below is one of their fruit stands with the sign announcing "Fruit for Sale—Harrisons' Nurseries." Although all types of peaches were grown on the nurseries, one of the most popular peaches was the Hale, named for one of the Harrison brothers, G. Hale Harrison. This is the peach for which Berlin was named Hale, Maryland, in *Runaway Bride*. The wagon delivering fruit to the stand is shown on the right. A customer is buying some of Harrison's delicious fruit. (Above, Ellis Wainwright Collection.)

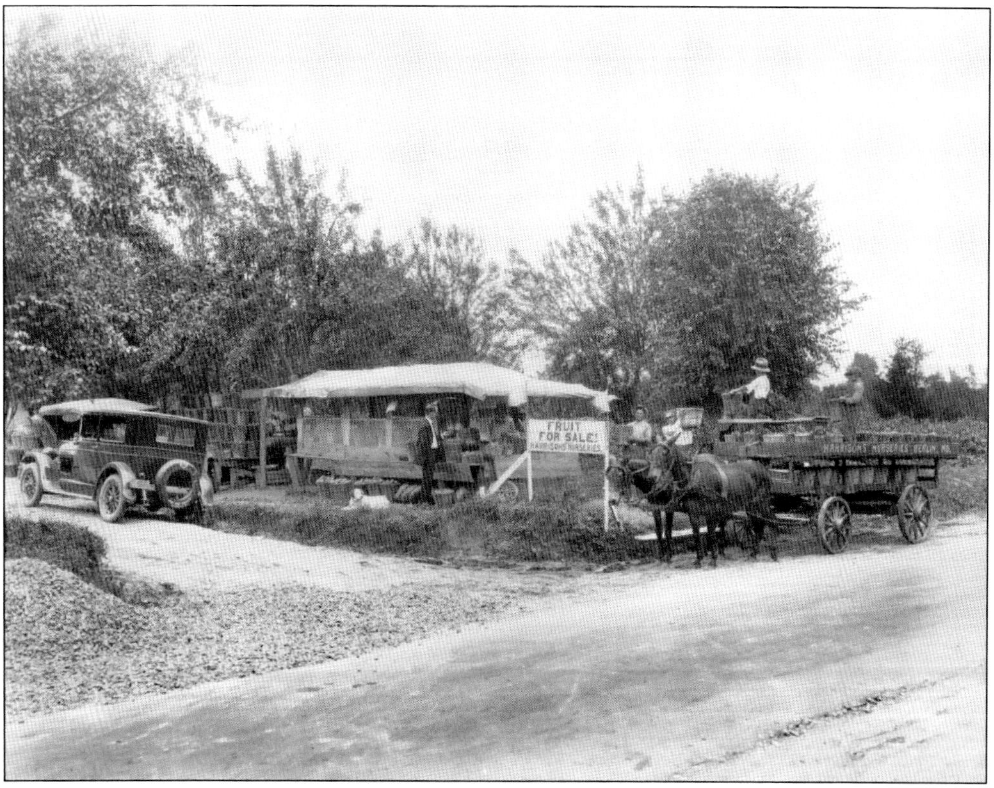

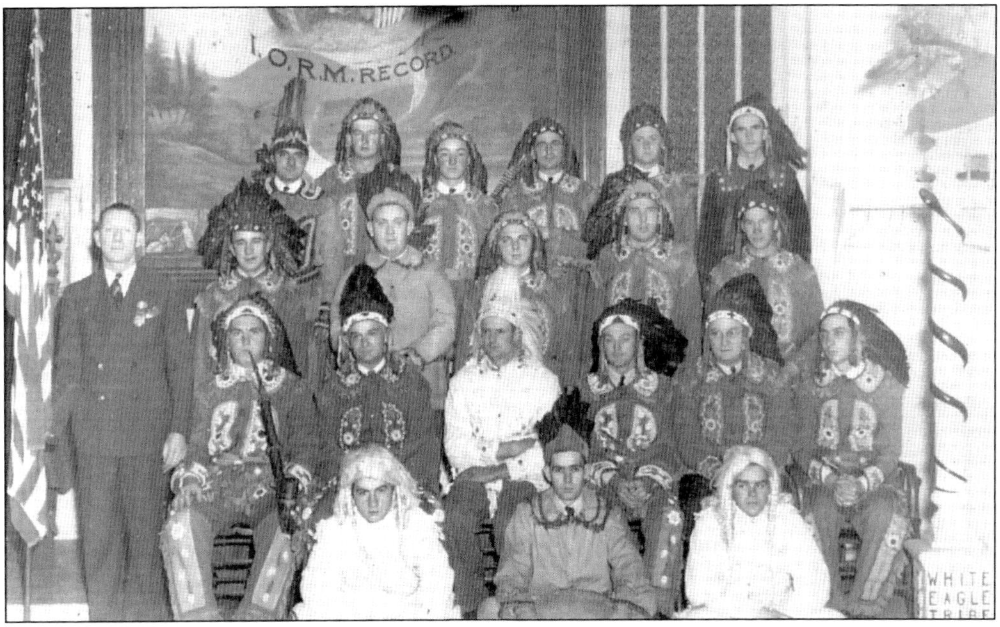


The Red Men, one of many organizations that flourished during the first half of the 20th century, met at the Odd Fellows Hall, where this photograph was taken in the 1940s. The White Eagle Tribe Improved Order of Red Men 101 are, from left to right, (first row) Johnna Davis, Colie Watts, and Irving McCabe; (second row) D. Howard Holsten (standing), Calvin Quillen, Thomas Taylor, Melvin Parker, John T. Bruehl, Calvin Cropper, and Herman Baker; (third row) Arthur Cathell, Everet Shockley, Billy Williams, Billy Purnell, and John Alvah Taylor; (fourth row) Angelo Villani, Bill Cropper, Edwin Jones, Harry Mitchell, Robert Cropper, and Lee Warren.

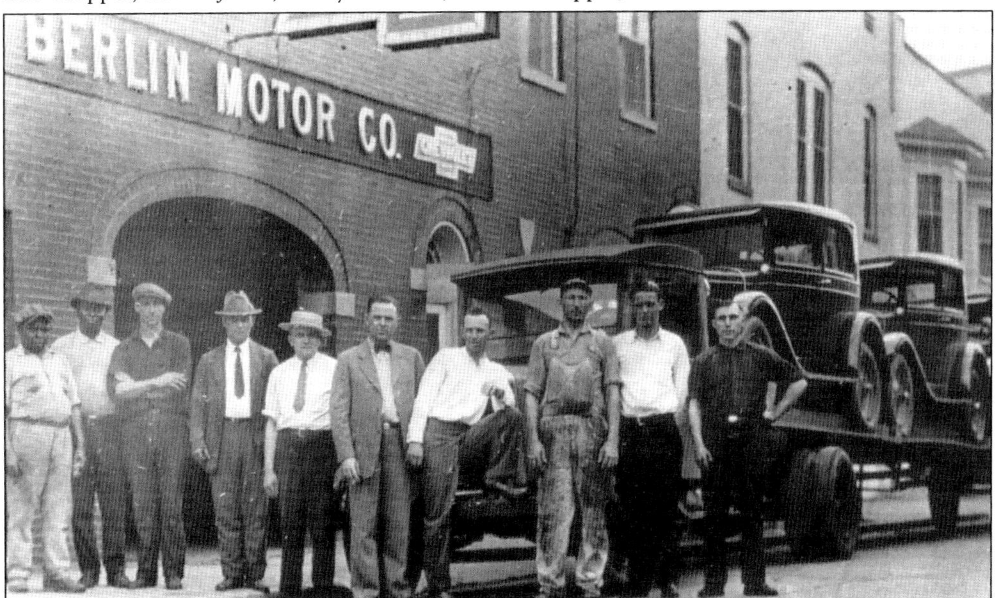


Employees of the Berlin Motor Company line up with a load of 1929 Chevrolets on their car carrier. Berlin Motor Company was situated on the property now occupied by Town Center Antiques II on North Main Street. (Matthews Collection.)

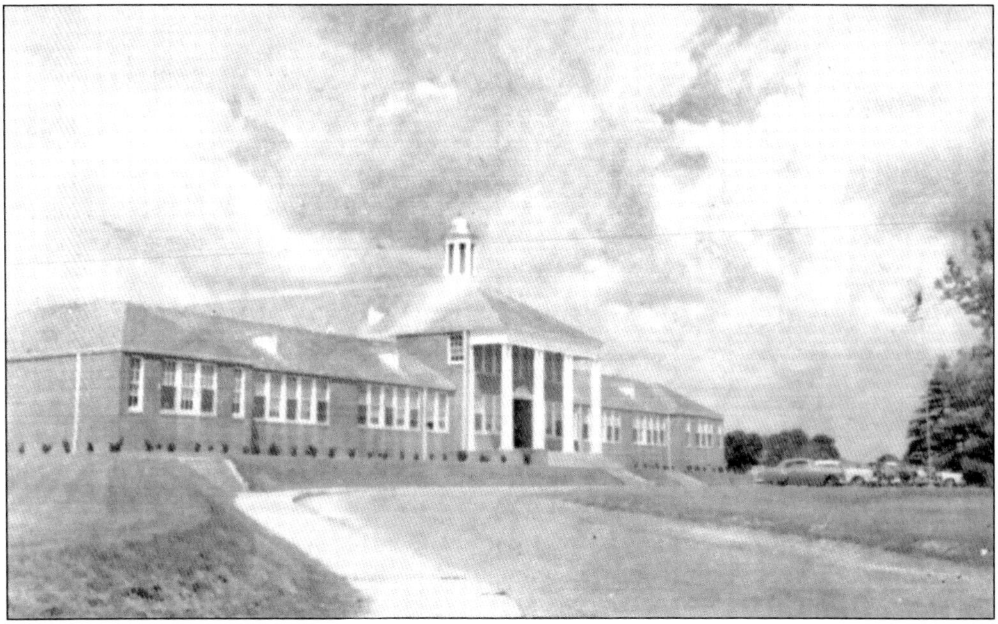

In 1930, Buckingham High School was built on South Main Street, serving grades 6–11 until 1942, then all grades until 1954 when Stephen Decatur High School opened. Buckingham then served as an elementary school until it was demolished in 1978; the distinctive cupola was preserved and sits in front of the old school site. The new Buckingham Elementary School, built slightly to the south, opened that year. Flower Street School served the African American population until its students began attending Buckingham and Stephen Decatur. Worcester Country School, the region's independent school, opened in 1970, changing its name to Worcester Preparatory School in 1999 to reflect its college preparatory mission. Below, Buckingham's 1946 May Day Court is comprised of a prince and princess from each junior and senior homeroom and later a couple chosen from each grade. Note the photographers at the base of the knoll. (Above, Mabel Rogers Collection.)

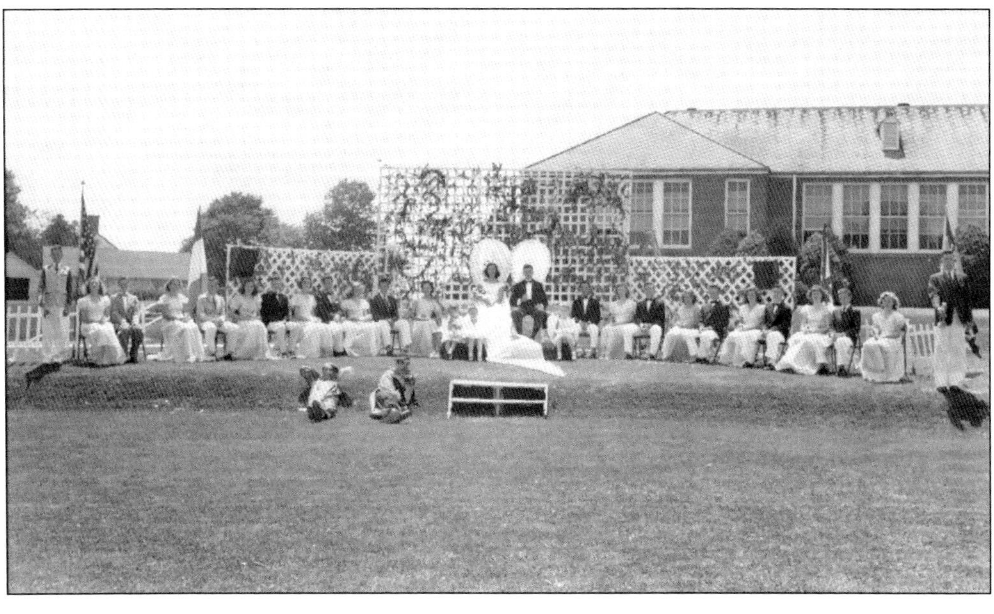

# *Five*

# "MODERN IN CIVIC GROWTH"

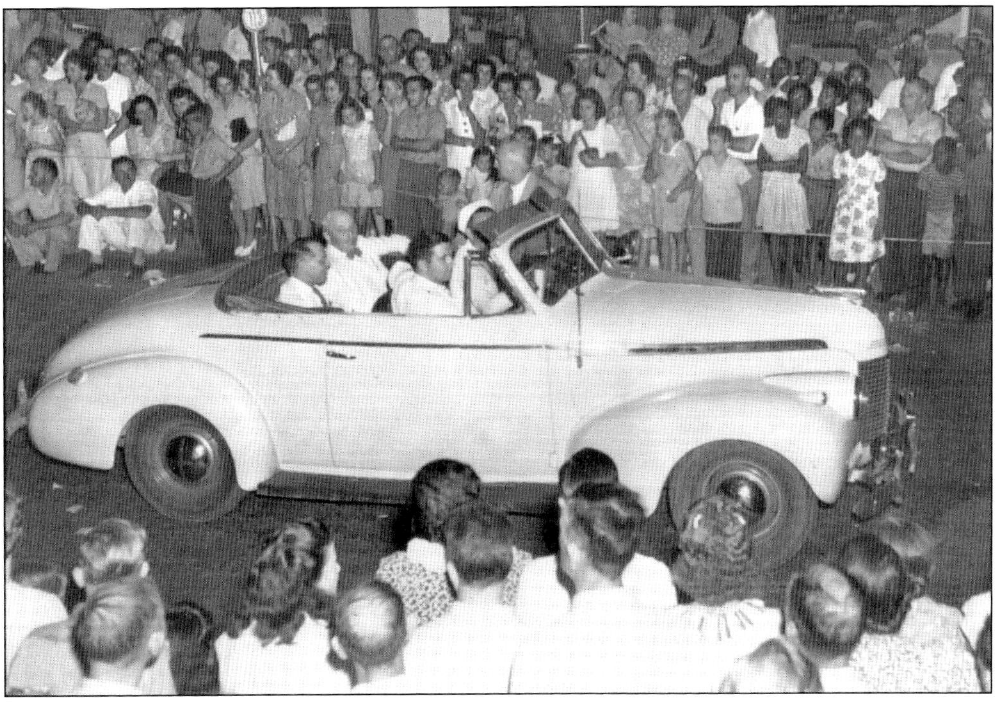

The townspeople of Berlin rode in cars like this pre–World War II convertible in the postwar era. This car was in the VE Day parade, appropriately leading Berliners into an era of prosperity, exemplified by the town slogan of the time, "Modern in Civic Growth." Riding in the backseat behind the driver is Mayor William Whaley; G. Hale Harrison is to his right.

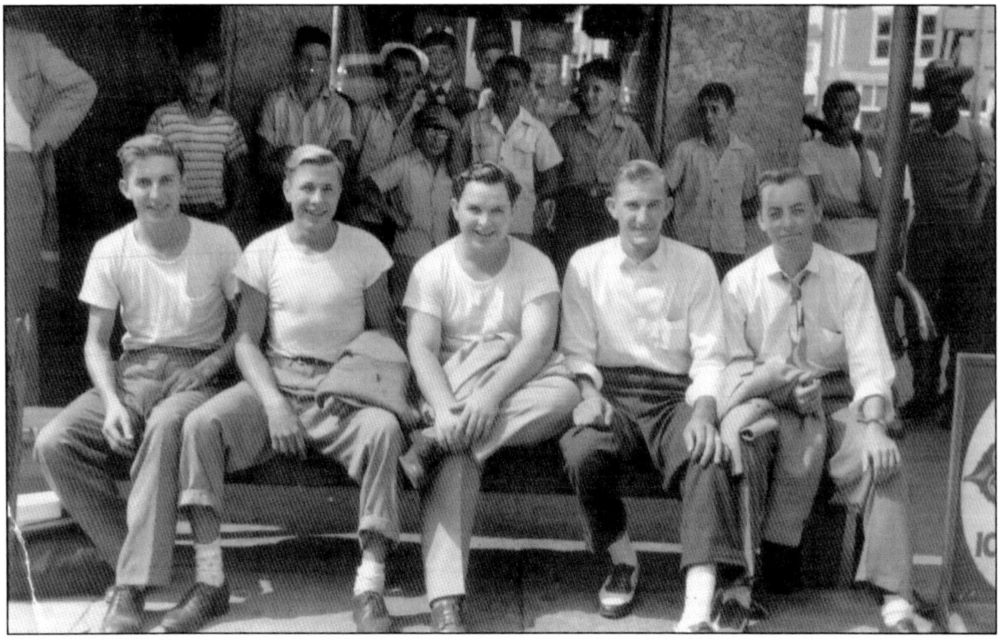

These boys are "sitting in front of Rayne's Corner Store, Berlin, Md, awaiting the bus to take us to Baltimore, we were all draftees, August 1943," according to the caption written by Tommy Mumford on the back of this snapshot. The draftees were Ellsworth Merritt, Mumford, John Walter Bishop, Clifton Gray, and George Godfrey. Mumford flew TBF Avengers from the deck of the carrier USS *Bismarck Sea* off Iwo Jima and survived its sinking.

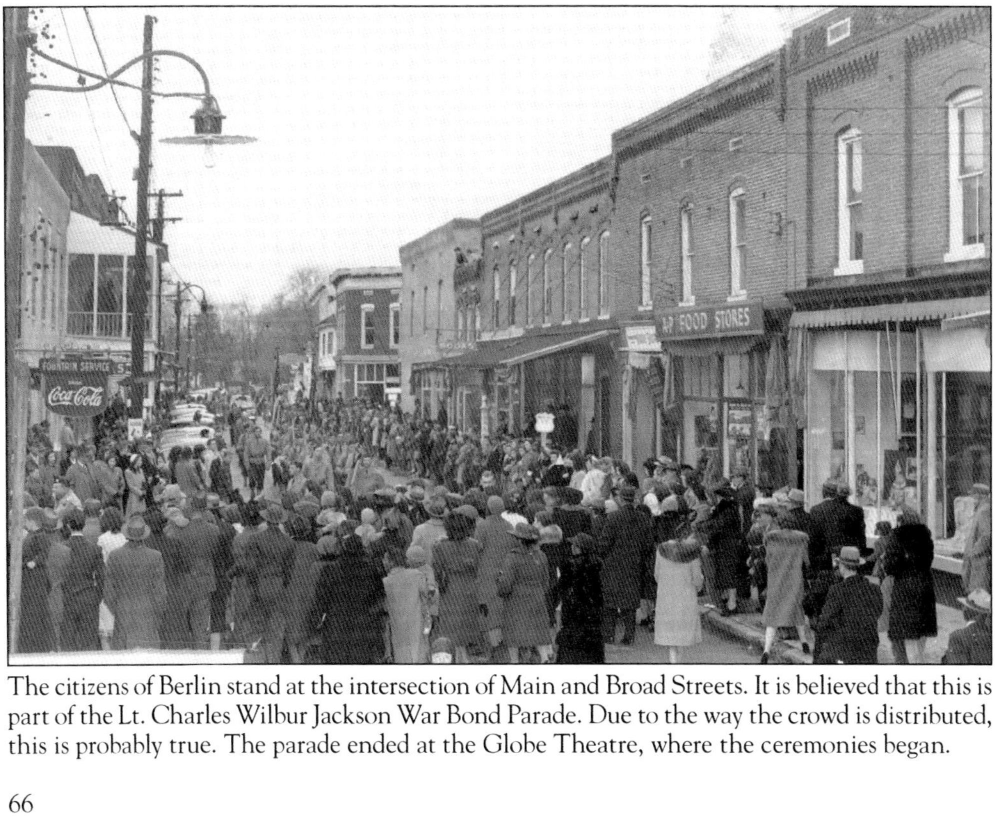


The citizens of Berlin stand at the intersection of Main and Broad Streets. It is believed that this is part of the Lt. Charles Wilbur Jackson War Bond Parade. Due to the way the crowd is distributed, this is probably true. The parade ended at the Globe Theatre, where the ceremonies began.

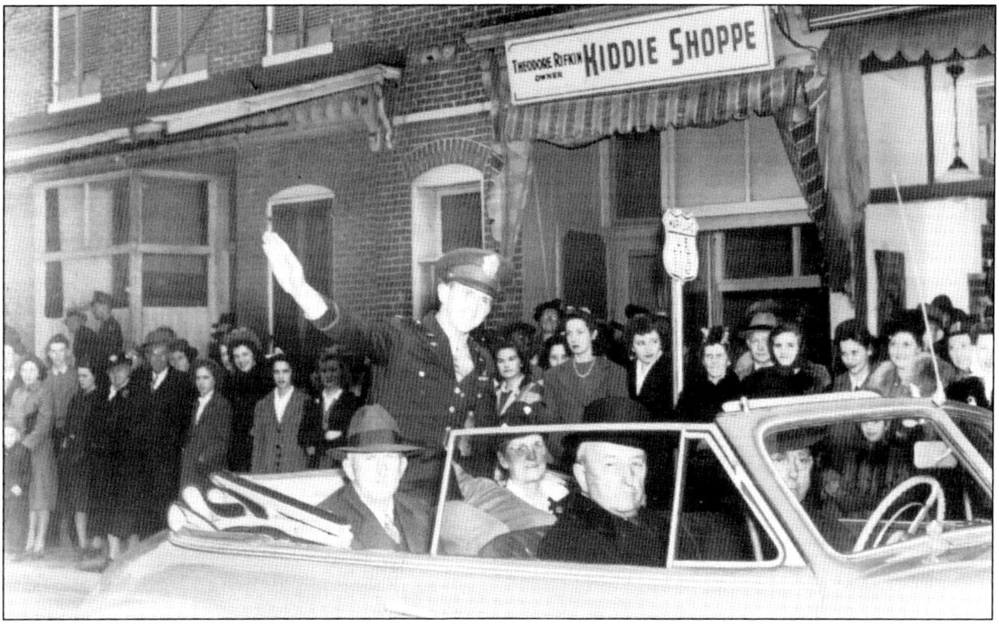


Lt. Charles Wilbur Jackson, fighter pilot and war hero, is the star attraction at a war bond drive in Berlin in late 1944 or early 1945. He is riding in a Main Street parade with his parents, Ben and Lea Jackson, in the backseat and Mayor William Whaley in the passenger seat. Carlton Powell is the driver. Prior to joining the Army Air Corps, Lieutenant Jackson was an oil truck driver for Magee Oil Company.

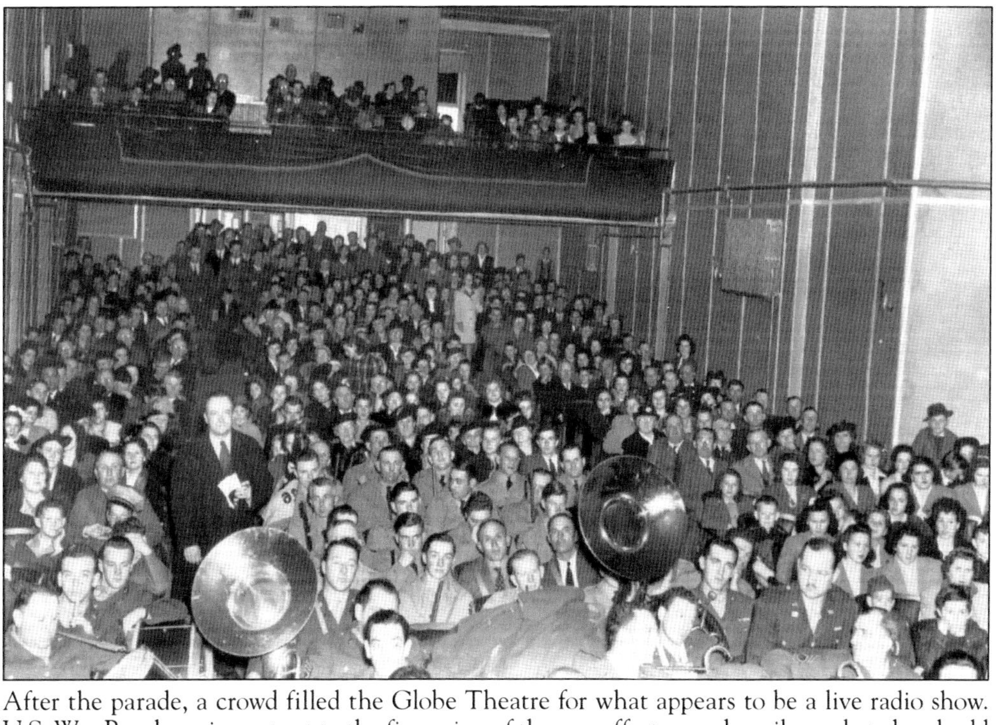

After the parade, a crowd filled the Globe Theatre for what appears to be a live radio show. U.S. War Bonds, so important to the financing of the war effort, were heavily marketed and sold at rallies like this one. Here banker Reese Cropper Sr., standing, makes an investment.

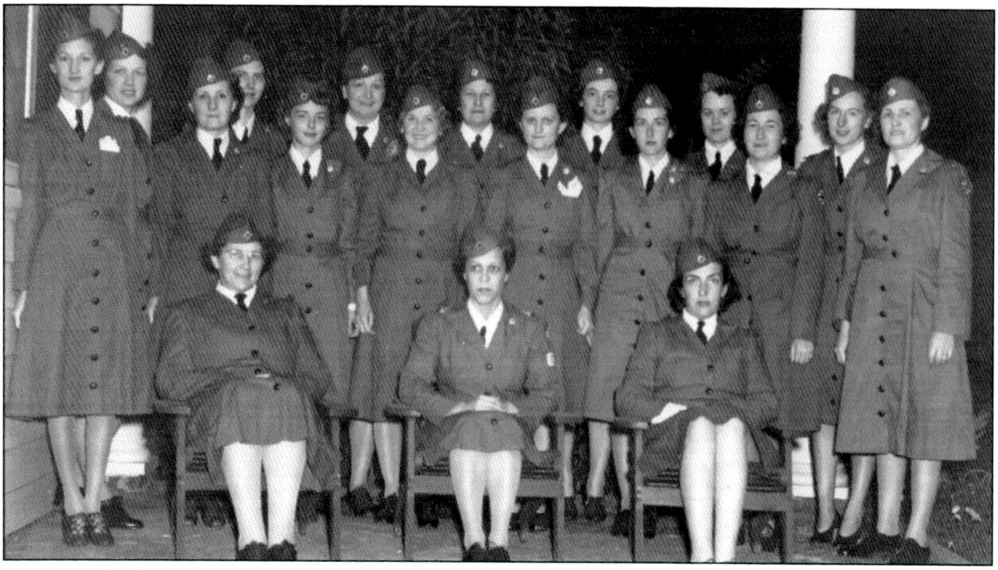

In 1942, the ladies of the town established an American Red Cross Motor Corps. Headed by Fran Quillin, seated right, it was complete with identity cards, uniforms, and technical manuals. Members were instructed and tested in first aid by Dr. Charles Law and Dr. Frederick Nicoll and also in basic automobile mechanics. It was the largest on the shore, boasting 45 vehicles supplied by members. This photograph includes Florence Rogers, Elizabeth Squares, June Quillin, Alma Pruitt, Ruth Warren, Josephine Scott, and Irma Hastings.

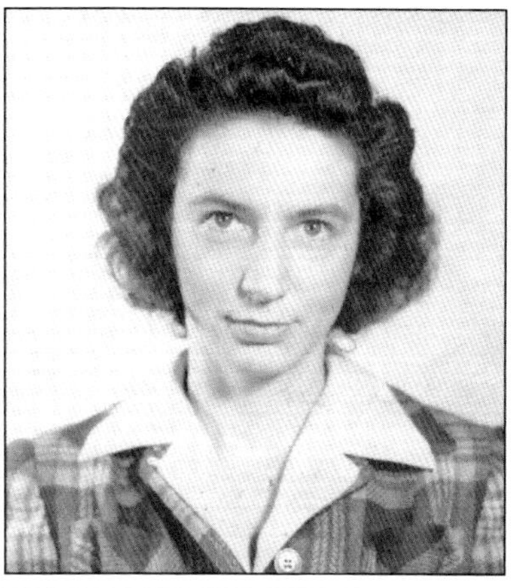

Ruth Warren is the holder of this American National Red Cross Motor Corps card. Members of the Motor Corps served as air raid wardens enforcing blackouts and as airplane spotters. They coordinated home sock knitting efforts, took coffee to troops defending the coast, and delivered telegrams.

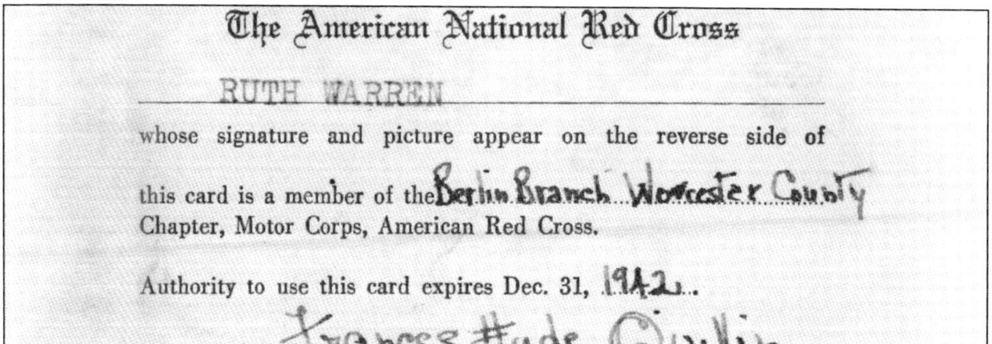

The American National Red Cross

RUTH WARREN

whose signature and picture appear on the reverse side of

this card is a member of the Berlin Branch Worcester County

Chapter, Motor Corps, American Red Cross.

Authority to use this card expires Dec. 31, 1942

Frances Hyde Quillin

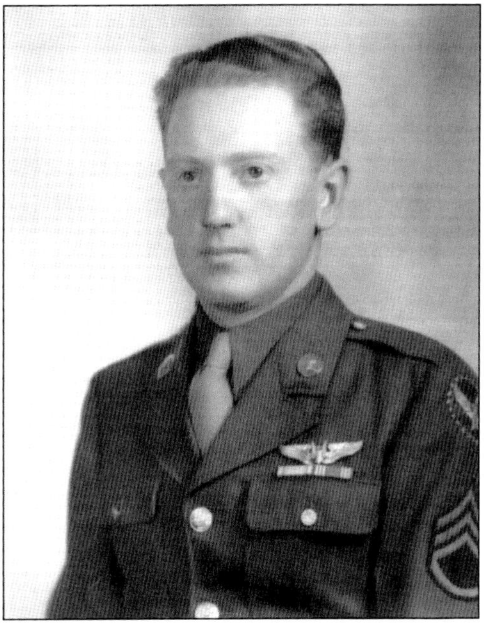

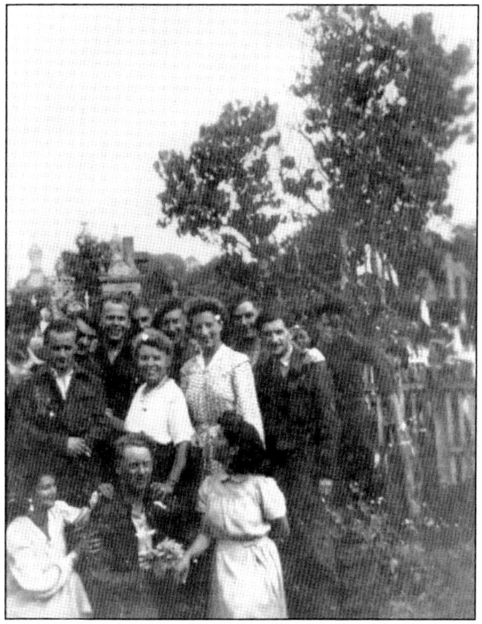

In June 1944, Fran Quillin (left) of the Red Cross Motor Corps delivered a terrible telegram to Edgar and Daisy Hudson. Their son, Willis, an Army Air Corps flier, was missing in action. He had been shot down and parachuted into German-held France. The French, however, found him before the Germans and hid him for two months until he was liberated. On the right is Hudson (center front) in France with the French women who risked their lives for him and other rescued Allied airmen.

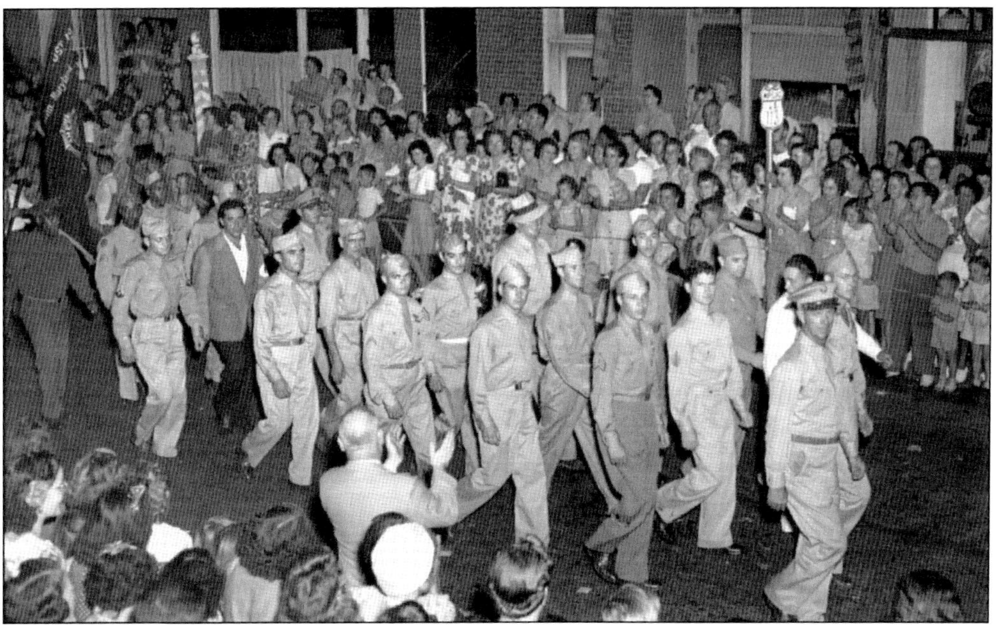

World War II ended in Europe in May 1945. Celebrations and parades were held all over the country. Berlin was no exception. This unit marching down Main Street is made up of soldiers home on leave. It was a happy time, but many of Berlin's boys were still in harm's way in the South Pacific and many of these soldiers expected to be shipped out soon to fight the Japanese.

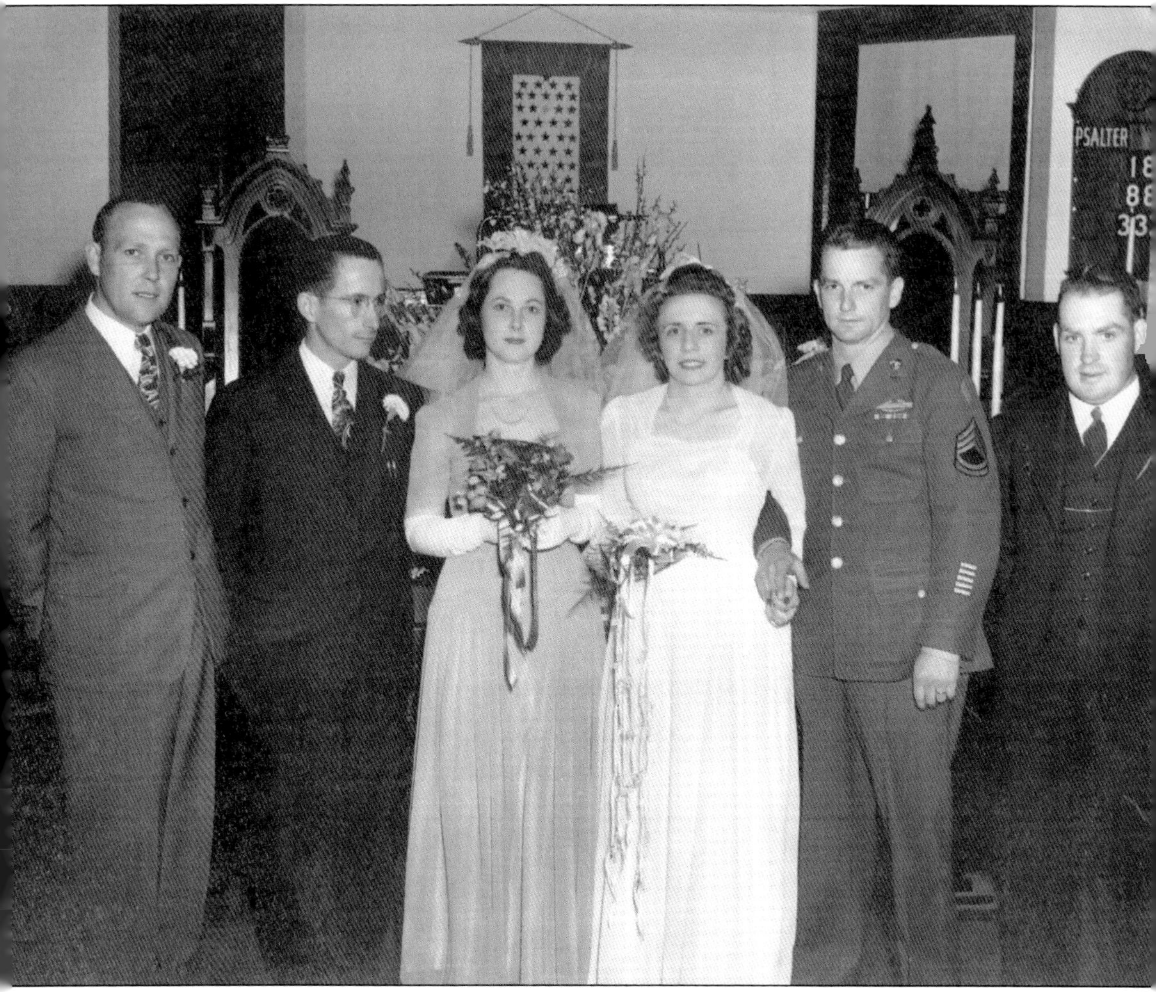


"Mr. and Mrs. Henry Ernest Onley request the honour of your presence at the marriage of their daughter Mary Ruth to Sergeant Wilson Davis Warren April 28 nineteen hundred and forty-five at half after two o'clock Buckingham Presbyterian Church Berlin, Maryland." The wedding had been delayed for two and a half years. In 1943, Mary Ruth Onley and her mother made the bride's gown and the maid of honor's gown. Wilson had come home on leave to get married, but because of a series of military foul-ups, he had to go back before the wedding could take place. He was in France when the brass asked him if he wanted leave in Paris or did he want to go home. Guess which he chose? Wilson and Mary Ruth are still happily married with three children, five grandchildren, and three great-grandchildren. The members of the wedding party from left to right are Paul Scott, Casher Hickman, Evelyn Hudson Bunting, Mary Ruth, Wilson, and John Ayres. The star-studded banner in the back of the chancel recognizes the men and women from Buckingham Church who served in the war. A gold star indicates that one of the members, Louis Jones, gave his life for his country. (Warren Collection.)

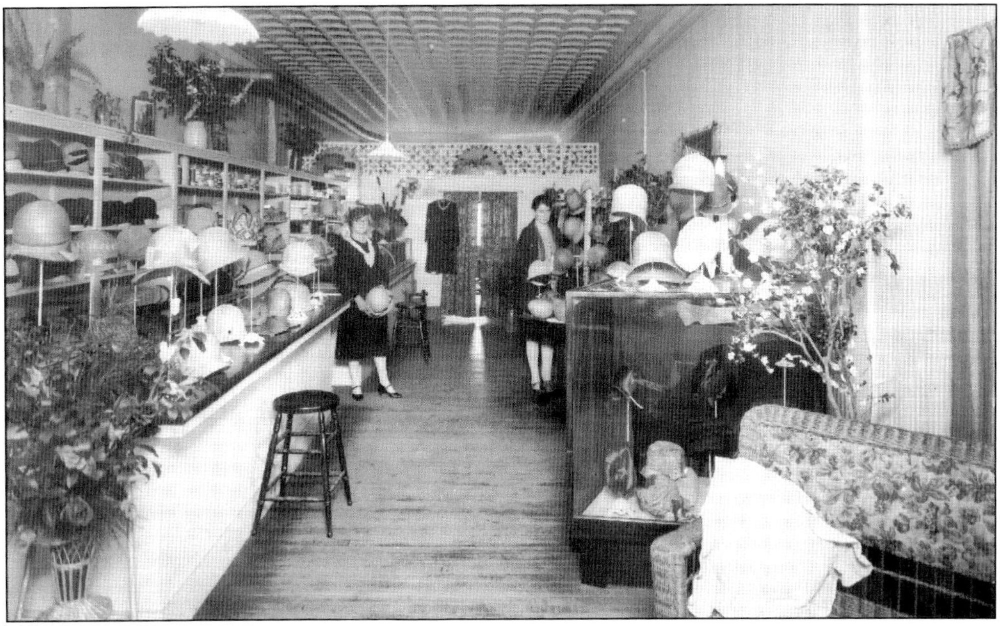

This lovely interior of Burbage and Burbage Millinery Shop was located on Main Street. Note the tin ceilings, the wicker furniture, and the many flower arrangements. It appears the notions for making hats may have been for sale. Spring must have been around the corner because the hats are mostly straw. The owner, Rydia Isabelle Burbage Richardson, stands to the left with a hat in her hand. (Cheryl Holland Collection.)

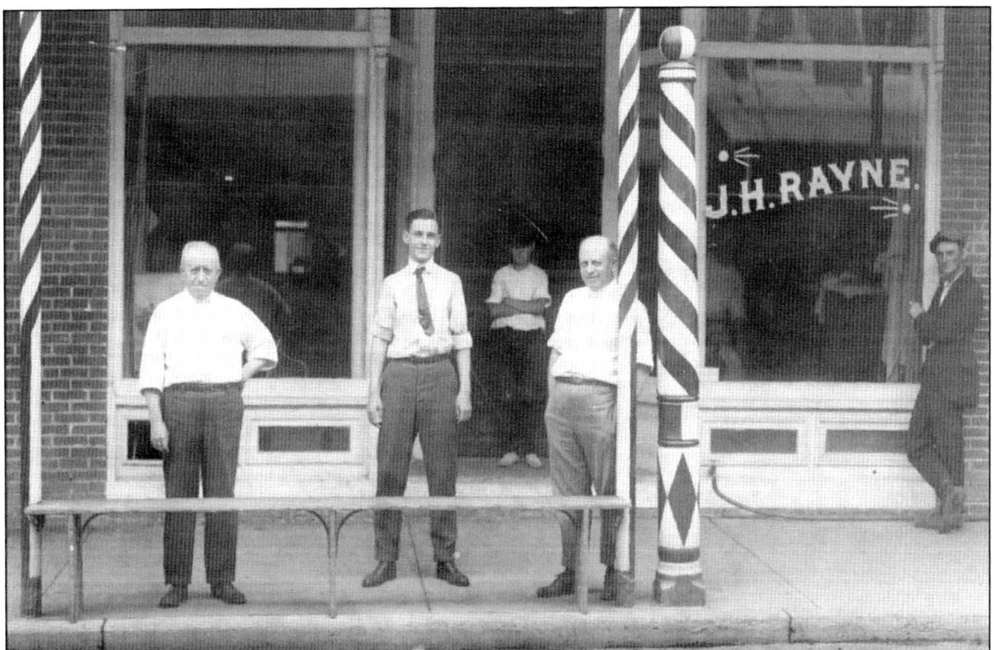


J. H. Rayne's barbershop was located just north of Conley and Rayne's Soda Fountain and was later owned by Howard Dill, also a barber. An early newspaper advertised the shop as the place to go "for an up-to date shave, haircut or shampoo—Best of Service Always."

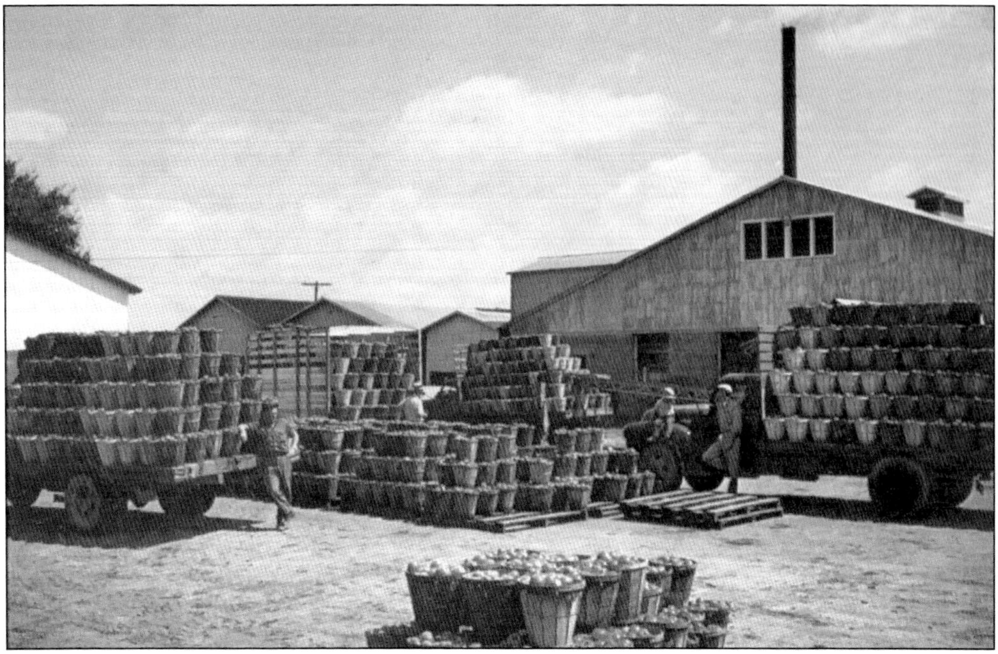

This canning company was built in 1906 by J. Richard Phillips and Levin E. Derrickson, doing business for six years. The original building burned, and Phillips built a new cannery, Phillips Canning Company. In 1930, new buildings doubled the size of the plant. With the major portion of its output going to the war effort, Phillips earned the War Food Administration "A" award in 1944. The cannery continued in business until the 1970s. The Phillips Canning Company Mother Goose label, below, was one of many labels affixed to Phillips's products. (Above, Mabel Rogers Collection.)

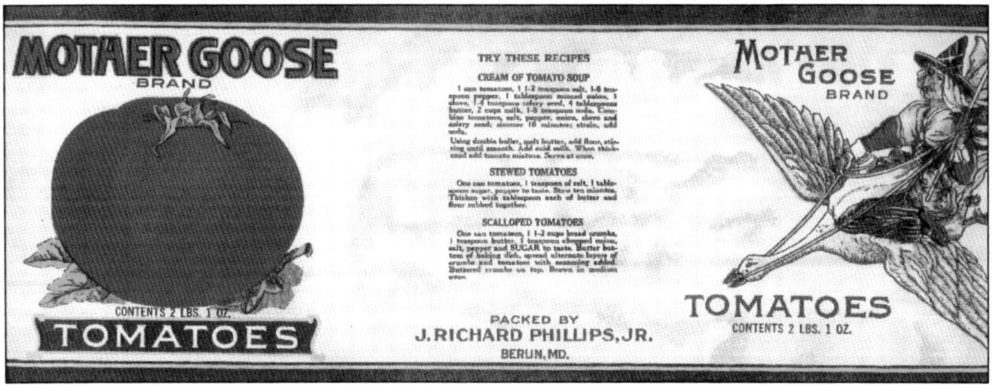

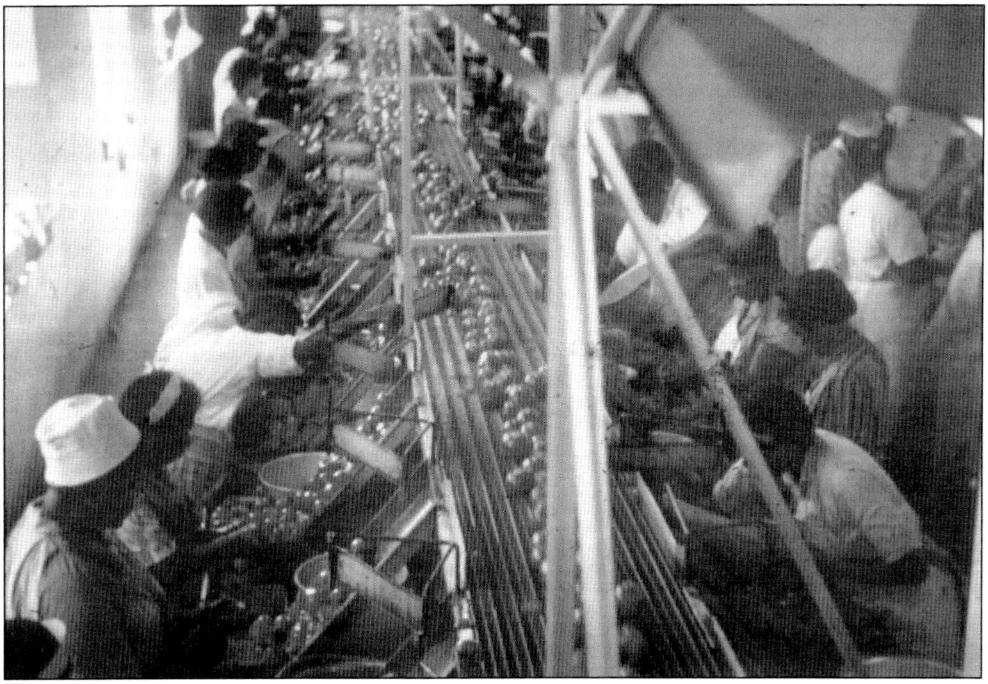

Inside the cannery, women workers sort and clean the tomatoes. Conveyor belts carry the tomatoes from one process to the next. As employers of over 180 people, Phillip's Cannery Company provided economic stability for many Berlin families.

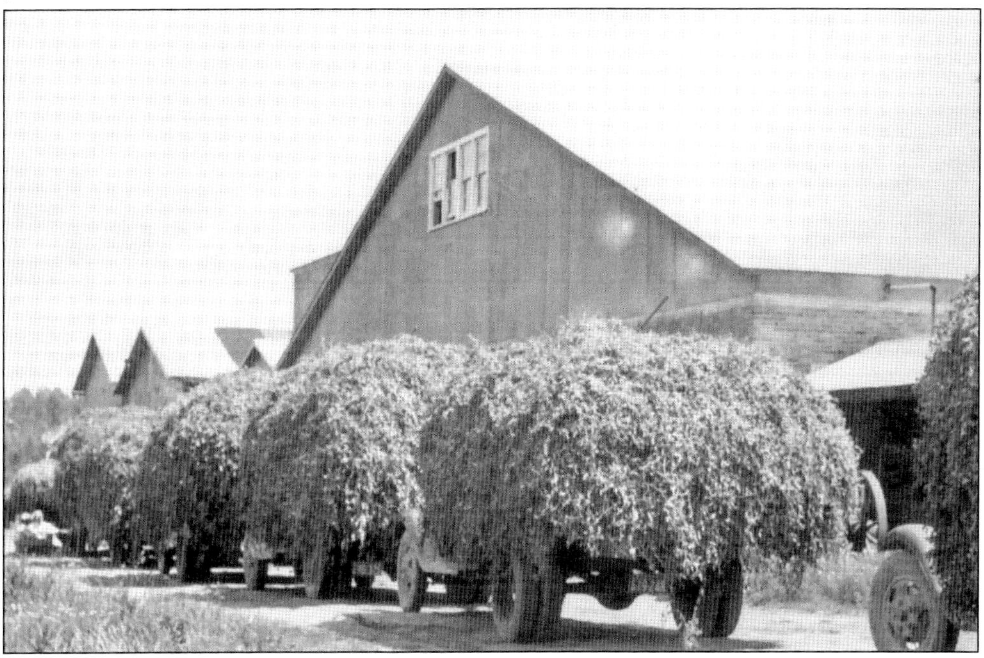

Tomato products—juice, puree, cubed, and later pizza sauce—were the staple products of Phillips. However, string beans and peas were also canned. Shown is a truck loaded with the local crop of beans. Some of these overloaded trucks came down local roads and highways to make their deliveries.

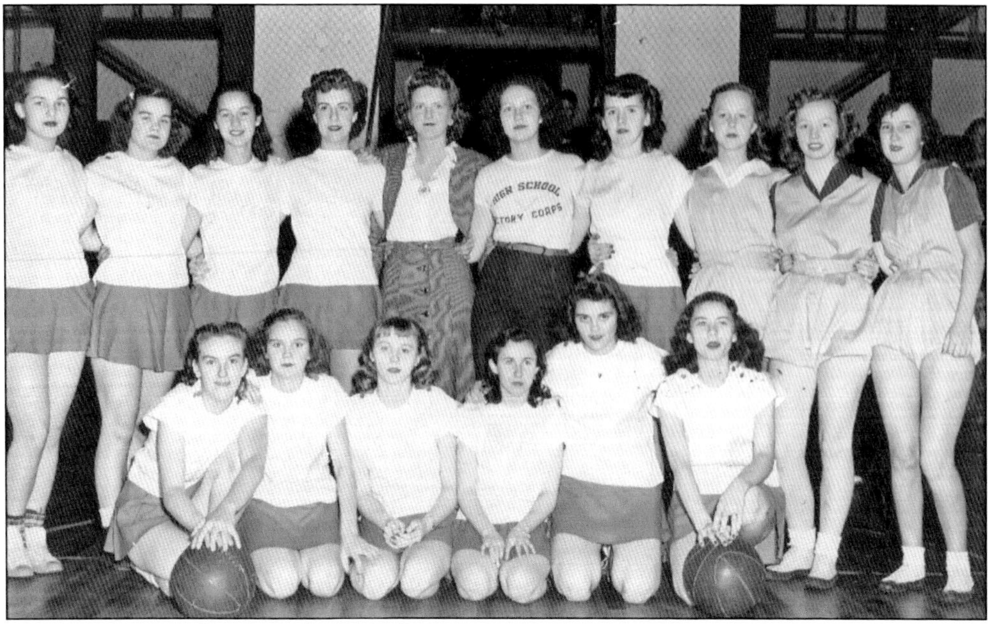

The 1947 State Champion basketball team from Buckingham High School is shown here. Pictured from left to right are (first row) Nadine Powell, Clara Baker, Odetta Cropper, Audrey Walters, Doris Baker, and Mildred Ann Tyndall; (second row) Delores Mogel, Betty Ann McCabe, Nancy Stosacker, Barbara Post, teacher Betsy Dennis, Oretta Wilkens, Nellie Baker, Ann Conley, B. Frances Magee, and Gloria Nottingham.

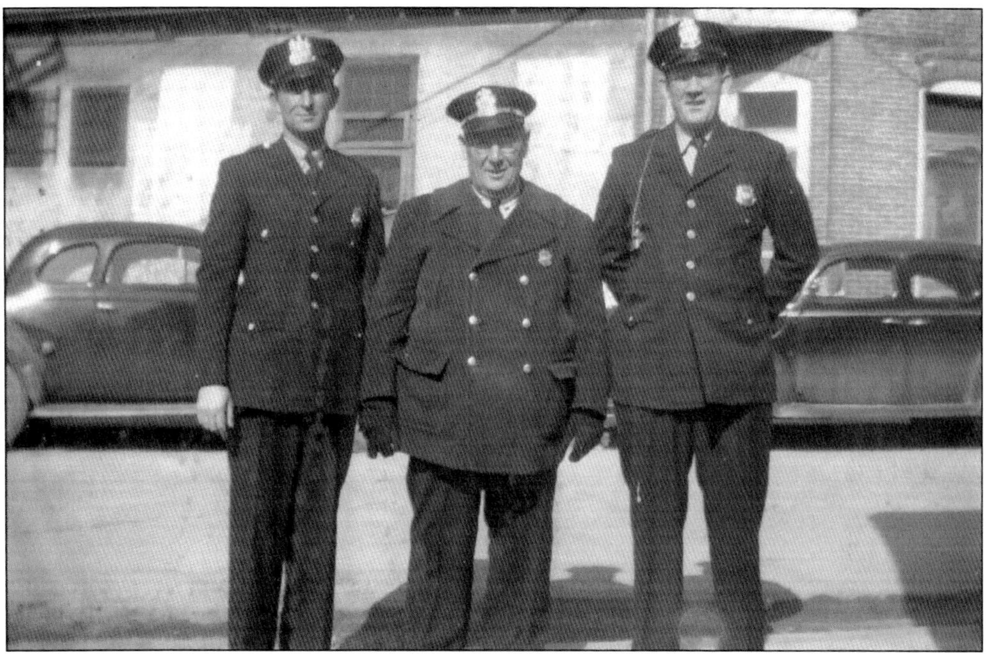

This 1946 photograph, taken outside the police station next to the Globe Theatre, shows Chief Elmer "Shock" Shockley (center), Bill Lynch (left), and Red Wheakley (right). One of "Shock's" favorite law enforcement methods was the "banishment" of drunks. His "Son, if you ever come back to Berlin, I'll lock you up!" was quick, efficient, inexpensive justice, which worked well.

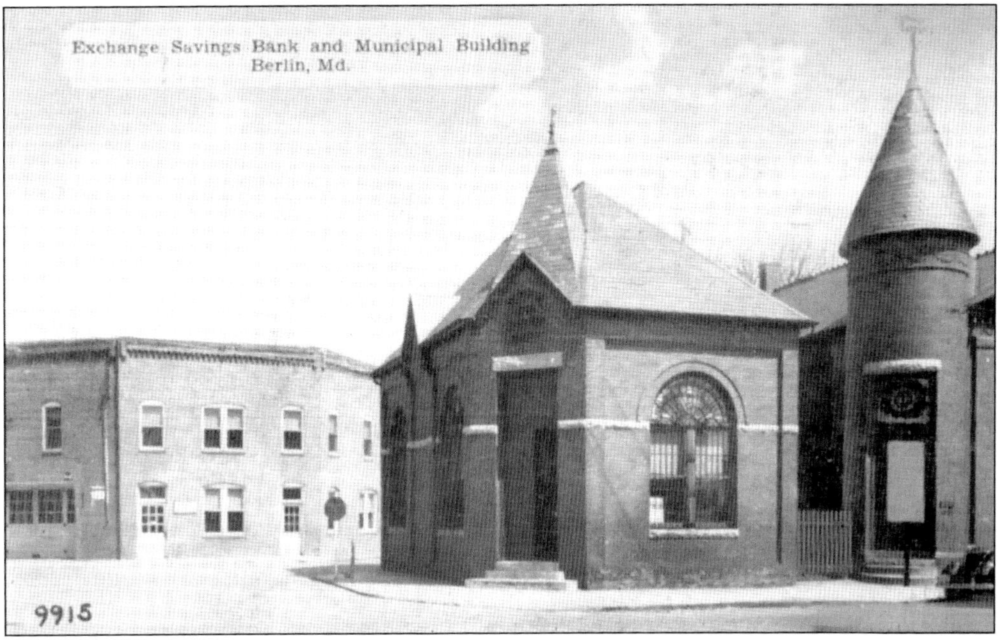


The Berlin Library Association was organized on January 25, 1910, when a group of public-spirited women met to start a library that was later built with donations from the Berlin Book Club, Rozelle Handy's "Friendly Library," and the Enoch Pratt traveling library. The library has moved through several locations, including a space in town hall, pictured on the left in the top photograph, and the Pruitt Parkway location, pictured below. Those who assisted in this 1961 Pruitt Parkway move are, from left to right, (seated) Harry Trimble, George Adkins, Donald Lyons, Mark Brueckmann, and Lewis Baker; (standing) Nelson Hudson, county librarian Dorothy Moore, Warner Foley, Berlin librarian Ruth Holland, Lionel Lyons, Jan Brueckmann, and Mrs. Warner Foley. The Berlin Library was moved to its present Main Street location on April 25, 1970. (Above, Ellis Wainwright Collection.)

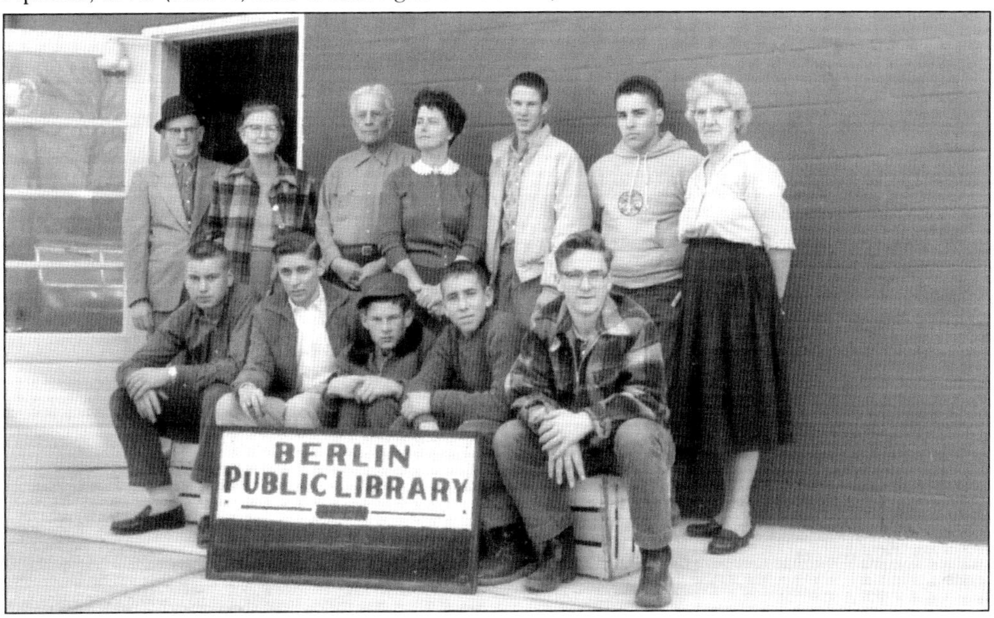

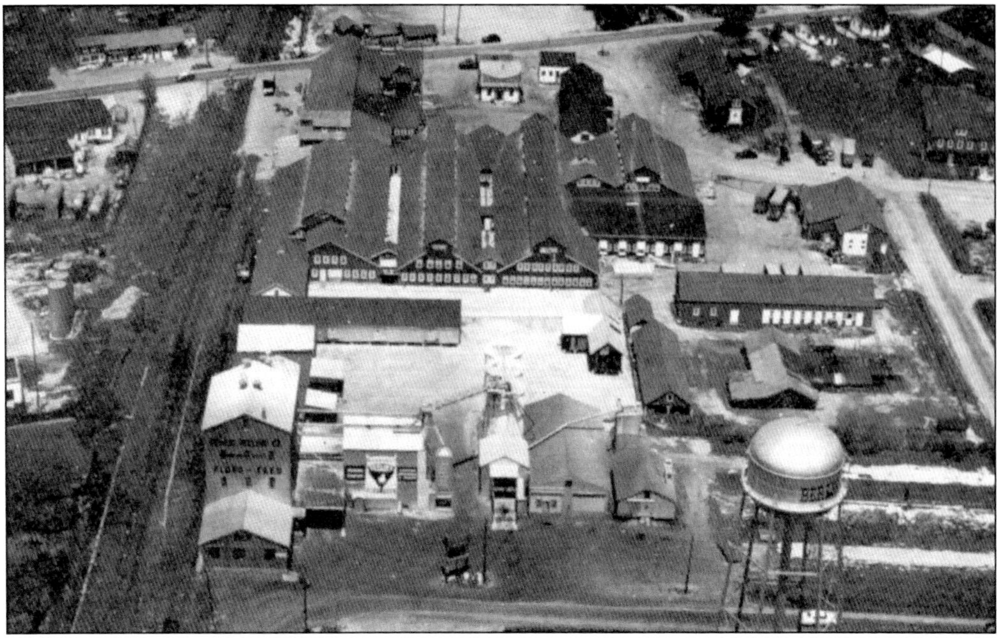

This 1940s photograph shows the Berlin Milling Company in the foreground and the Acme Poultry Company in the center. The mill operated from 1898 to 1969. Acme advertised "Something to Crow About!" and offered cash for market-ready fowl. The photograph below shows the mill after it burned in April 1956. Several brave people tried to get to the mill's books but to no avail. Fire companies from up and down the Delmarva Peninsula came to join with the beleaguered Berlin Fire Company. The wind was very strong; it had snowed that day. Fire engines surrounded the building, especially on the railroad tracks, trying to protect the homes on Main Street. The homes were saved but not the mill. Lights were out in the northern end of town; nearby houses had only hot water for a few days.

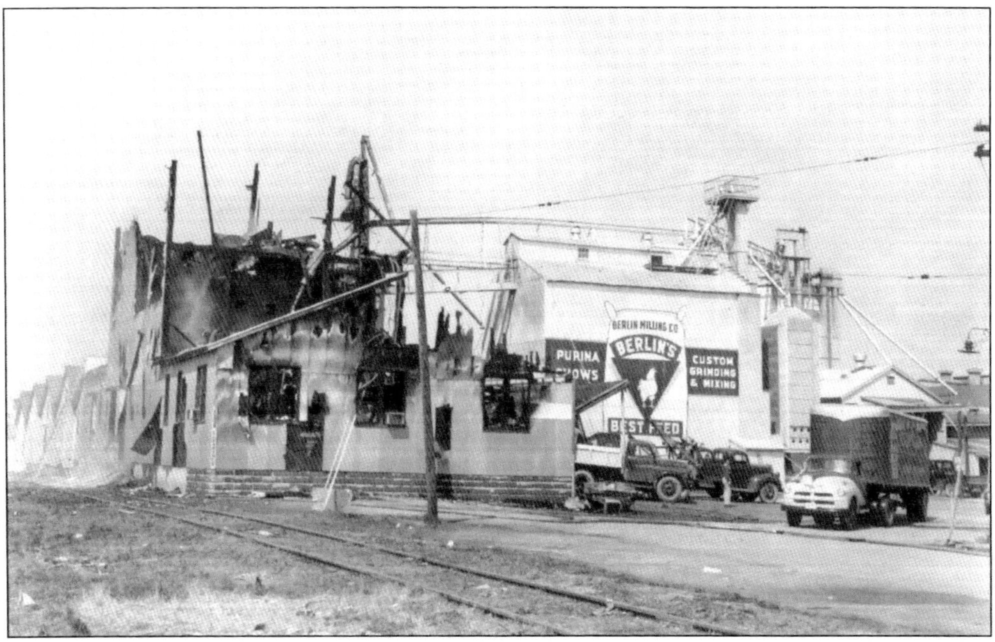

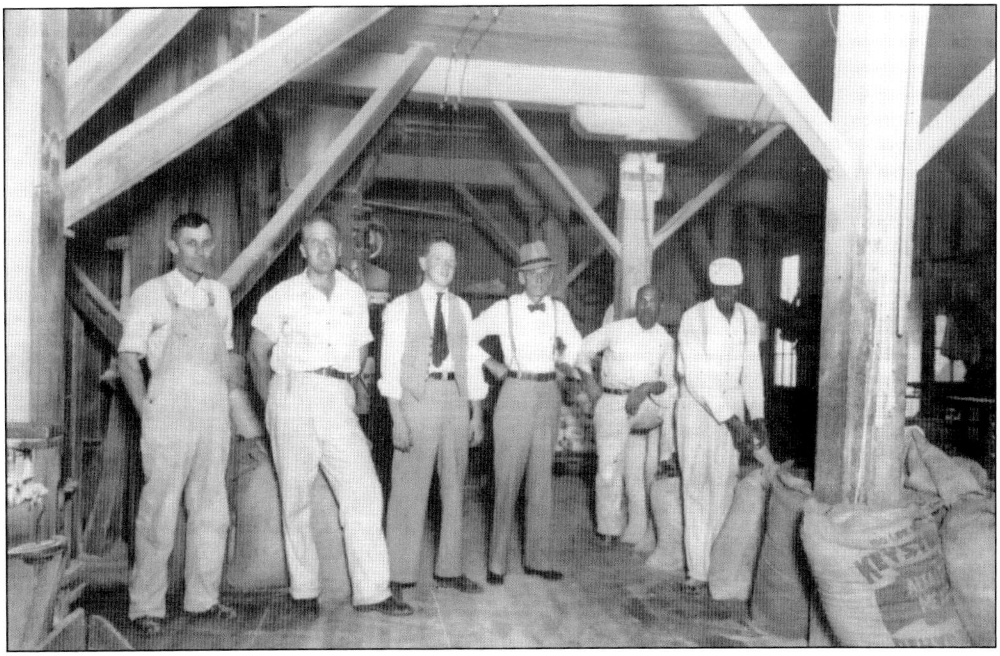

E. Bowen Quillin, one of the owners of the Berlin Milling Company, stands with a group of workers. "Bo" is in the middle with his fedora hat and bow tie; Willis Hudson, the *facto factotum* for the mill, can be identified by his tie and vest. Willis can be remembered as one of the town's war heroes pictured on page 69. Lloyd Lynch, a mill worker, is far left.

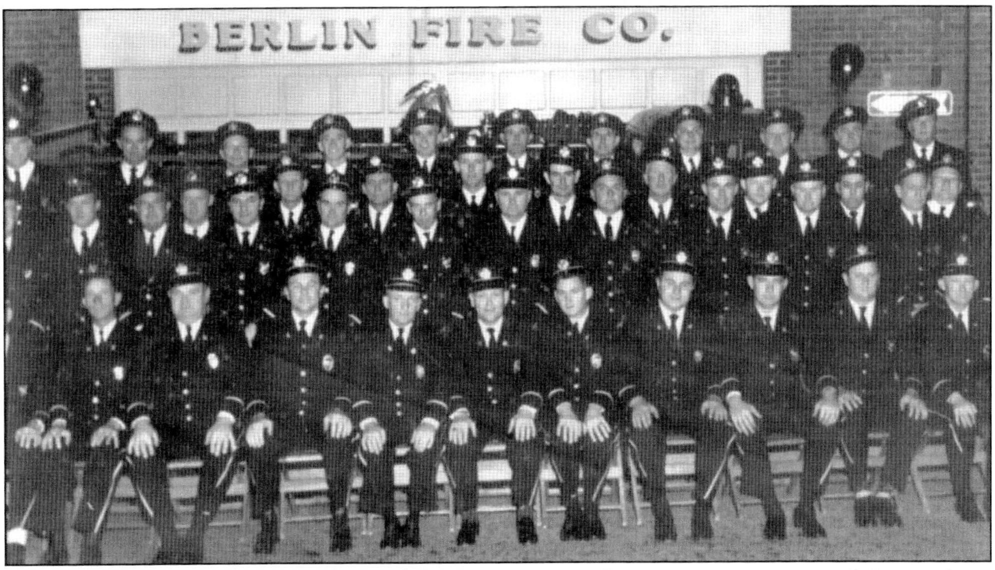


After the 1904 fire, the town authorized the construction of a town water system and the purchase of effective firefighting equipment. A volunteer fire company was organized with 26 volunteers in 1910. The 1936 newly renovated Berlin City Hall on William Street included space for fire equipment and a firemen's meeting room and social hall. The social hall also was used by the community. A new Berlin Volunteer Fire Department building was built on North Main Street in the 1970s. Many of the firemen in this photograph participated in fighting the Berlin Milling Company fire in 1956.

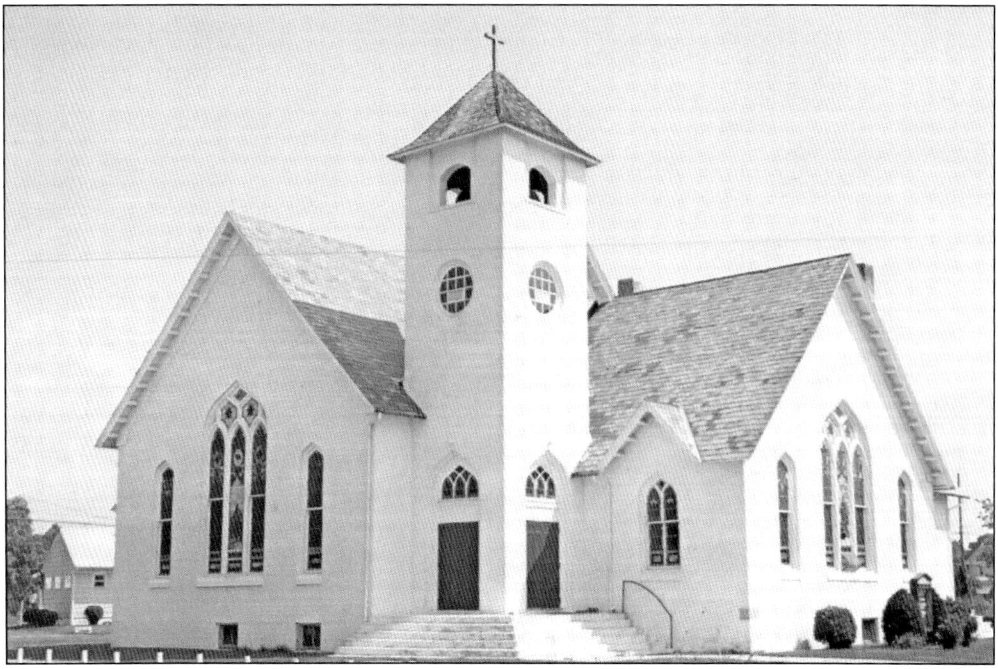

St. Paul United Methodist Church was the daughter church of Bethel Methodist Episcopal Church in Germantown. In 1876, a group was organized to build a new wooden church in north Berlin to accommodate the rapid growth of that area. On October 31, 1915, the cornerstone for this new brick church was laid on Flower Street, a short distance from the first north Berlin church, and the old church was converted to a church hall. A group of St. Paul's young people are pictured below. (Above, Ellis Wainwright Collection.)

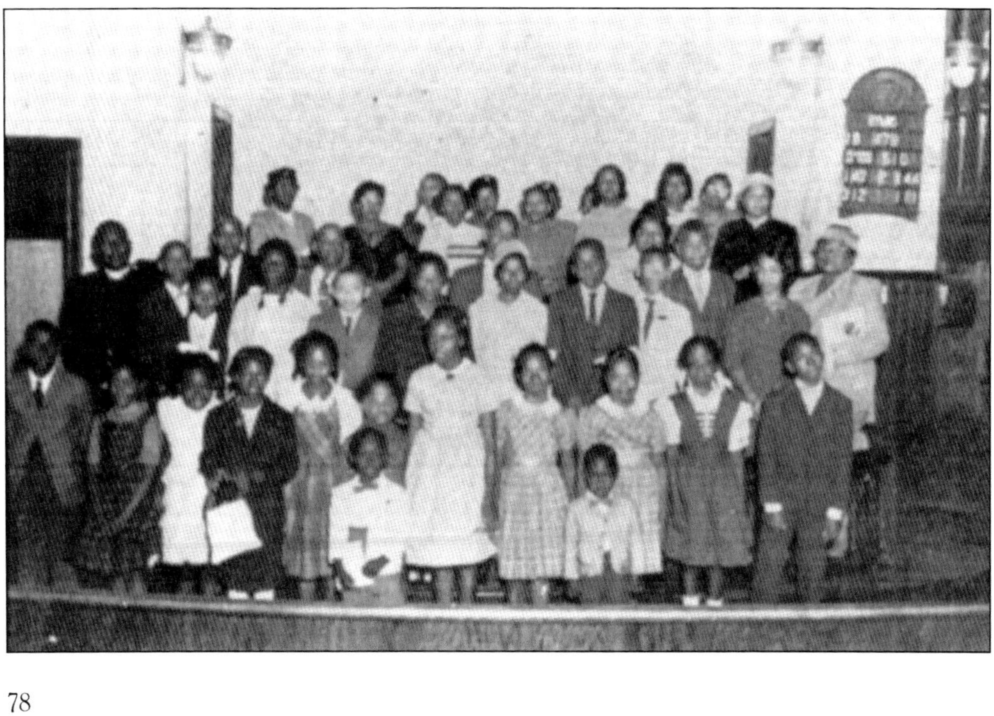

# *Six*

# SONS AND DAUGHTERS

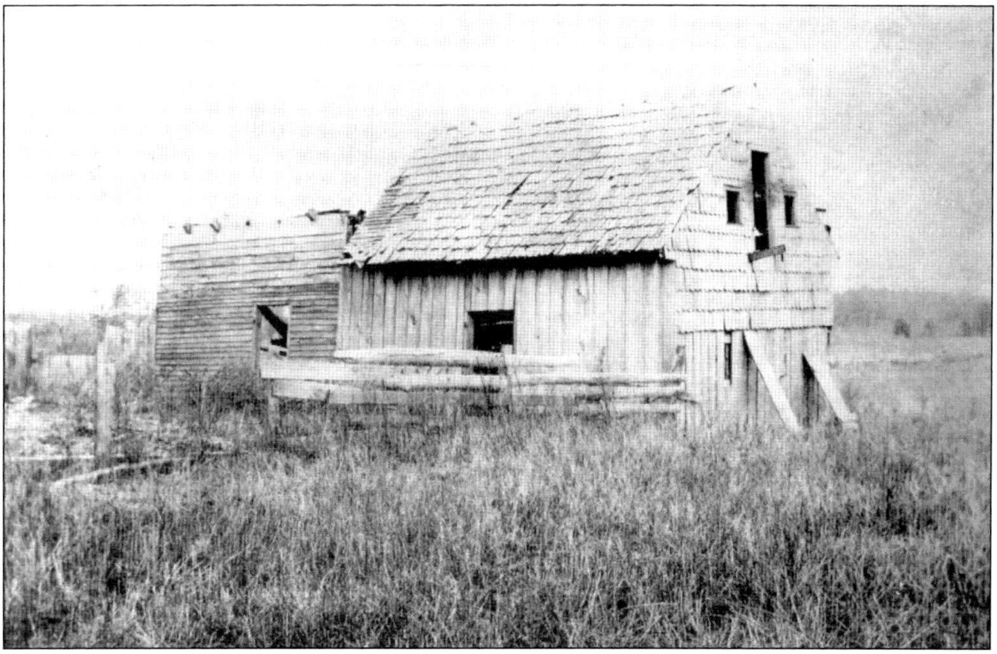

Stephen Decatur was the first of many locals to achieve fame. Fortunes of war brought his family to the Berlin area in 1778. Decatur's father, a patriot privateer, operated under authorization of letters of marque issued by the Continental Congress to prey on British shipping in the waters along America's East Coast, sailing out of Philadelphia. In September 1777, Philadelphia fell to British forces, and the Decatur family fled to Maryland's Eastern Shore, which provided the first inlet from the barrier island not controlled by the British. The captain's ships continued their privateering operations from the sheltered coves of the coast east of what is now Berlin. Decatur's mother, Ann Pine Decatur, gave birth to the future American naval hero on January 5, 1779, in this house owned by local farmer Isaac Murray and located on property now across Route 113 from Berlin's Stephen Decatur Park. After Philadelphia had been freed from the occupying British forces, the family returned to the northern city when young Stephen was three months old. (Margaret G. Phillips Collection.)

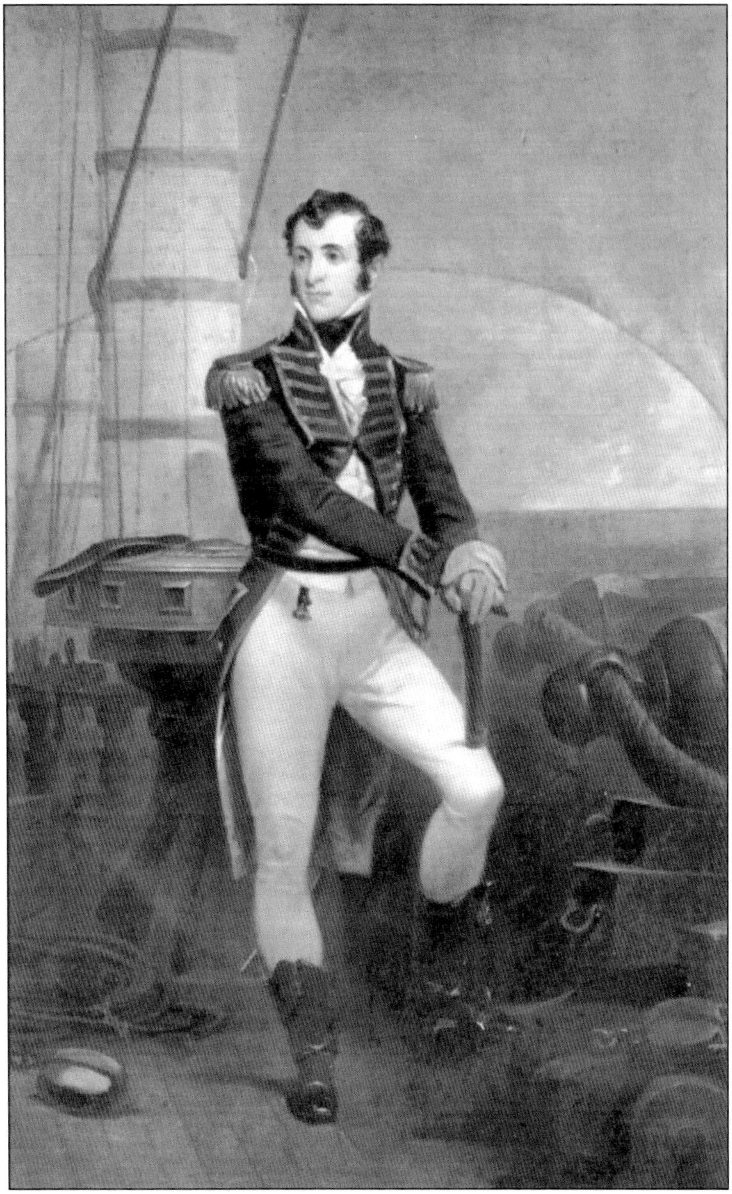

In 1798, nineteen-year-old Stephen Decatur entered the navy as a midshipman, serving with distinction in the country's actions against the Barbary pirates, leaders of nations along the African coast of the Mediterranean who demanded tribute of American shipping for the privilege of trading in their waters. Later serving in the War of 1812, at age 25, he received the highest rank recognized by the navy at that time. Decatur's life was cut short by a senseless tragedy. Because of personal animosity resulting from an incident that contributed to the War of 1812, Decatur was challenged to a duel by a fellow naval officer, Commodore James Barron, over Barron's allowing the boarding of the U.S. ship *Chesapeake* by British naval forces. The two officers met on the field of honor on March 22, 1820, at Bladensburg, Prince George's County, and Decatur fell, dying the next day. He is buried in Philadelphia. He is remembered for his toast: "Our country: In her intercourse with foreign nations may she always be right; but our country, right or wrong." (Portrait by Alonzo Chapel; Range Collection.)

John Postley served with the Synepuxent Battalion during the Revolutionary War, becoming colonel in June 1782. Postley was a soldier, a planter, and an elder in Buckingham Presbyterian Church. After his death in 1815, funds from his estate were used to start the Postley Fund for educating needy students of Worcester County. This granite marker was erected on Postley's grave site in 1909. The Postley Award is still given by the board of education.

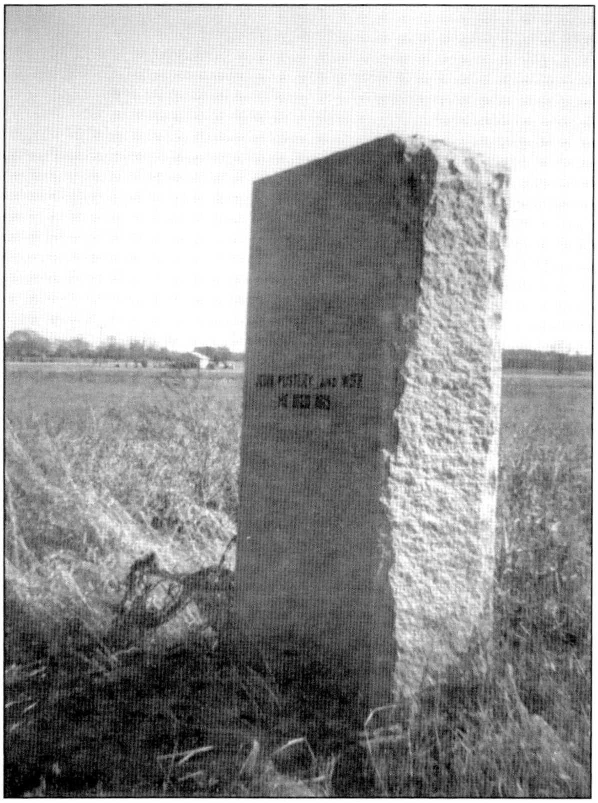

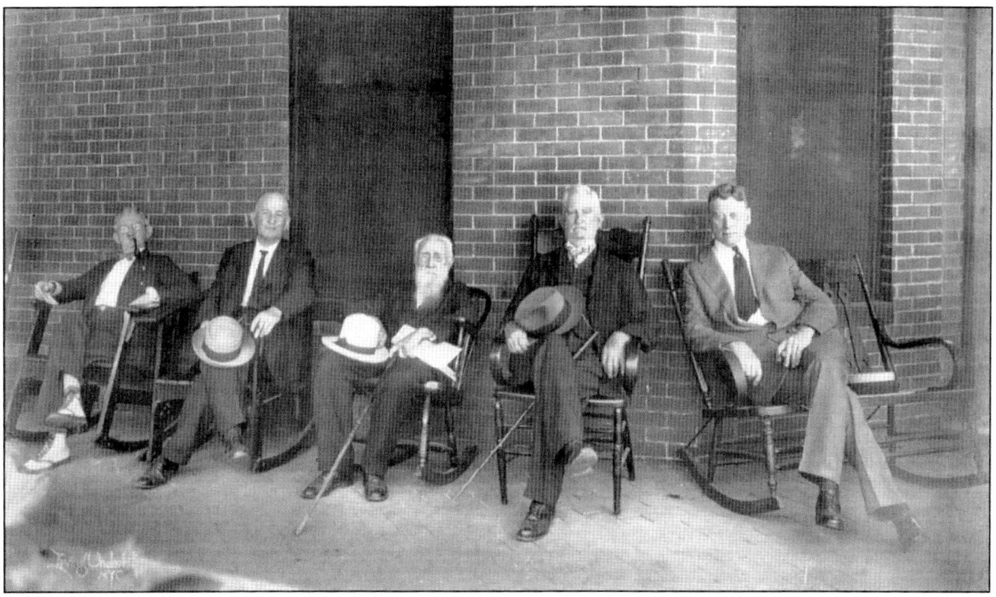

Littleton Purnell Bowen (1833–1933) was a preacher, poet, lawyer, historian, and author of many books. As a historian, Bowen took great interest in Francis Makemie, the founder of organized Presbyterianism in America, finally finding Makemie's desk and later his grave in Virginia. Bowen's memorial at Buckingham Cemetery was dedicated in June 1936. He is pictured in the center of these Berlin businessmen on the porch of the Atlantic Hotel about 1930.

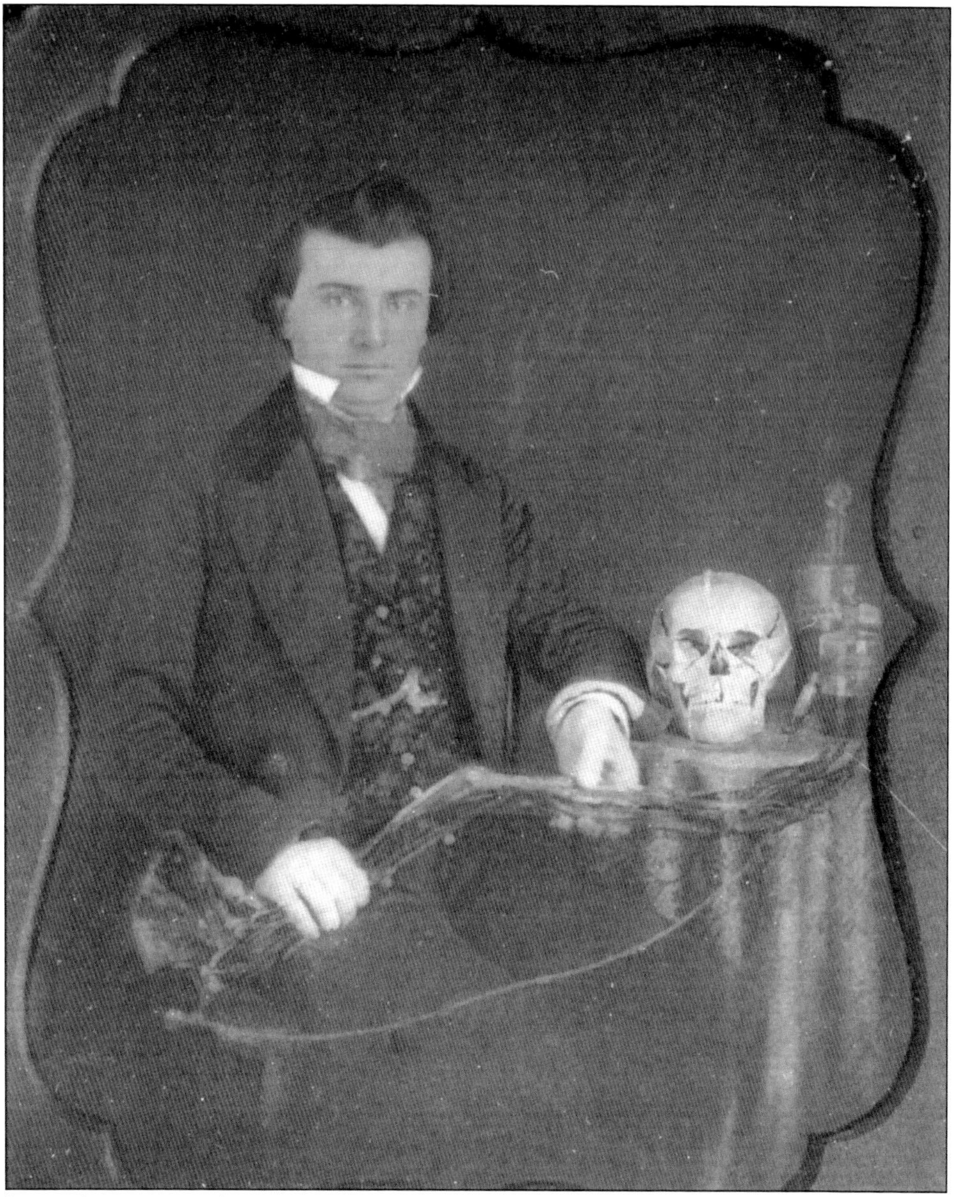

John Taylor Hammond, M.D., was born in 1832 in Queponco, on lands that his ancestors had owned since 1677, west of present-day Newark, Maryland. That year, his father, Edward, died, and his widowed mother, Elizabeth, moved with her four small children to a newly built house in Berlin, now known as Burley Manor. John, like his brother Thomas Edward, graduated from the College of New Jersey at Princeton. He matriculated at Jefferson Medical College in Philadelphia and graduated in 1854. He returned to Berlin, married Esther Priscilla Toadvine of Salisbury, and became a horse-and-buggy doctor. He tended the community for 50 years and never sent a bill, most certainly because of family income from the farms in Queponco. He was an overly trusting and gullible man who unfortunately never refused to co-sign promissory notes. The default of the markers led to the sale of the better part of the ancestral lands in Queponco. It was not until his son, Thomas Victor Hammond, M.D., intervened that the losses stopped. Dr. Hammond the elder, who died in 1902, was, however, known as "the Kindest of Hearts."

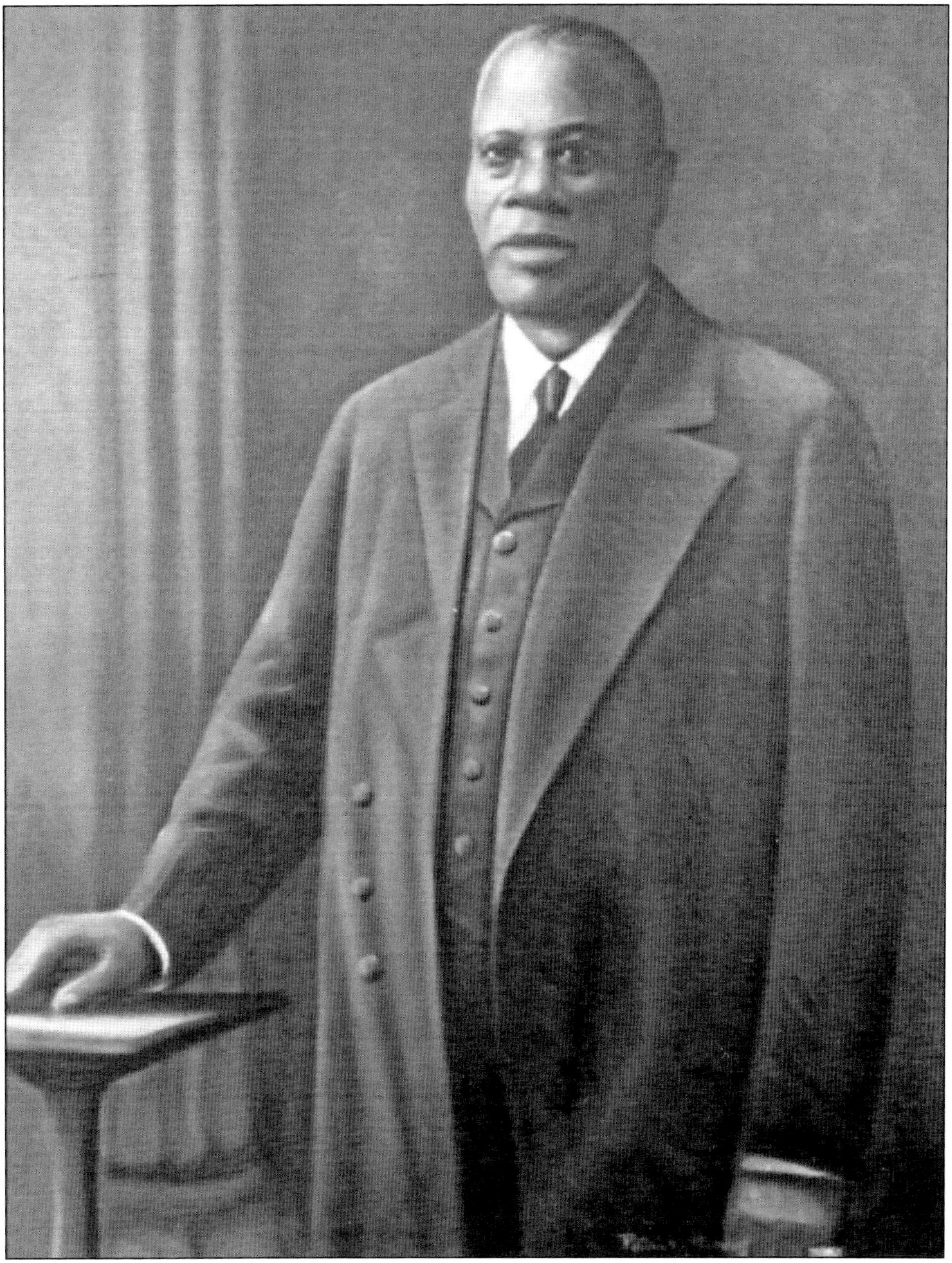

Charles Albert Tindley was born in Berlin on July 7, 1851, to a slave father and a free mother. He was orphaned at an early age. He learned to read and write at the age of 17 while working as a hod carrier during the day and studying correspondence lessons at night. One of the most famous African American Methodist ministers of his time, Tindley served several congregations, including the Bainbridge Street Church and the Calvary Methodist Episcopal Church in Philadelphia, which was later renamed Tindley Temple Methodist Church in his honor. As one of the fathers of gospel music, Tindley wrote the words and music of several hymns, including "Stand By Me" and "I'll Overcome Someday," which moved Pete Seeger to write "We Shall Overcome," the famous anthem of the civil rights movement. (Painting by Patrick L. Henry.)

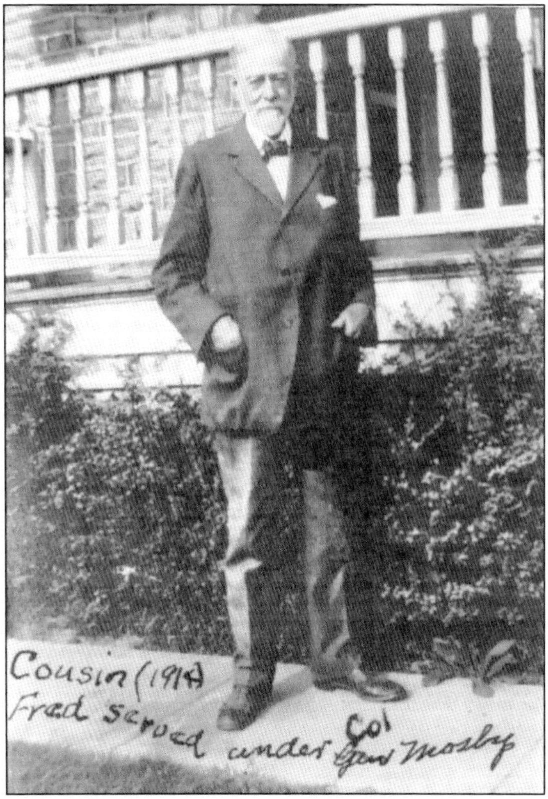


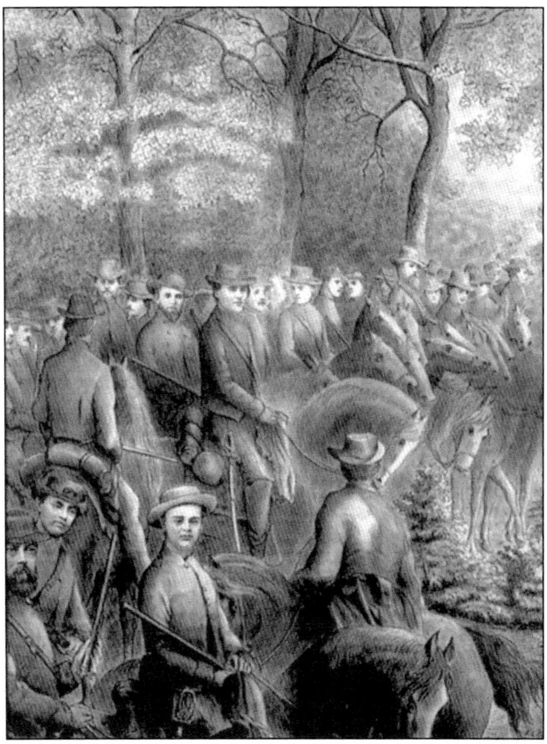

In the 1862 Civil War Enrollment Records, Fred Pitts was noted as being 19 years of age and "In Rebel service." Pitts enlisted in Company K, 1st Virginia Cavalry on May 25, 1862, and served honorably until Lee's surrender at Appomattox Courthouse in April 1865. His moment in history came on May 11, 1864, at Yellow Tavern, north of Richmond. He was mounted along a fence line awaiting a Yankee cavalry charge when the famous cavalry general, J. E. B. Stuart, riding alone, came up just as the charge began. Stuart was wounded, and Pitts caught him as he reeled from the saddle, using his own horse to help the general to the rear. After the war, Pitts frequently regaled his friends with this tale in the Berlin blacksmith shop. Pitts executed the lithograph, below left, "In Reserve," of his unit during the war. (Above, Joseph Moore Collection.)

Born a slave in 1844, Isaiah Fassett's manumission on November 11, 1863, required he enlist in the Union Army, U.S. Colored Troops. In the 9th Regiment, he fought in the battles of the Wilderness; St. John's Island, South Carolina; Deep Bottom, Virginia; the siege of Petersburg; and the entry into Richmond. After the Battle of the Crater, Fassett was reported "Dead" until he yelled he was "jist creased." Discharged in 1866, Fassett returned to Berlin a free man, becoming a loyal member of the G.A.R. Post 51 in Berlin. He died in 1946, one of the longest-surviving Civil War veterans in Maryland. (Patrick L. Henry Collection.)

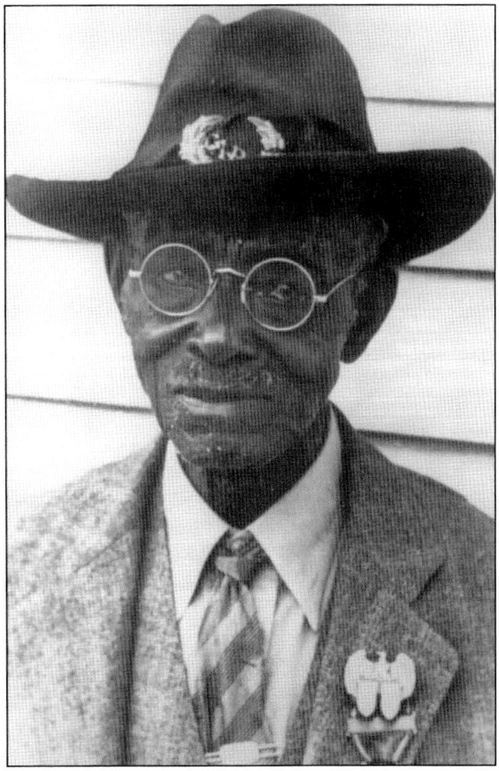

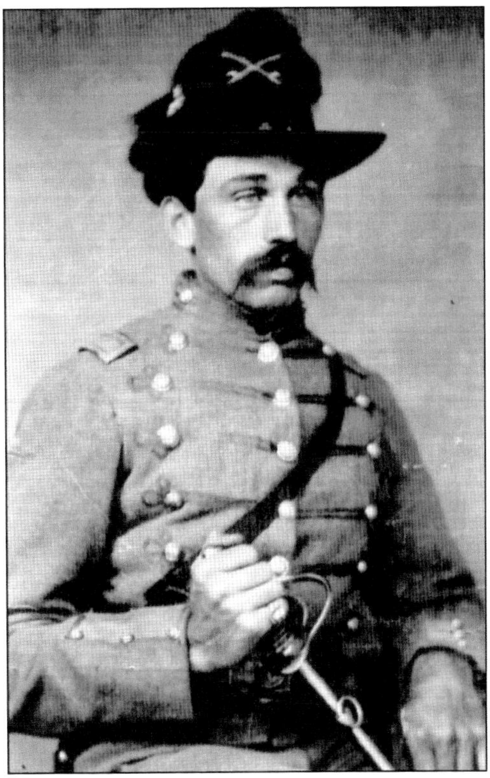

Dr. John W. Pitts (1842–1910) served in the Confederate infantry and later under Gen. J. E. B. Stuart in the 1st Virginia Cavalry. After the war, he practiced medicine in Berlin for more than 40 years. A community leader, Dr. Pitts was Berlin's first mayor, a vice president of the Calvin B. Taylor Banking Company, an elder of the Buckingham Presbyterian Church, and a district deputy grand master of the Independent Order of Odd Fellows. (Joseph Moore Collection.)

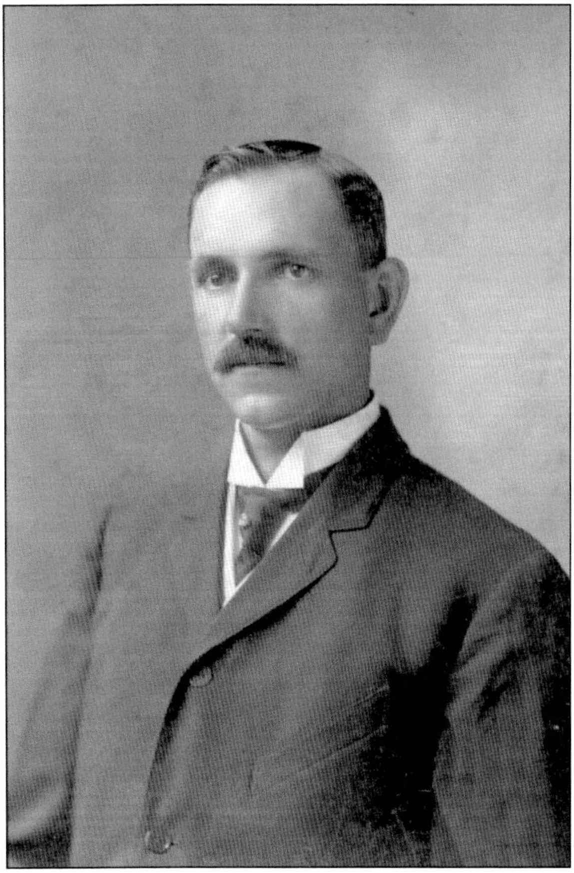

Orlando Harrison was born in Delaware on January 27, 1867, and moved to Berlin in 1884. His family started Harrison's Nurseries, which, by the 1920s, had become the largest grower of fruit and shade trees in the world. Harrison served in the Maryland House of Delegates in 1906, was mayor of Berlin from 1900 to 1908 and again in 1910, and was elected to the Maryland Senate in 1912. During his administration as town mayor, Berlin built its water and light system and paved its streets. Harrison's efforts in the state senate made possible the Ocean City and Pocomoke bridges. He also supported a new north-south highway from Dover, Delaware, to Cape Charles, Virginia, which later became today's Route 113. (Below, Ellis Wainwright Collection.)

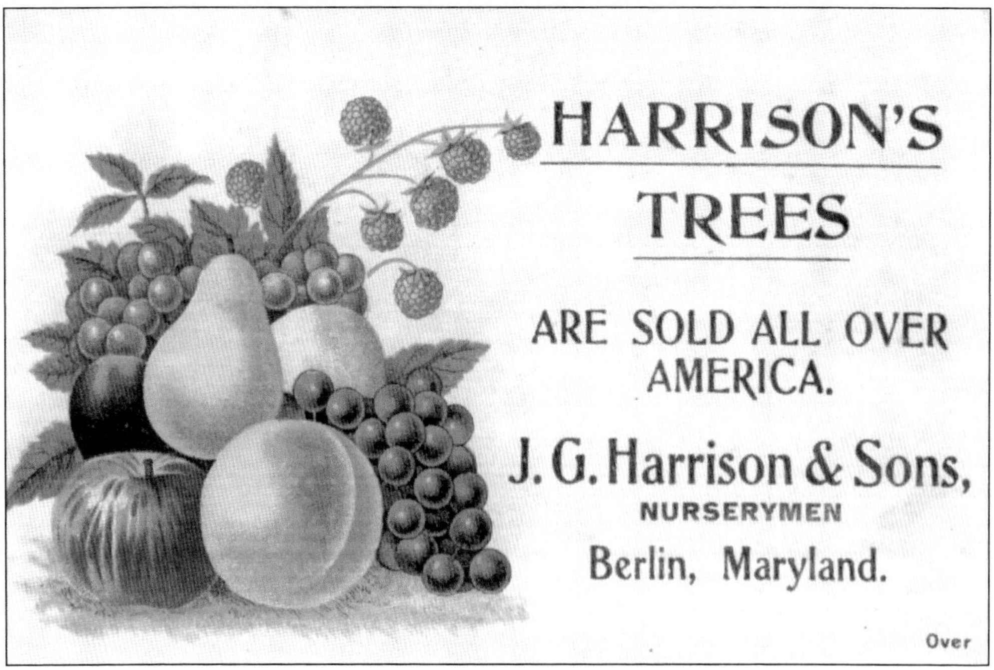

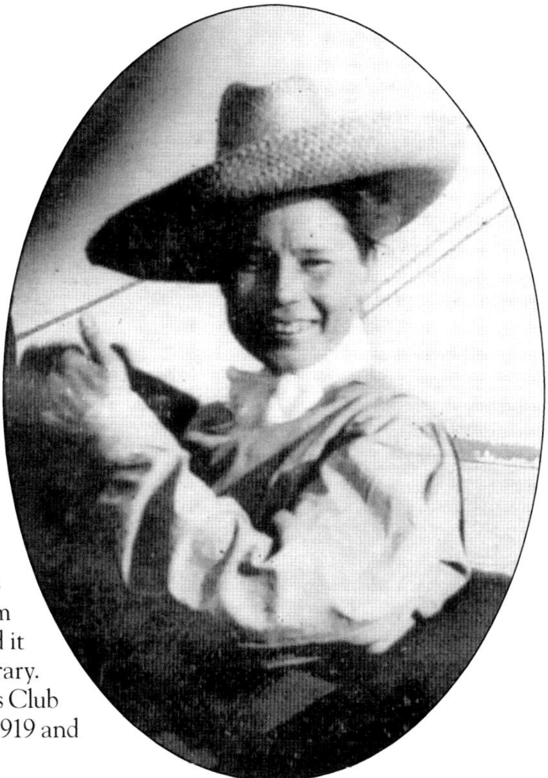

Rozelle Purnell Handy (1871–1920) was born in Richmond, Virginia, and moved to Berlin with her mother after her father died in 1893. Immersing herself in the local community, Handy started the "Neighborhood Sunday School" on her family's Ayres Creek property. This building, pictured below, was also used as a community center during the week, providing programs to educate and benefit young people. Believing everyone should have access to good reading, Handy began a book-lending system using her family's extensive library. After obtaining use of a room in Berlin's Community Building, she stacked it with her books and opened the Friendly Library. Handy was the first president of the Women's Club of Worcester County on its organization in 1919 and actively supported women's suffrage.

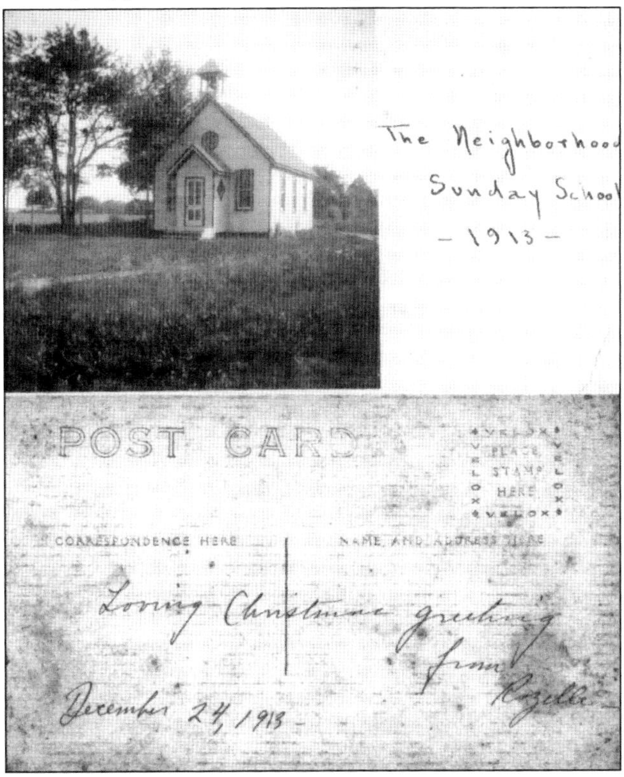

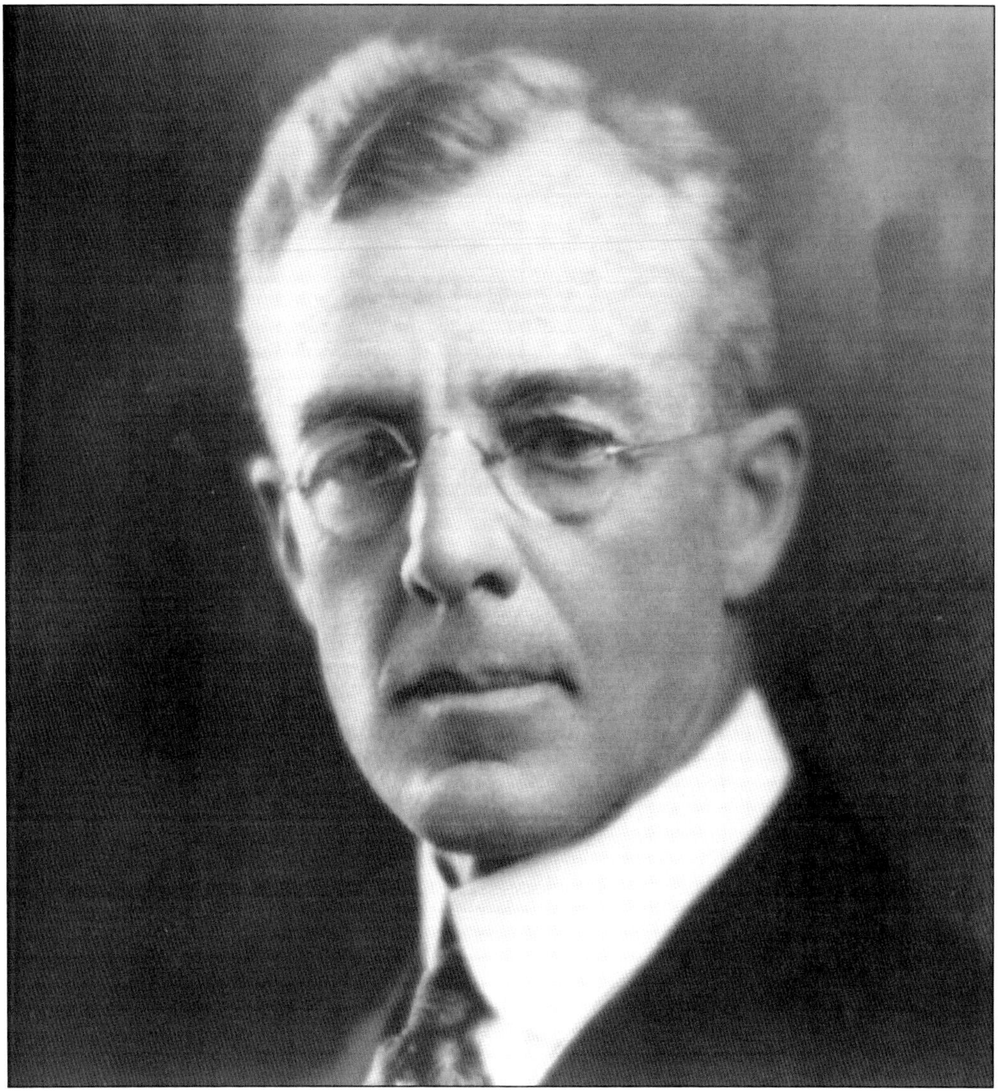

Calvin B. Taylor is most widely known as the founder of Taylor Bank, which he started in 1890. Taylor, born on Trappe Creek Farm in 1857, became a teacher and lawyer, principal of Berlin High School, and superintendent of Worcester County Schools. He served on the Berlin Town Council for four years and as mayor for two years. Taylor was a two-term member of the Maryland House of Delegates and a 25-year member of the Worcester County Democratic State Central Committee. An elder of Buckingham Presbyterian Church, Taylor served as Sunday school teacher and superintendent for more than 25 years, donating a new social hall and infant care room. He died in 1932 in his home, which has now been restored as a historic house and town museum, the Calvin B. Taylor House Museum on North Main Street.

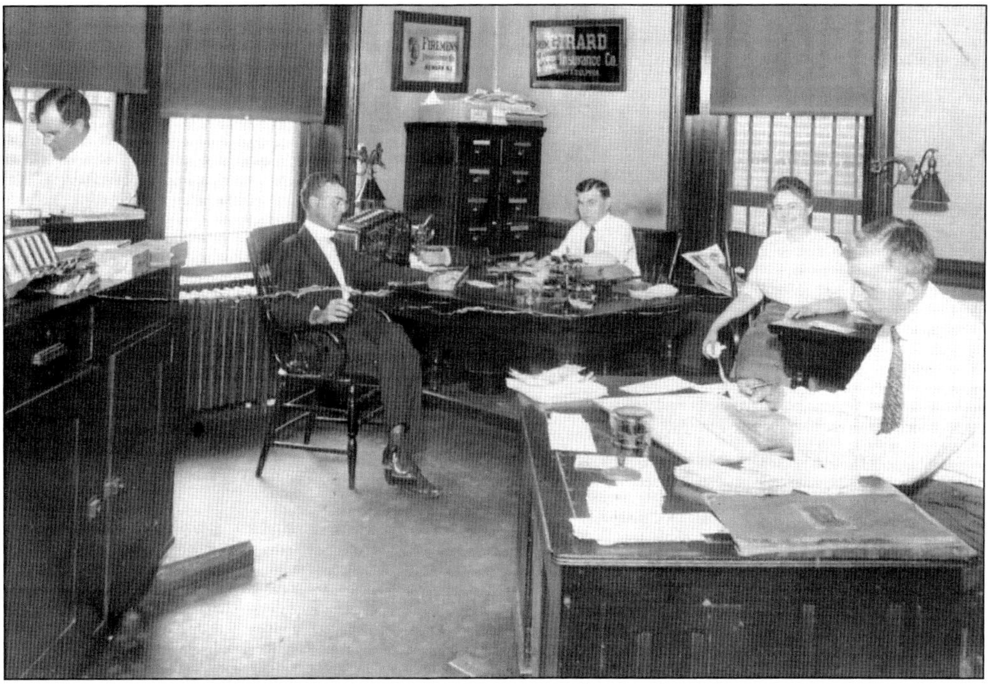

This interior photograph of the original Calvin B. Taylor Banking Company on Main Street was taken in 1915 and shows Calvin B. Taylor in the chair in front of the window. Raymond Boston, clerk, is seated in the back; assistant cashier John E. Smith appears at the counter; and William L. Holloway, cashier, is seated at the front desk. Miss Lillian Bowen, clerk, is seated behind Holloway.

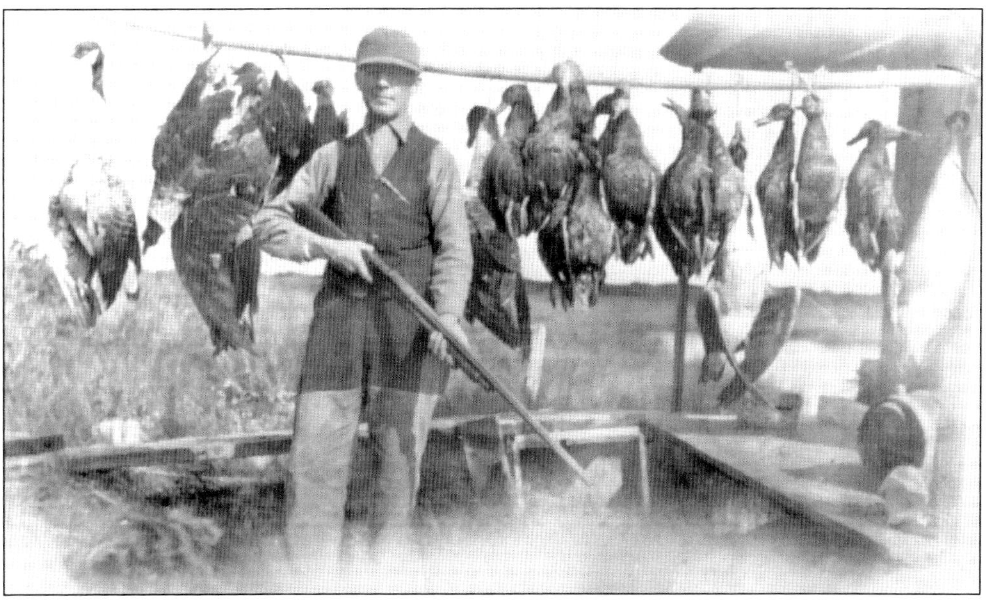

An upstanding member of the community, Calvin B. Taylor was known to fish in the surf in his necktie, high collar, and suit coat, but barefoot with his pant legs rolled up. This picture of Taylor was taken at the North Beach Clubhouse on Assateague Island in the 1920s when there were no "bag limits" on hunting.

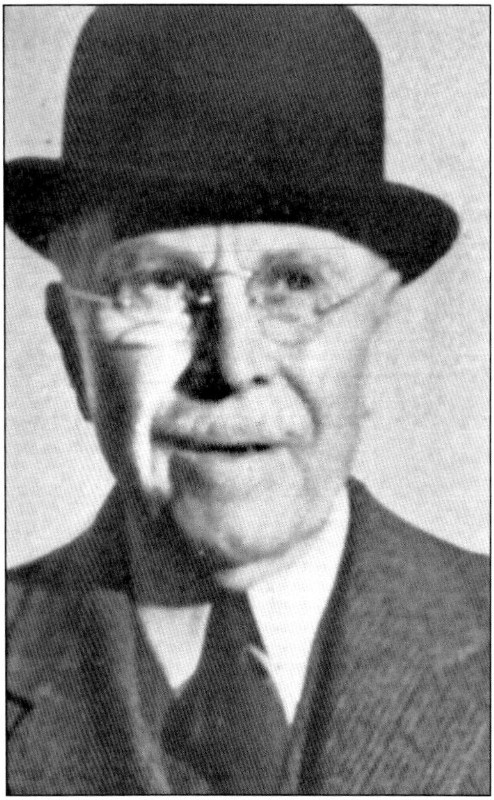

Glen Riddle Farm, east of Berlin, was the winter headquarters of Samuel D. Riddle, known as the owner of the greatest racehorse of the 20th century, Man o' War, pictured below. The extremely successful stud horse sired Triple Crown winner War Admiral, another great horse of the era. Both Man o' War and War Admiral trained on the Riddle Farm. In the 1930s, War Admiral was a contender in every major race on the East Coast. Seabiscuit, Man o' War's grandson, (although a year older than War Admiral) was a favorite on the West Coast. The two horses finally came together in a match race at Pimlico, Maryland, on November 1, 1938. Billed as the "Race of the Century," the head-to-head was featured in Universal Studios' 2003 movie *Seabiscuit*.

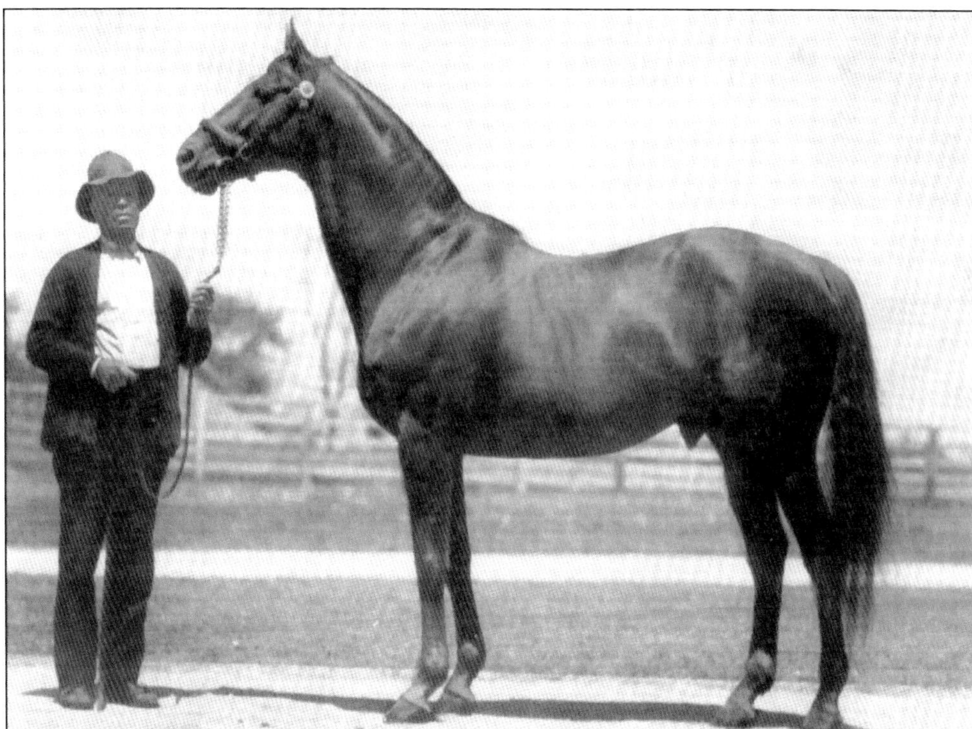

Dale Wimbrow, the "Delmarva Songster," was a local composer and musician who gained national notoriety in the 1930s. He is best known for composing the poem "The Man in the Glass," which is used extensively to this day by Alcoholics Anonymous. Another of Wimbrow's songs, "The Good Old Eastern Shore," was dedicated to the people of the Delmarva Peninsula.

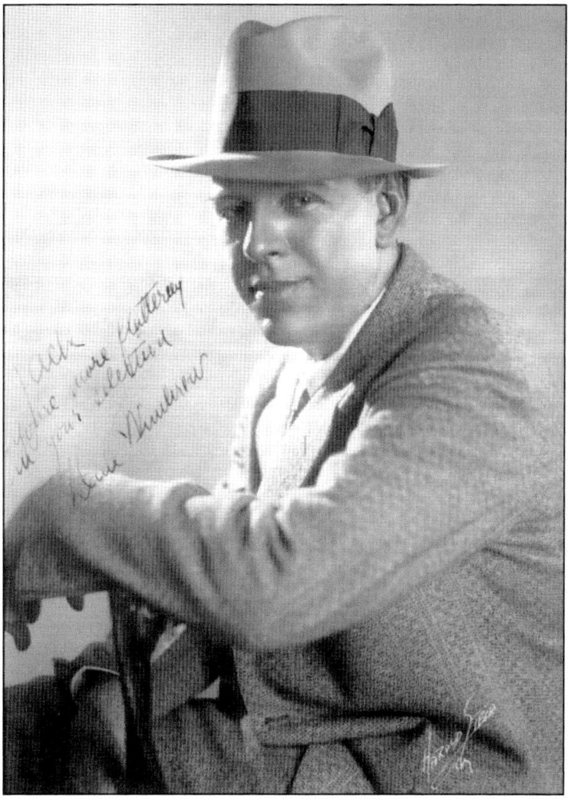

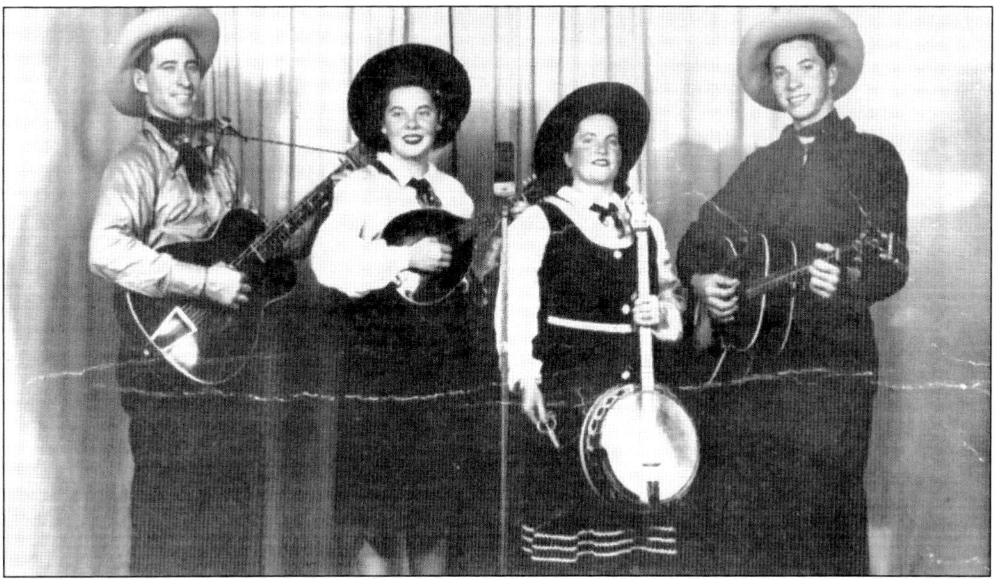

William Hurdle's childhood ambition was to be a musician, but it wasn't until 1929 that he published his first songs, "I Like My Bootleg Man," and "Love Like Mine." He became famous on the Eastern Shore as the One-Man-Band, playing at charity parties and barn dances. When his wife, son, and daughter joined him, the Hurdle family was billed as the "Southern Hillbillies." (Mabel Rogers Collection.)

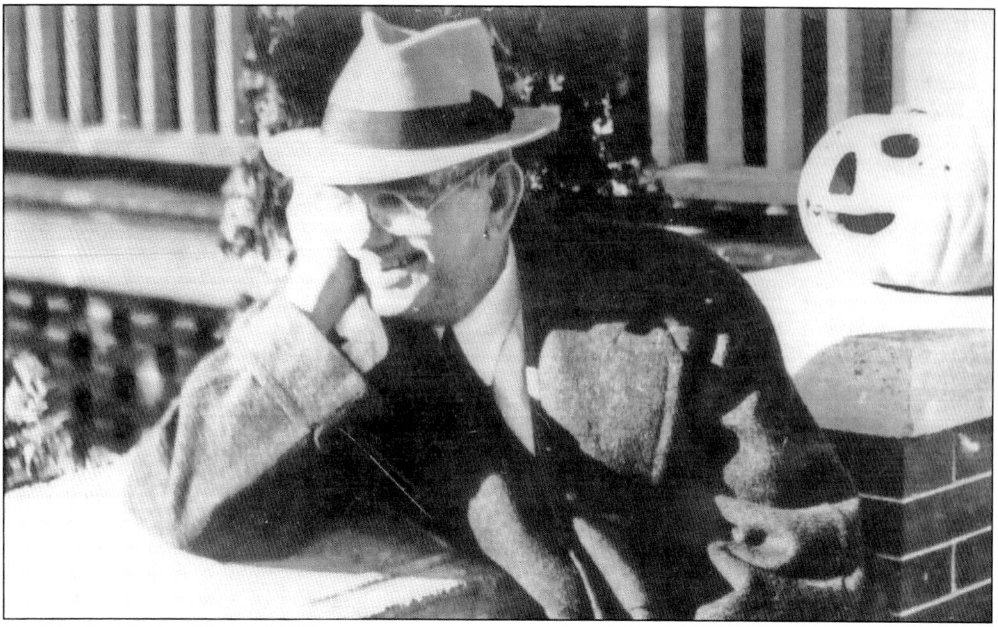

Dr. Charles Holland (1877–1937) is shown on the steps of the Holland House in the 1930s. Dr. Holland received his medical degree from Baltimore's Homeopathic School of Medicine in 1904, practicing in nearby Powellville and Whaleyville before moving to Berlin in 1916 to take over his brother's, Dr. Ebe Holland's, medical practice. When he retired in 1936, Dr. Frederick Nicoll took over the practice at the Holland House on Bay Street.

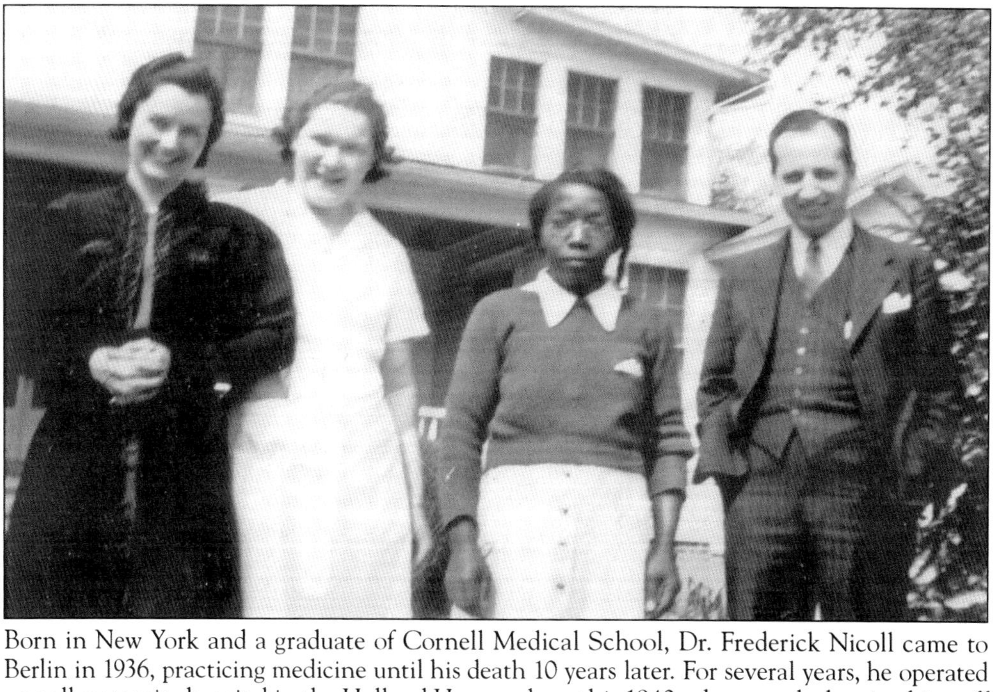

Born in New York and a graduate of Cornell Medical School, Dr. Frederick Nicoll came to Berlin in 1936, practicing medicine until his death 10 years later. For several years, he operated a small maternity hospital in the Holland House, where this 1940s photograph showing his staff was taken. Virginia Holland Nicoll, his wife, is pictured on the left beside Mary Brittingham and Mamie Davis.

Dr. Charles R. Law, born in 1886, was mayor of Berlin from 1926 to 1928. A prominent physician, Law was nationally known as a leading sportsman in the eastern United States. According to him, Worcester County's deer had become extinct in 1857; so in 1922, working with state game officials, he released several deer into the area, enough to repopulate the deer on the Eastern Shore.

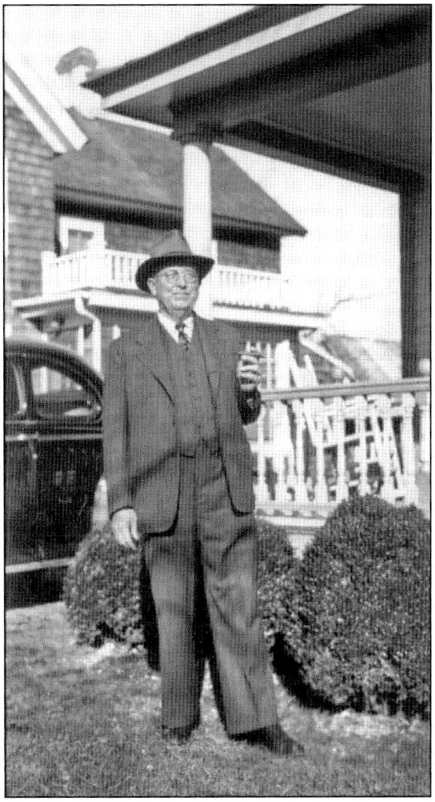

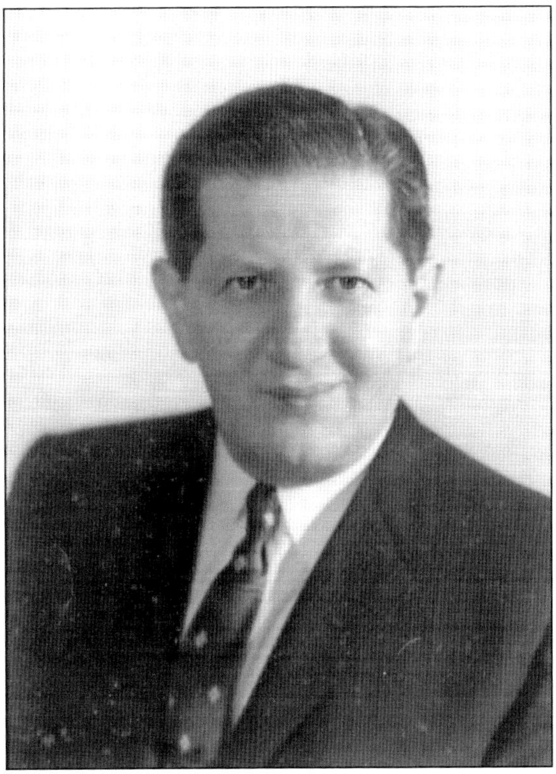

Jesse Hollins was born on October 21, 1905. His father was a trader in hides and his uncle Joseph a leading Berlin merchant. During his life as an inventor, the younger Hollins was granted over 100 patents and was internationally recognized as a major contributor to automotive safety. He was a pioneer in electrically operated directional signals, inventing the traffic hazard warning device and developing the thermally activated flasher. His family created the Signal-Stat Corporation. Hollins died in 1979 on his 74th birthday.

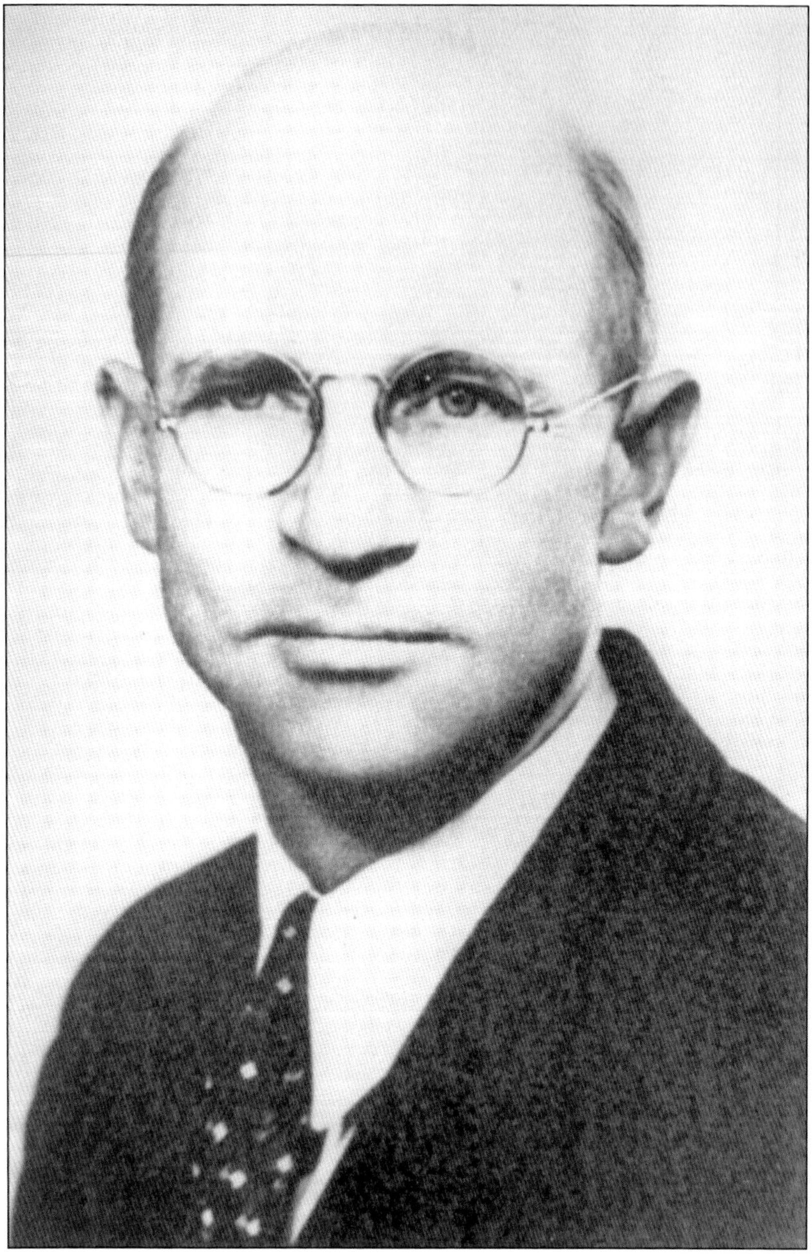

William Pitts, born in Berlin on August 14, 1889, was a local land surveyor, county surveyor, and amateur historian for many years. His William D. Pitts Collection of Survey Records, housed in the Worcester County Library, is considered the most complete set of such records in the country. He served the community in his profession and as a historian, counselor, and friend to many for more than 70 years. Meticulous and accurate to a fault, if Pitts surveyed it or said it, then it was true and correct. His memory was phenomenal. Once, when asked about the ownership of a property, he advised the enquirer, "Son, your dad owns that; I mean your grandad; I mean your great-grandad. Let me check." In fact, the enquirer's great-great-grandmother bought the property in 1838. Pitts was incredibly fit and actively surveyed until shortly before his death. He had a spring in his step until the day he died.

# *Seven*

# JUST PLAIN FUN

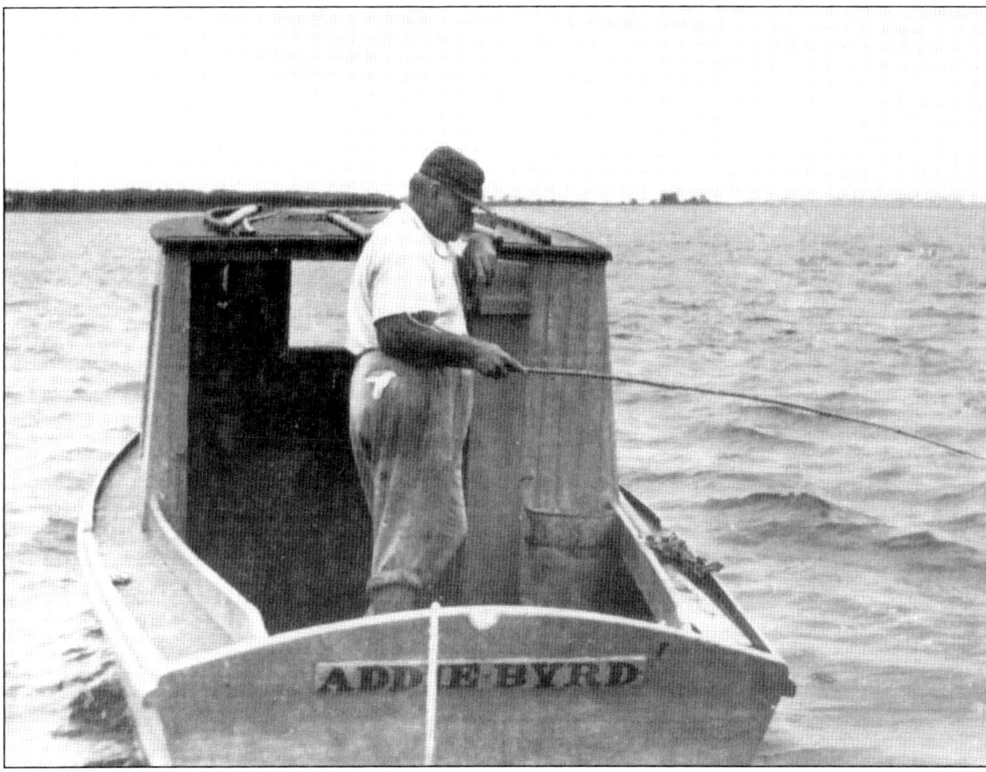


The *Addie Byrd* was a scow, a blunt-nosed boat typical of the bay workboats in the first half of the 20th century. Because of the shape of the bow, it was less likely to get stuck on the bay's shoals or sandbars and easier to free if stuck. Small gasoline inboard engines, often from automobiles, powered these boats, which were around 20 feet long. The "house," as the cabin was called, provided protection from the elements, particularly the sun, and was stocked with several glass, one-gallon jugs of potable water, as well as fishing poles, crab nets, clam rakes, nets, and sometimes life preservers, collected on beachcombing expeditions. This gentleman, Ethan Allen Carey, is a waterman, a "progger" in local parlance. He could handle this boat, named for his beloved wife, by himself and scull it (propelling the boat with one oar by stroking in a circular, side-to-side motion from a notch in the stern) at a speed equal to its engine speed. Proggers could live off the bay and a little farming at a time when life was simple and uncomplicated.

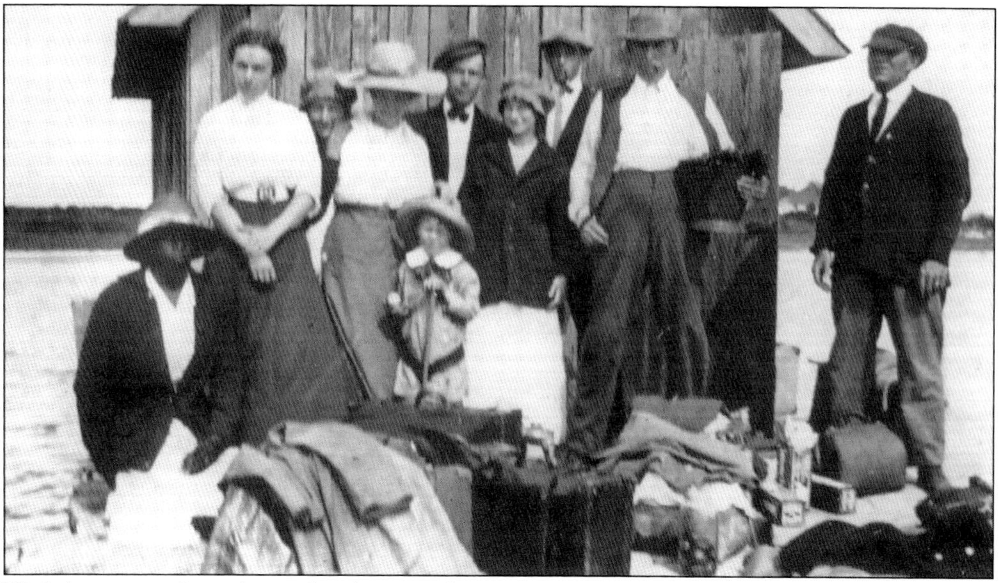

With luggage and supplies, a family awaits boat transportation to North Beach for a stay at the "Hotel" in about 1930. There were no paved roads on the island, and beasts of burden were employed. Beach buggies in those days were truly buggies, or more likely carts and wagons. The peace, quiet, and fresh air were worth the effort, and the pounding surf was a soothing and relaxing tonic for "modern day life."

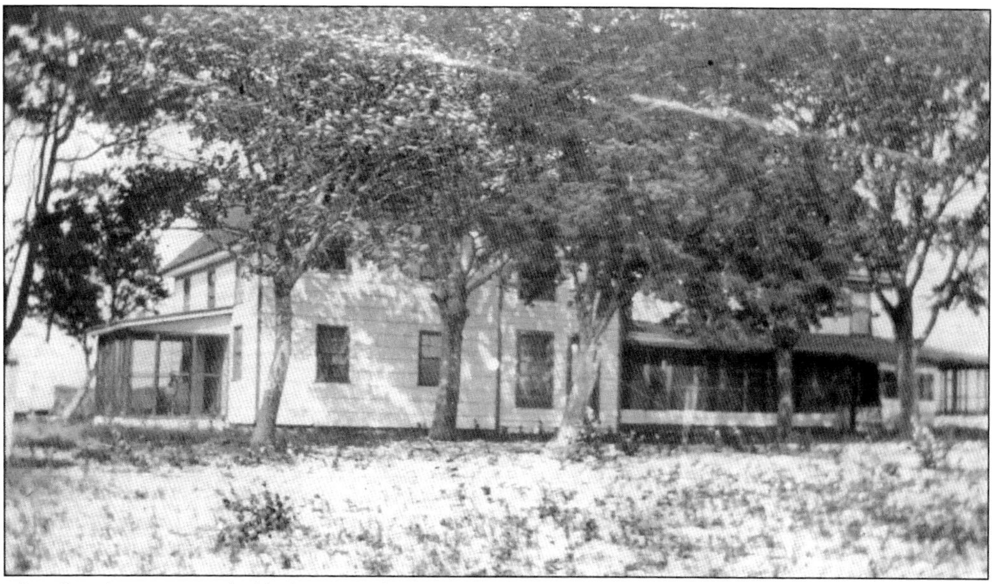

This farmhouse provided lodging and meals for guests during the summer and was known as the "Hotel." The acquisition of the island by the state and federal governments in the 1960s preserved a great natural heritage closely associated with the town, but the townspeople lost a wonderful playground that they could enjoy without significant regulation necessitated by increased public use of the island. Thankfully the island has retained some of its peacefulness.

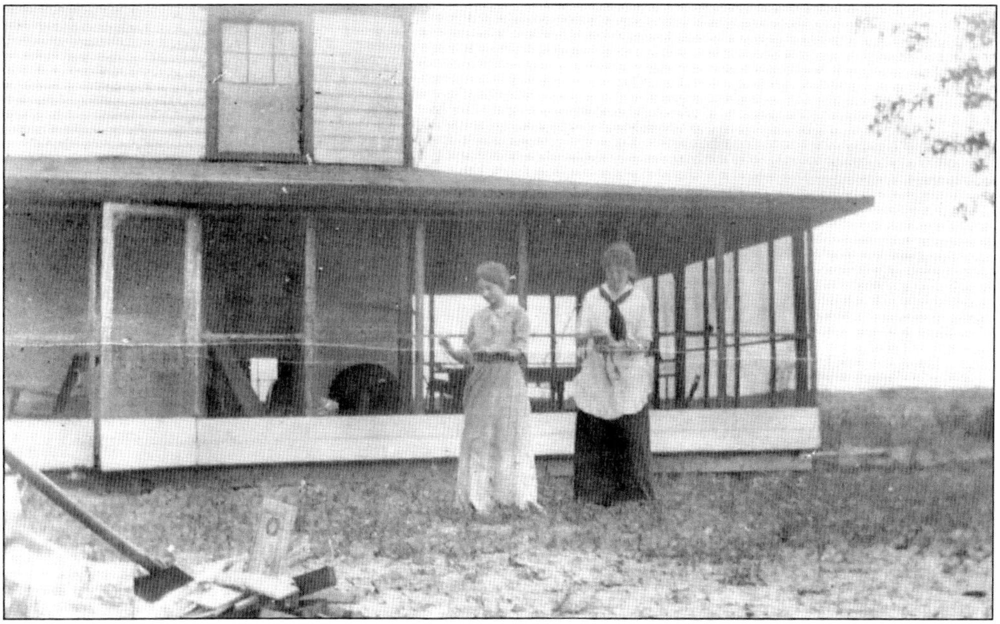

Here are two guests at the Hotel. They appear to be engaged in food preparation. Note the woodpile and axe, which served the cook stove. Screened porches on Assateague Island were not an amenity but a necessity. The Assateague mosquitoes were as virulent or perhaps more virulent then as now. These ladies are wearing the latest in beach vacation casual wear.

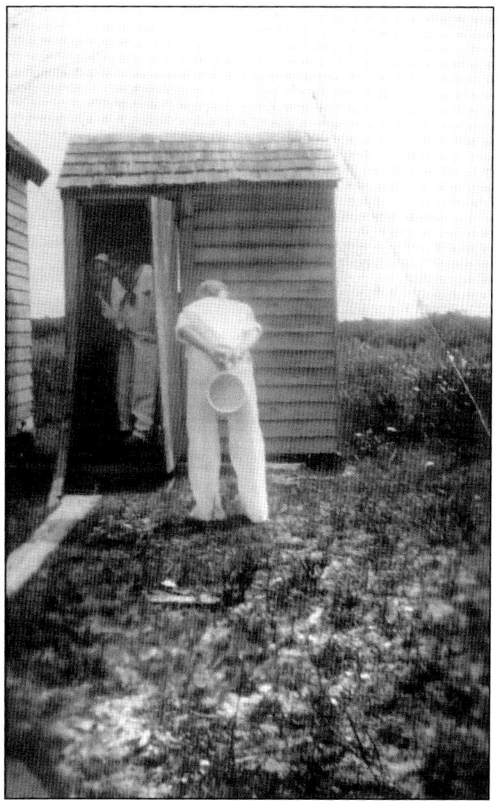

This is not a woodshed or a dairy. It is the privy and was apparently very much in use on this vacation. By the time of this photograph, the Town of Berlin had indoor plumbing and a municipal sewer system, having prevailed in a lawsuit filed by a citizen, John Keas, attempting to prevent such governmental extravagance.

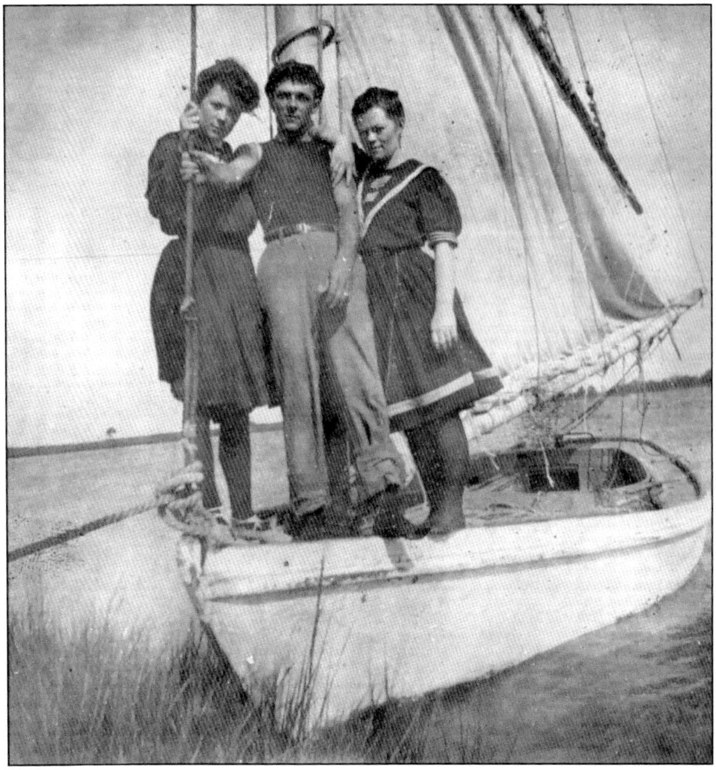

Before 1900, to go boating "down the bay," sailing, sculling, or rowing skills were necessary. Mechanical engines were not generally found in bay craft prior to that time. Bay sailboats were kept stable with adjustable centerboards, there being far too many shoals and sandbars in the bay to accommodate boats with keels. This is Kendall and Mabel Jarvis and one of Mabel's sisters (left).

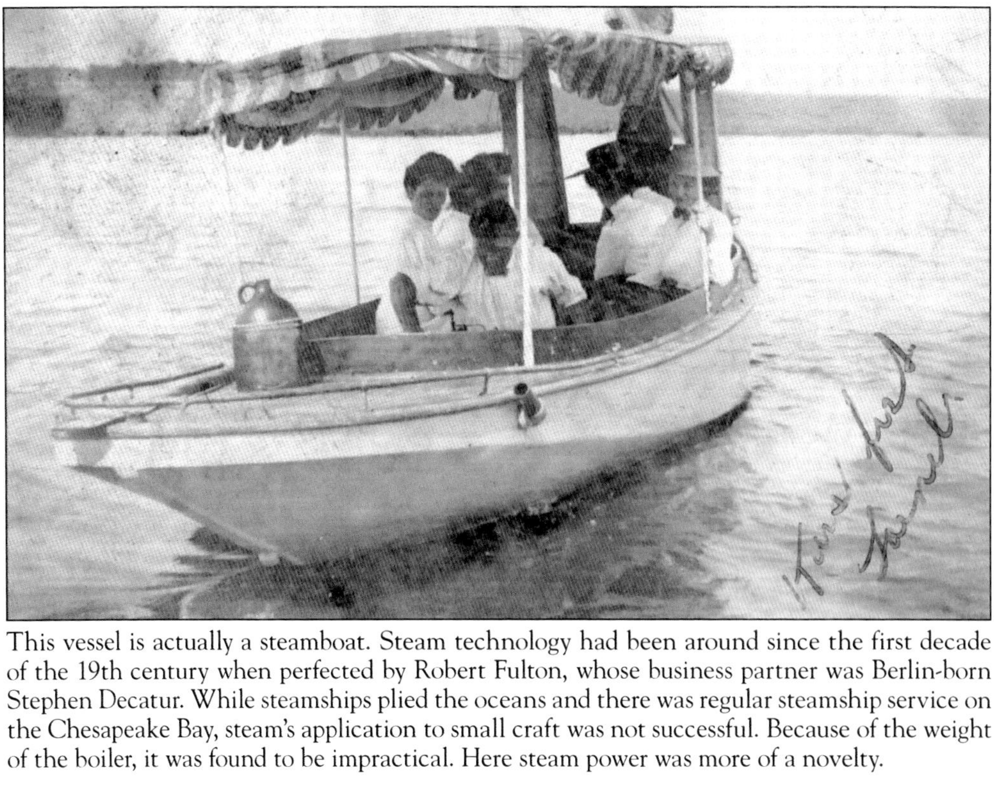

This vessel is actually a steamboat. Steam technology had been around since the first decade of the 19th century when perfected by Robert Fulton, whose business partner was Berlin-born Stephen Decatur. While steamships plied the oceans and there was regular steamship service on the Chesapeake Bay, steam's application to small craft was not successful. Because of the weight of the boiler, it was found to be impractical. Here steam power was more of a novelty.

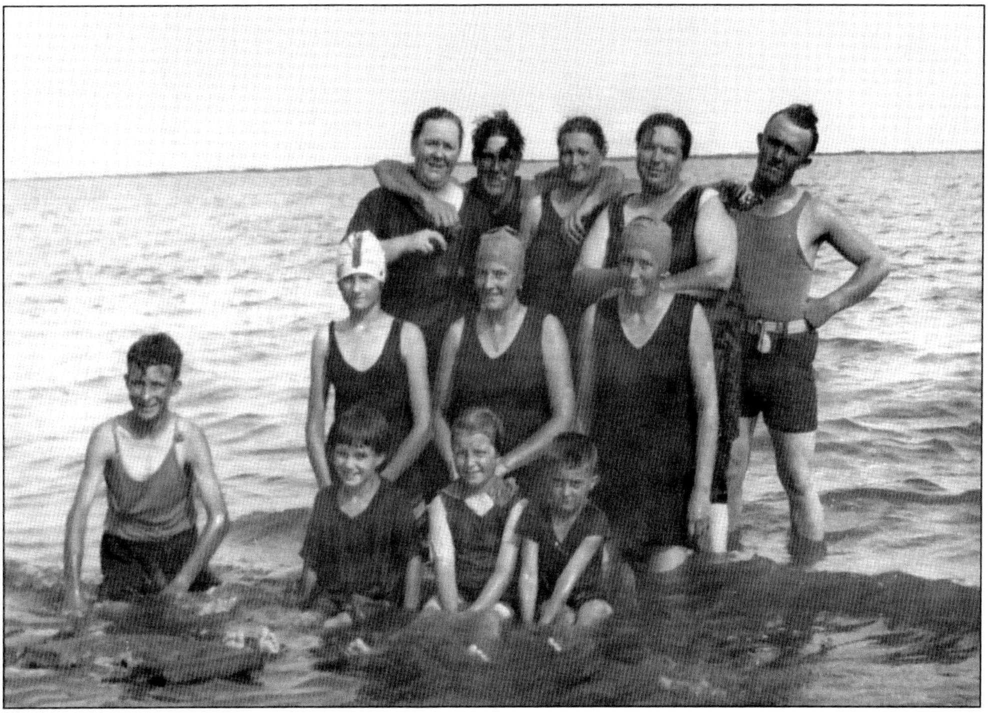

Bathing suits have changed, but the joy of "bathing" has not. This group in their woolen suits appears to be bathing in the bay. The water was too shallow to swim in, so bathing was a more accurate description. The wool suits must have been extremely uncomfortable and, despite the attempt to cover a lot of bare skin, were apparently quite revealing when wet. (Cheryl Holland Collection.)

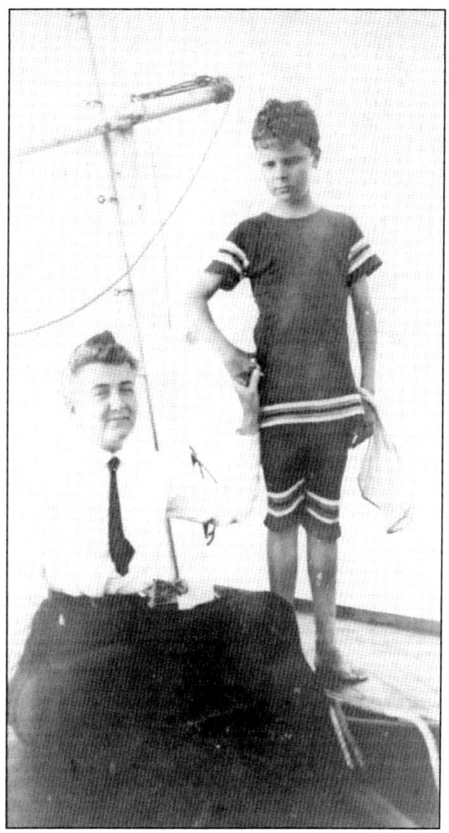

This photograph, taken about 1903 on the deck of a small sailboat, shows a young Berlin boy, Edward H. Hammond, and his governess. Note the governess's attire. This young man later became an accomplished sailor.

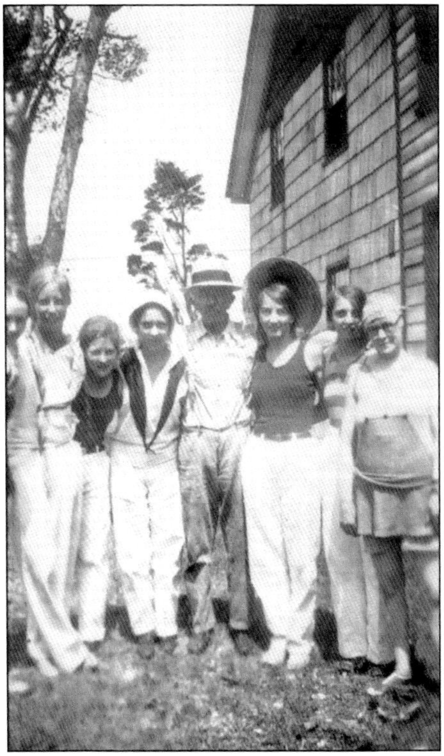

This is another group of vacationers posing at the Hotel about 1935. Unfortunately their identities are unknown, a situation that cries out for labeling, dating, and preserving photographs. Today's digital shots are tomorrow's antique photographs.

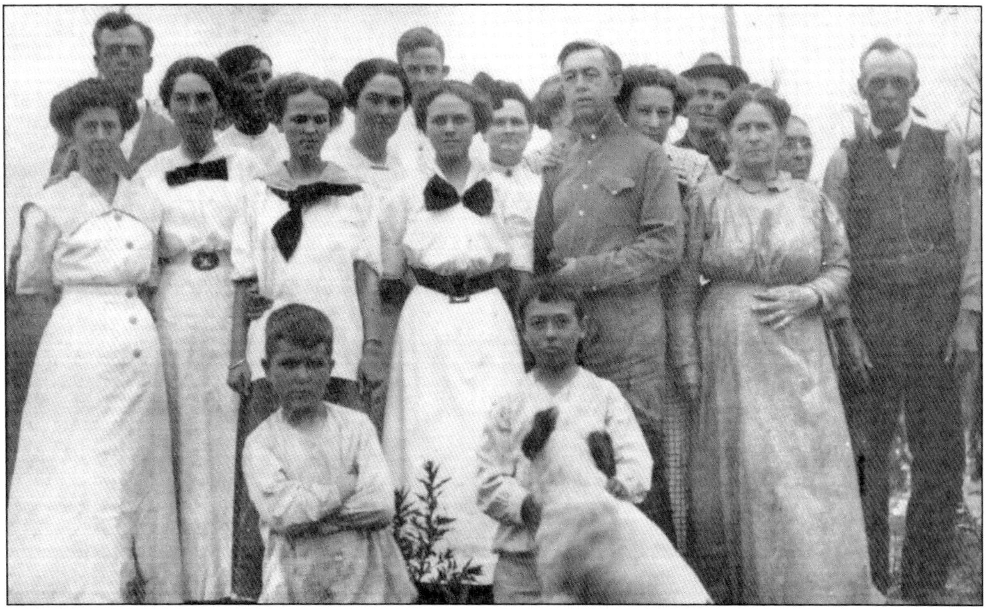

This picture is dated and labeled "Picture taken about 1910–1912 at North Beach at Gunning Lodge, near old Coast Guard Station." From left to right are (first row) Roland Purnell and Lee Burbage; (second row) Lydia Richardson, unidentified, Nell Boston, Elva Burbage Mitchell, William Holloway, Mrs. Cecelia Burbage, and William Burbage; (third row) Calvin B. Taylor, three unidentified, Annie Purnell, unidentified, Minnie Holloway, William Purnell, and unidentified. (Cheryl Holland Collection.)

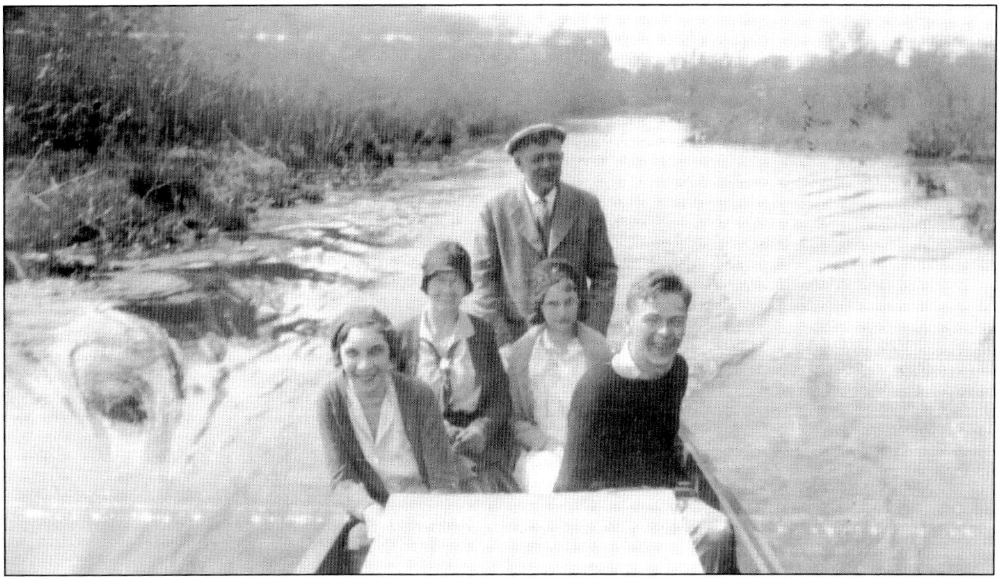

When speedboats first appeared on the bay, Kendall Patey Jarvis (center) was one of the first to have one. Here he is with his wife, Mabel Powell Jarvis (second from left), Mary Louise Taylor (far left), Elizabeth Taylor, and son Kendall Powell Jarvis going out Hayes Landing Creek, perhaps heading for the amusements at Public Landing. The trip from Hayes Landing to Public Landing was quicker by boat than by automobile. This photograph was taken about 1925.

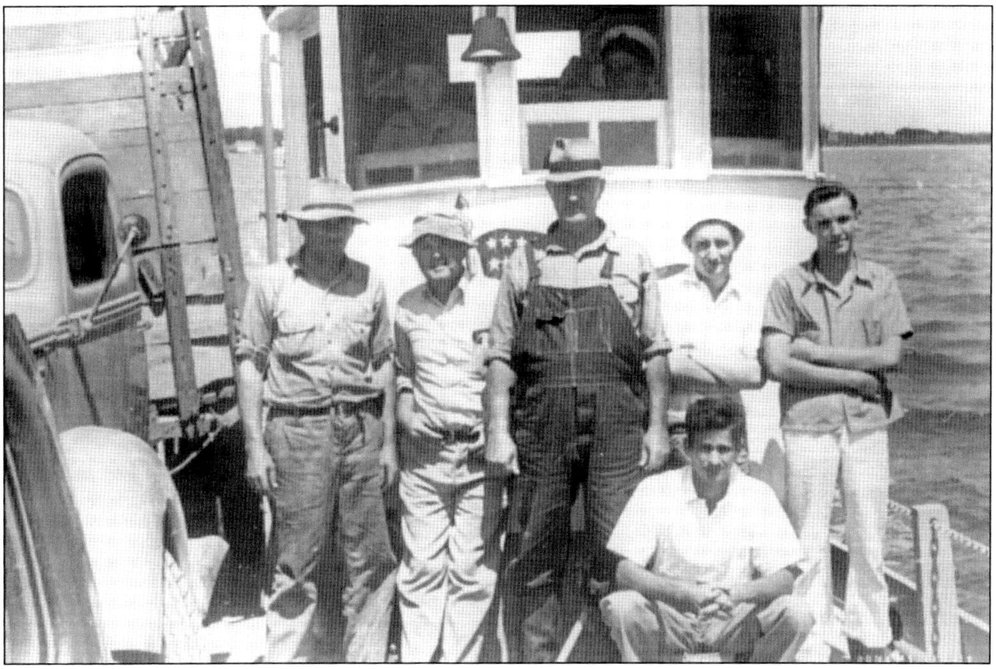

A small ferry served Assateague in the mid-20th century. Mainland farmers grazed cattle on the open range. For about 40 years, a ferry served the island. Here cattlemen, including Sheriff Ned Lynch (in bib overalls) ride the ferry to check on their cattle. They are, from left to right, (kneeling in front) Chuck Willis; (standing) Raymond Massey, Raymond Bounds, Lynch, Ralph Selby, and E. R. "Skeeter" Bounds; (in the cabin) Ike Jones and Walt Watson.

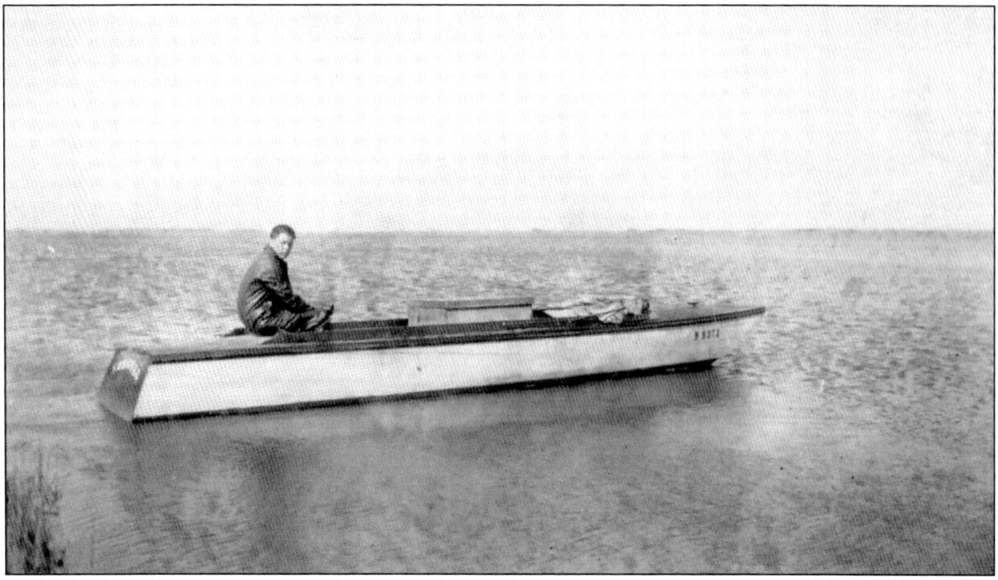

The bucolic life "down the bay" began to change in the 1930s with the coming of the speedboats, expensive polished mahogany craft with powerful inboard engines capable of running at a rate of speed never before experienced on the bay. When the outboard motor was perfected, it became a less expensive alternative to the speedboat but almost as fast and noisy.

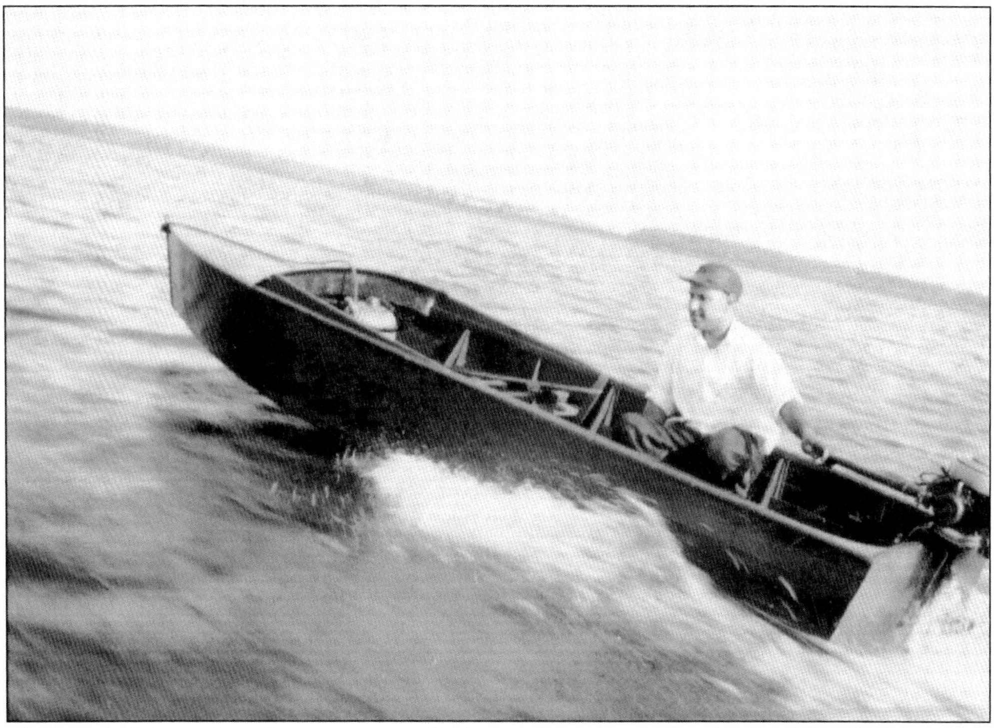

The drone of the outboard motor or actually the gasoline engine was the death-knell of the peace and quiet of the bay, but it ushered in a whole new era of enjoyment of the bays and Assateague. The next threat to pristine bays is over-development of real estate on the shoreline, providing a great challenge for the people of Berlin.

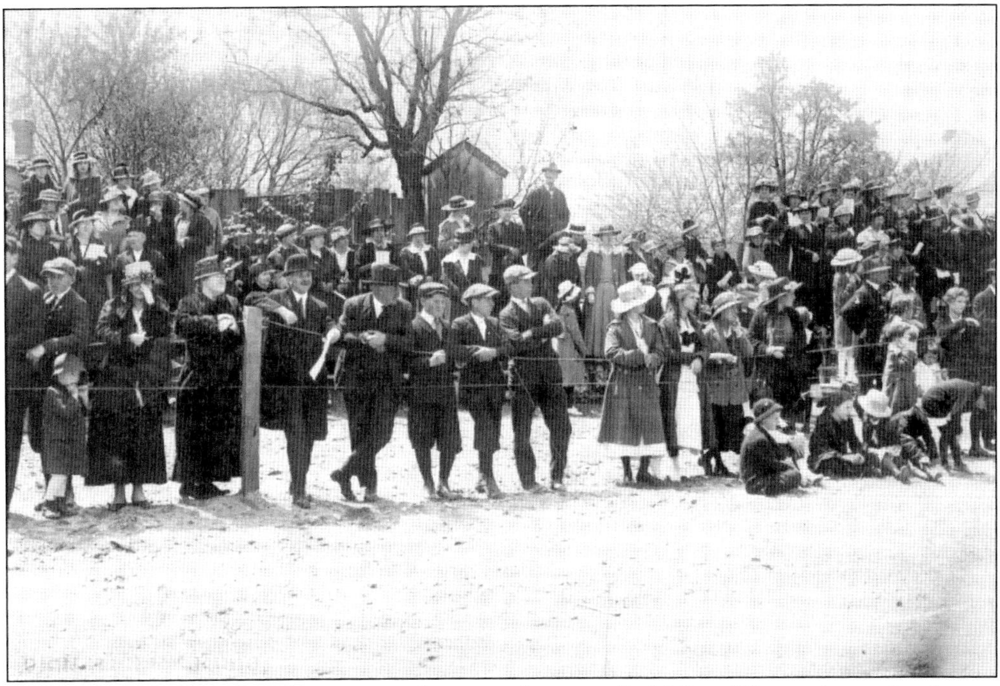

Spectators cheer on their favorites at the annual county Field Day. The various schools sent teams. There were track and field events as well as hit ball, dodge ball, field ball, and touchdown pass ball. There were boys' events, girls' events, and mixed events.

This scene depicts an early-1900s "honey-do" chore. She appears to be providing a lot of sidewalk supervision. This photograph was taken for fun with a box camera. Prior to about 1900, photographs were taken by professional photographers and mainly in studios. When box cameras became commercially available, snapshots became popular and the camera was used just for fun. This snapshot was taken on Washington Street about 1910.

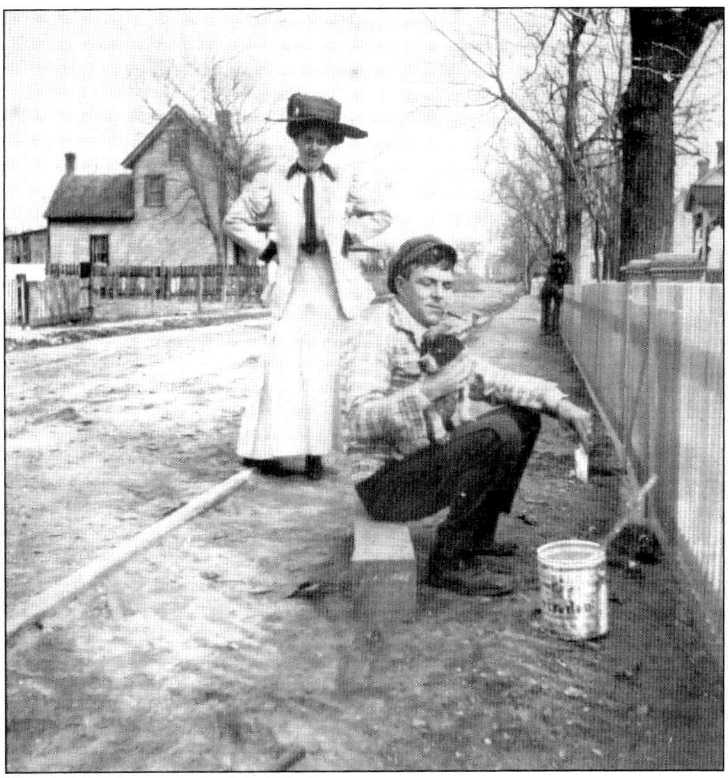

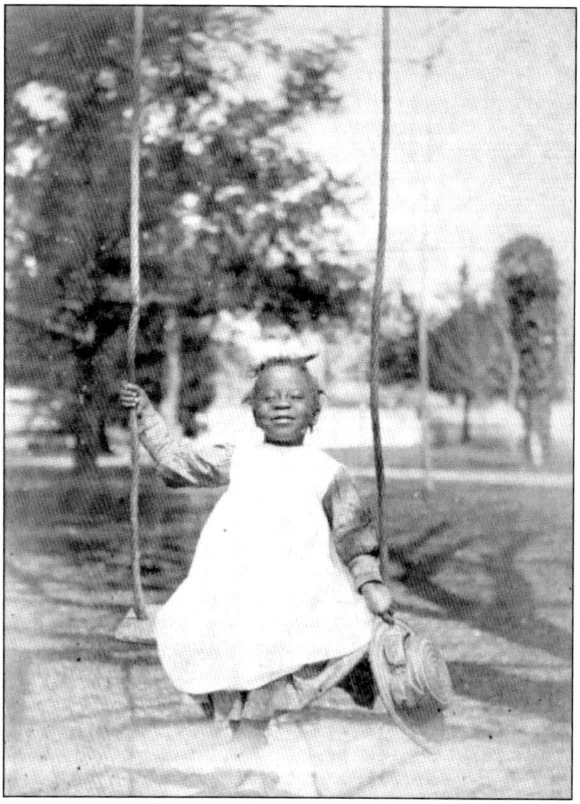

Sadly we do not know the name of this adorable little girl. The photograph dates from about 1900 and is from Burley Manor. Note the straw bonnet in her left hand.

Virginia Hammond is pictured in her bonnet in a rustic gazebo at Burley Manor around 1900. These gazebos were a style very much in vogue at the time. Note the cinched waist, also very much in vogue.

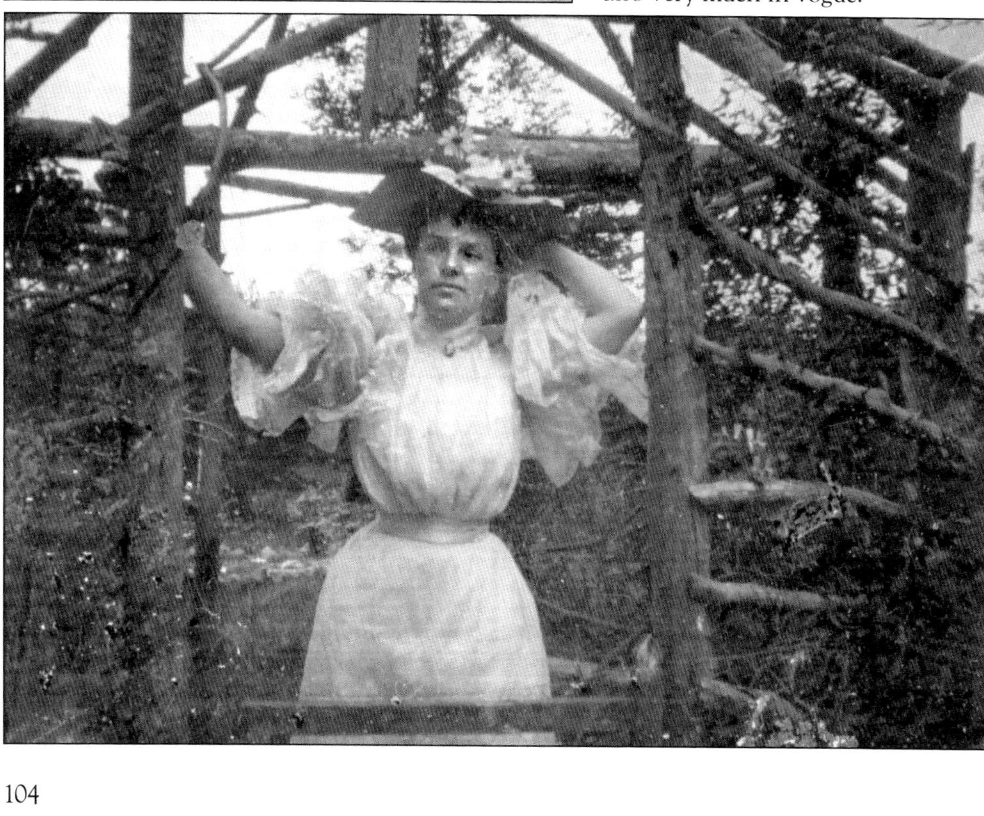

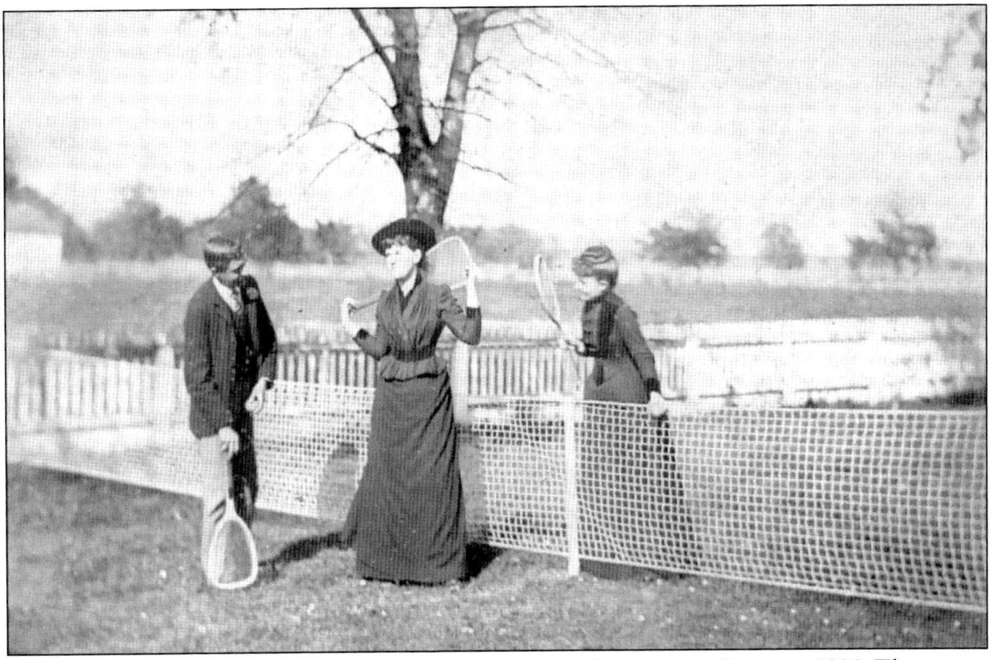

This photograph shows tennis being played on a lawn on South Main Street in 1890. The tennis outfits bear little resemblance to those of today and would seem to be a little confining, but then these players did not have coaches or sports psychologists.

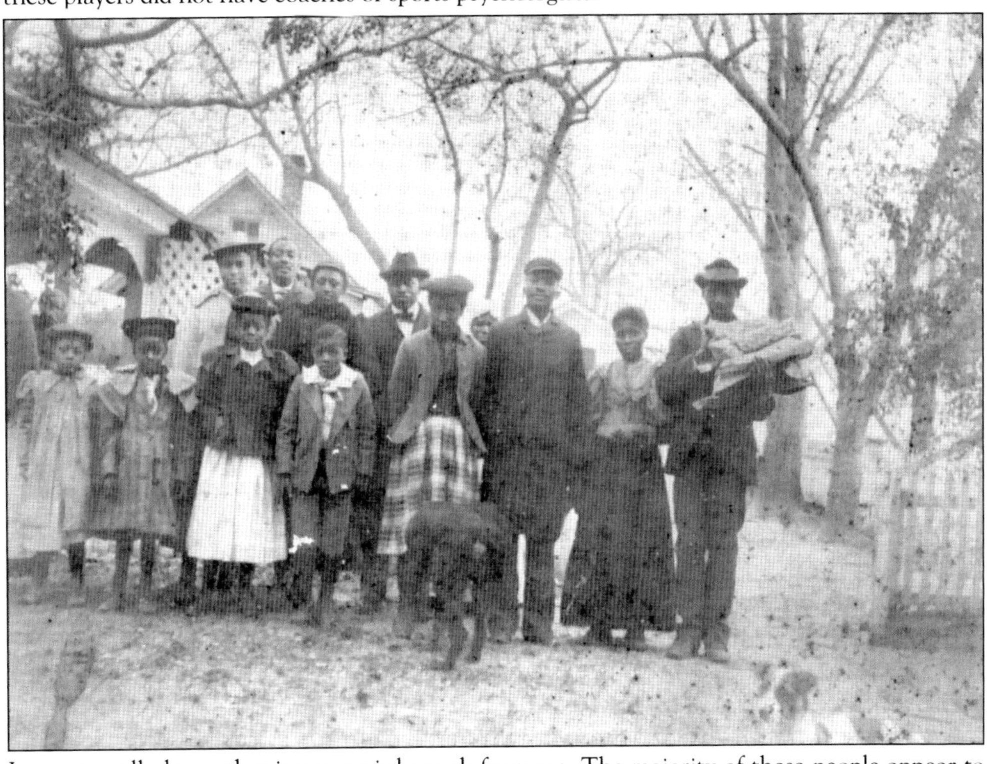

It was not all play; rather it was mainly work for some. The majority of these people appear to be dressed for church.

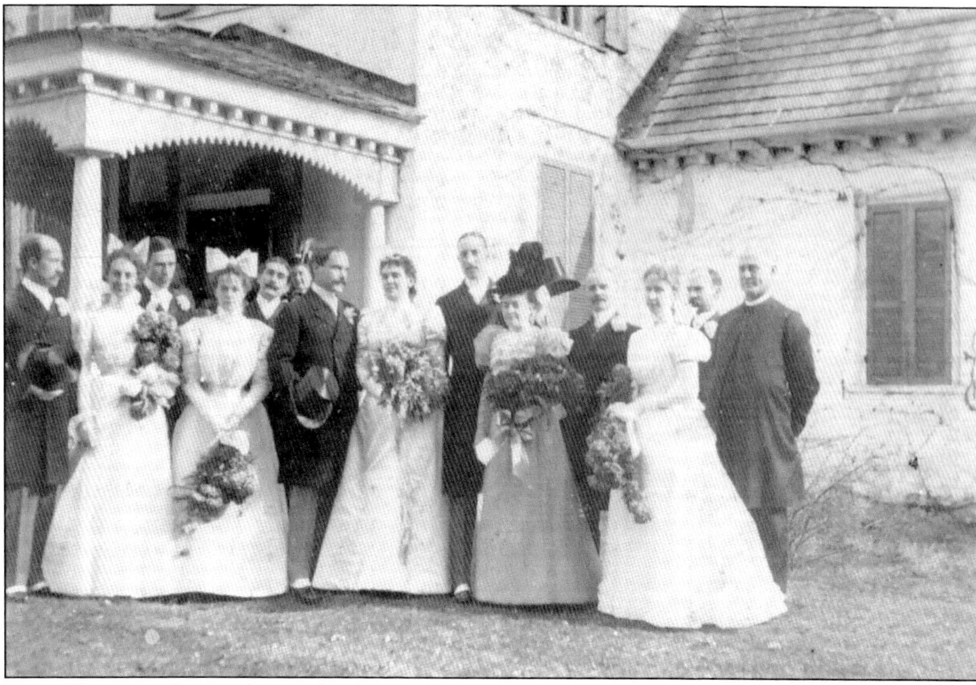

December 2, 1897, was a happy day for Virginia Hammond of Burley Manor and William L. Fleming of Harrisburg, Pennsylvania. Members of the wedding party pose on the lawn after the ceremony at St. Paul's Episcopal Church. The reception was held here at the bride's home.

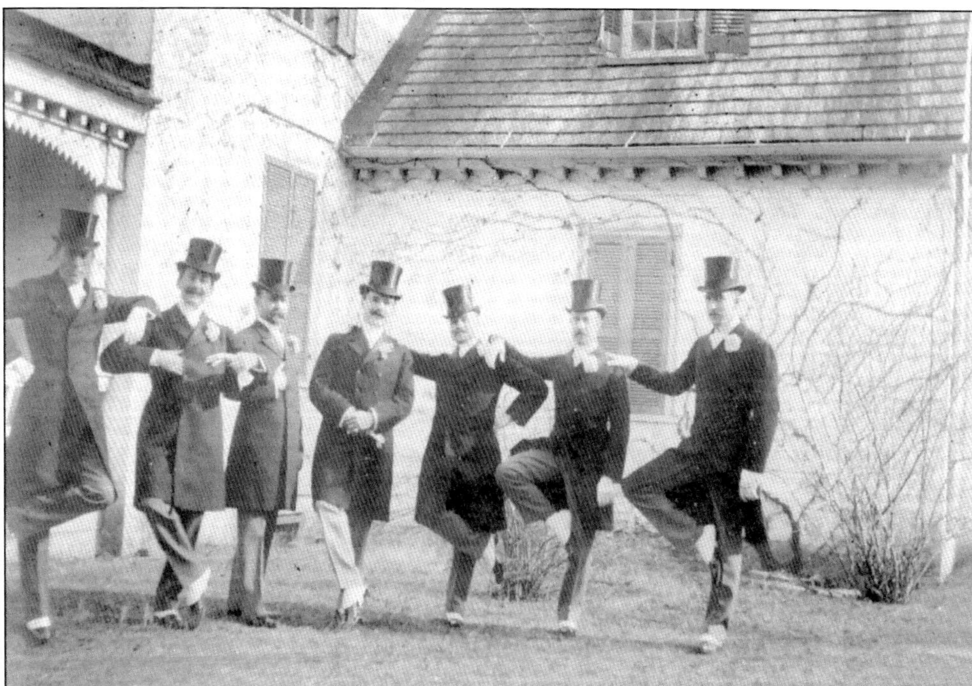

This photograph from the Hammond-Fleming wedding proves that groomsmen were just as goofy 100 years ago as now.

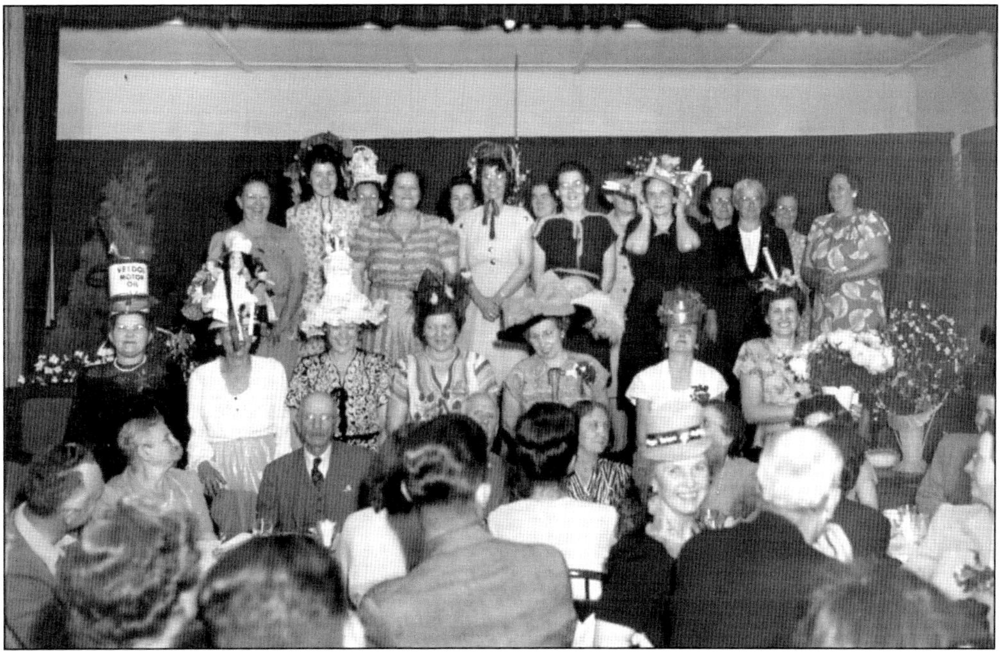

These ladies are contestants in a hat contest held at Stevenson United Methodist Church in about 1950. Churches in the 1950s were social as well as religious centers, and the social aspects of church life were as important in those days as they are now. One very popular and continuing social event in local churches is the church supper.

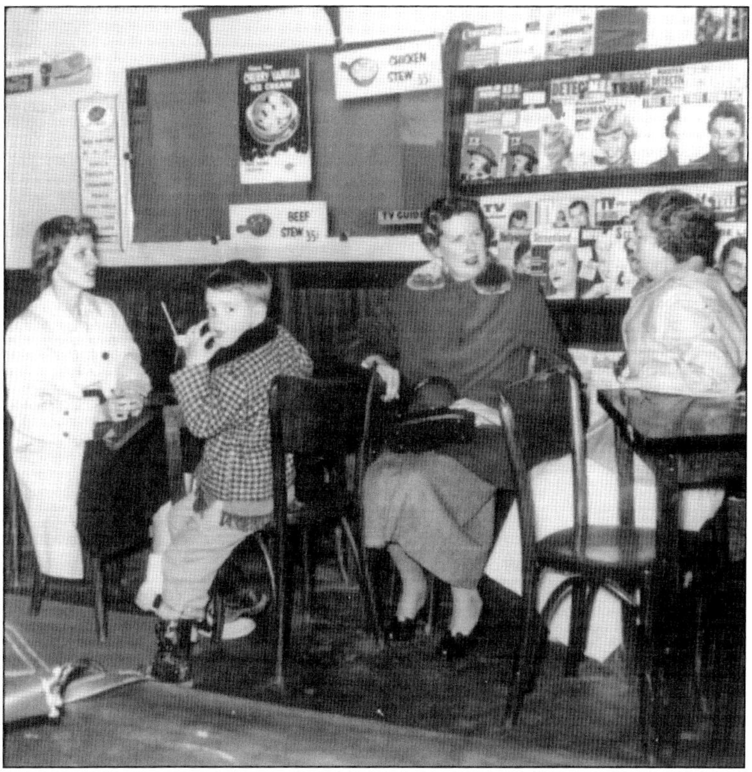


Churches weren't the only social hot spots; so were soda fountains. Around 1950, Berlin boasted three such establishments: Conley and Rayne, the Cove, and the Kozy Korner. They served light fare, soft drinks, and sweet concoctions like chocolate zips, ice cream sodas, milk shakes, and all flavors of ice cream. Inside Conley and Rayne, Anna May Shockley, in the coat with the fur collar, chats with a friend.

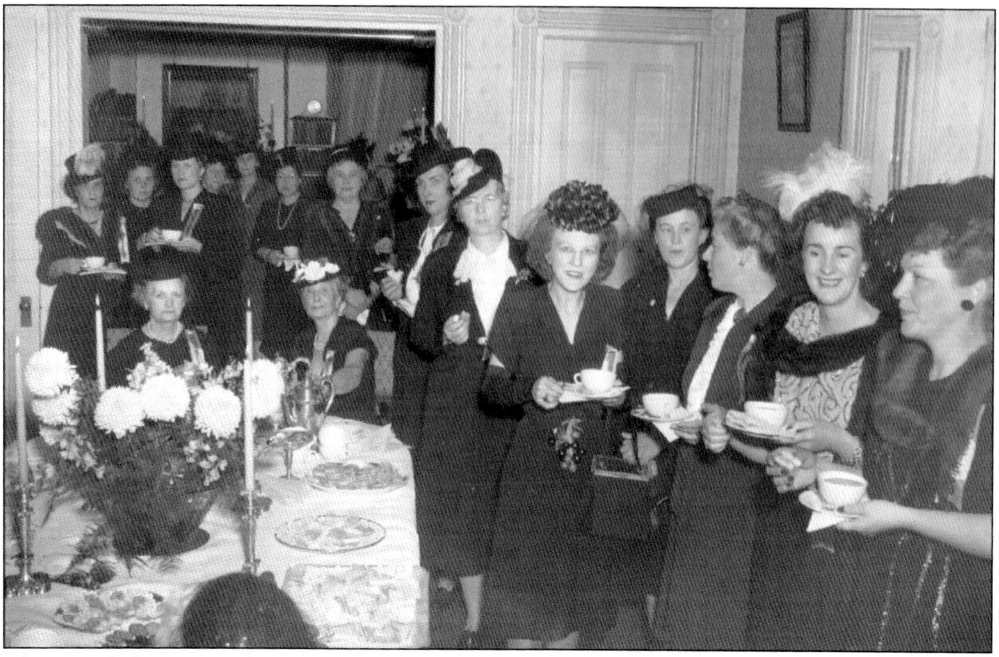

This 1946 ladies tea was held in the old Lions Club building on Route 113 just south of Main Street. This building later burned and a new Lion's Den log cabin was built on the same site. Some of the ladies can be identified as Mabel Purnell, Violet Culver, Irma Hastings, Fran Quillin, Macon Chandler, Virginia Richardson, and Lois Harrison.

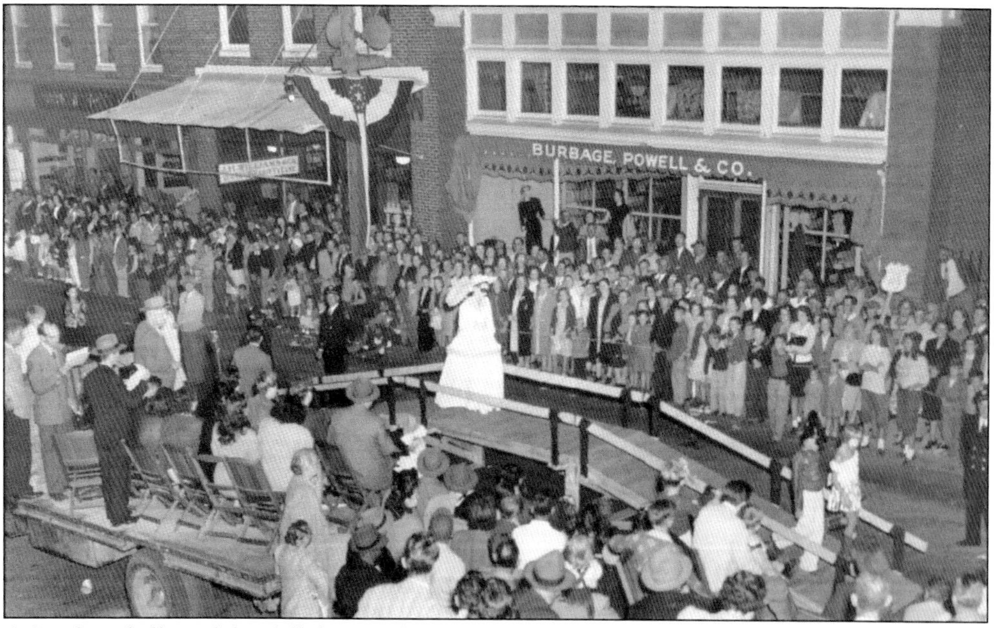


A Southern belle with her full skirts and parasol is center stage for the judges at a 1940s Halloween parade on Main Street. The building with the white canopy is William's Five and Dime, affectionately known as "Ralph's," after J. H. Williams's son-in-law, Ralph Davis. Right after Thanksgiving, Ralph would invite Santa Claus to put some toys in his upstairs so the town children could have toys to pick for Santa to bring on Christmas Eve.

# *Eight*

# Preservation, Restoration, and Reward

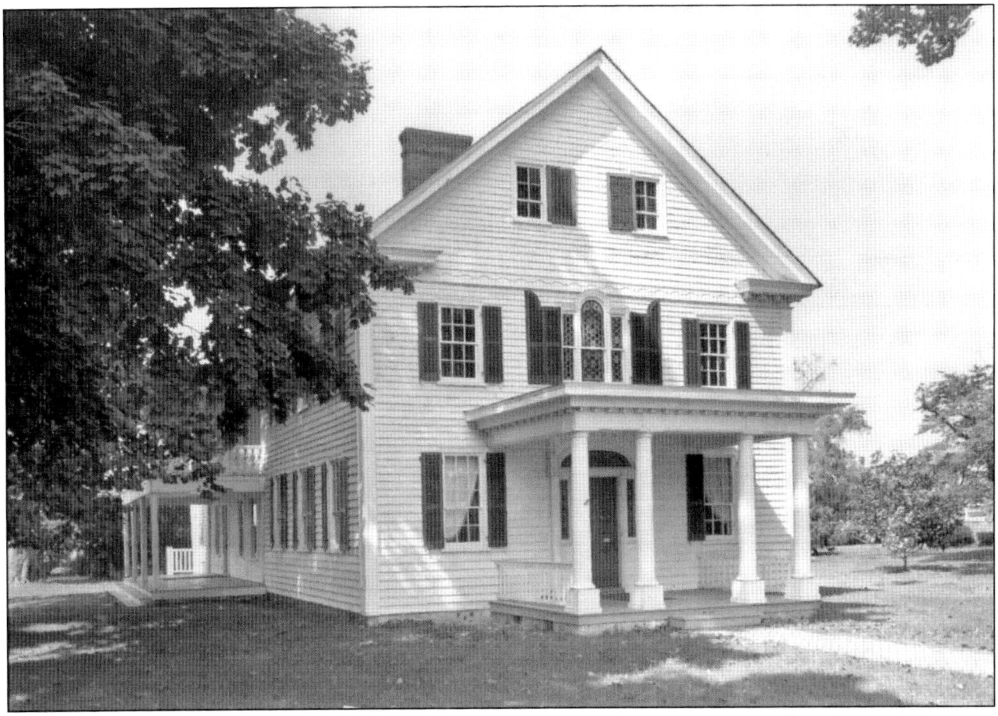

Public awareness of the great importance of preservation and restoration was heightened when, in 1981, the U.S. Postal Service set its sights on the Calvin B. Taylor House (built 1832) to demolish and alter its grounds to construct a new post office. A group of citizens convinced the mayor and council to purchase the property and turn it over to the newly formed, nonprofit Berlin Heritage Foundation for restoration with privately donated funds. The structure was in deplorable condition, but the foundation raised substantial funds and began restoration as the Calvin B. Taylor House. As restoration progressed, small groups of citizens, realizing the benefits of preservation and restoration, began to look at the downtown, already on the National Register of Historic Places, as having great potential. The downtown, parts of which were destroyed by the fires of 1895, 1901, and 1904, had all been built between 1895 and 1905. It had not been changed much structurally, only inappropriately fixed up, and in some cases was falling down.

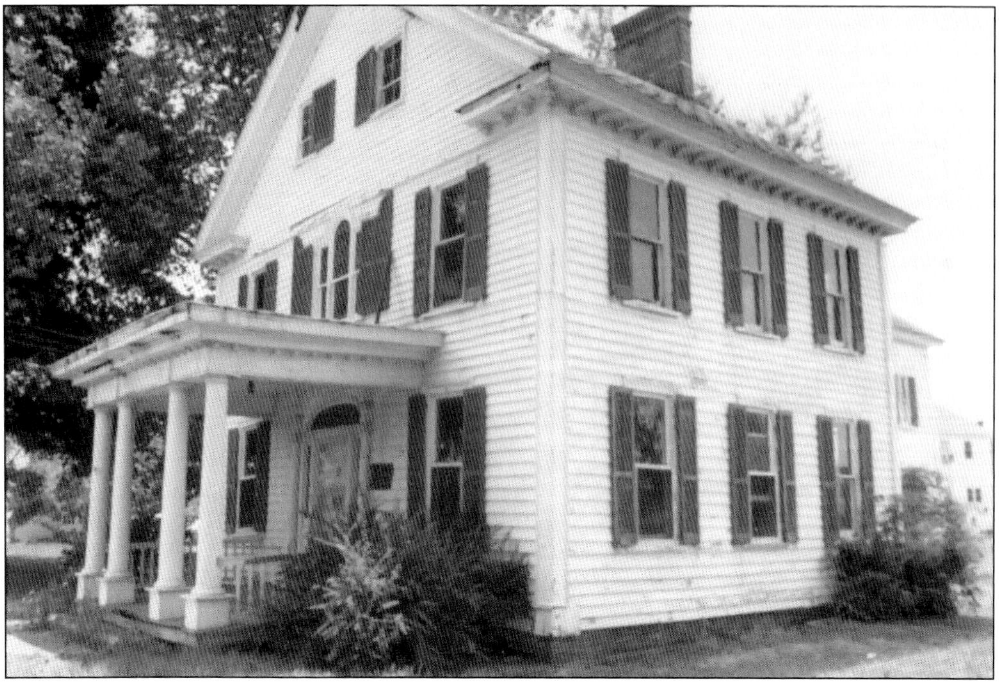

After Calvin Taylor's death in 1932, the house went through several changes of ownership and occupancy. Immediately prior to its acquisition by the town, it contained apartments. Termites were getting fat on its sweet gum framing and yellow pine floors. It was treated and stabilized, and work on making it into a house museum and gallery as planned by the foundation began.

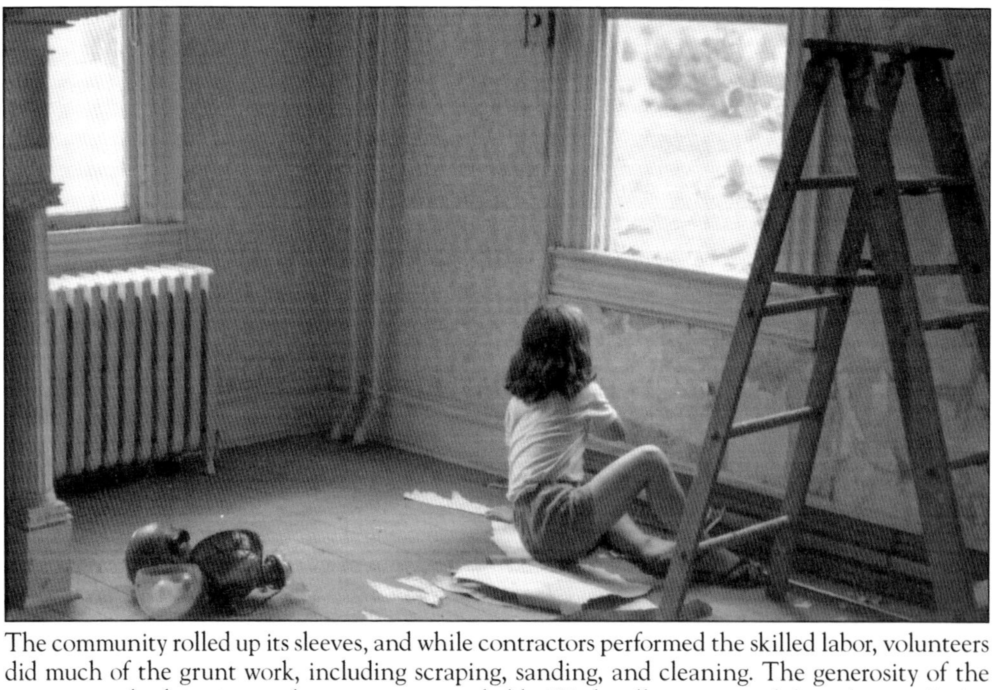

The community rolled up its sleeves, and while contractors performed the skilled labor, volunteers did much of the grunt work, including scraping, sanding, and cleaning. The generosity of the community, both in time and money, was remarkable. Work still goes on, and the volunteer Berlin Heritage Foundation still gratefully accepts donations.

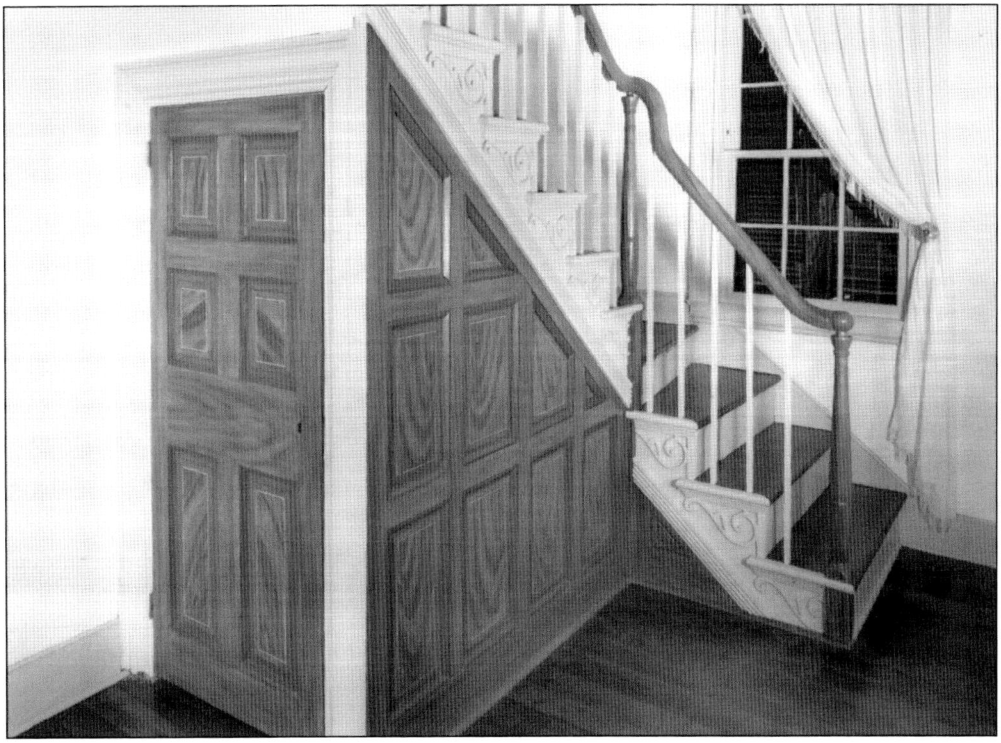

The original block of the house, built in 1832 by Isaac Covington, is a typical gable-fronted Greek temple with double parlors, a transverse hall, and a small office. This view from the front entrance shows the graining on the pine woodwork that has been restored to its original mahogany and maple appearance by Phillip Ward and Linda Croxson, who are among the foremost grainers in America today.

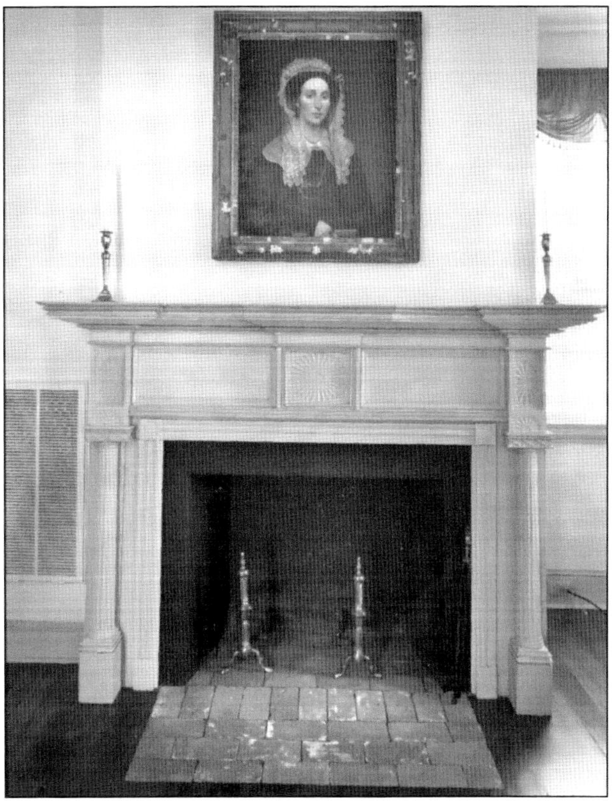

As funds permit, the house is being properly appointed and great care is taken by the board of directors to be historically correct. Soon floor coverings of period design specially loomed for the double parlors will be installed. In the north parlor, a portrait of Mary White, who lived in Robin's Nest, hangs restored above the fireplace. Architectural patterns on this mantle repeat those of the exterior front entrance.

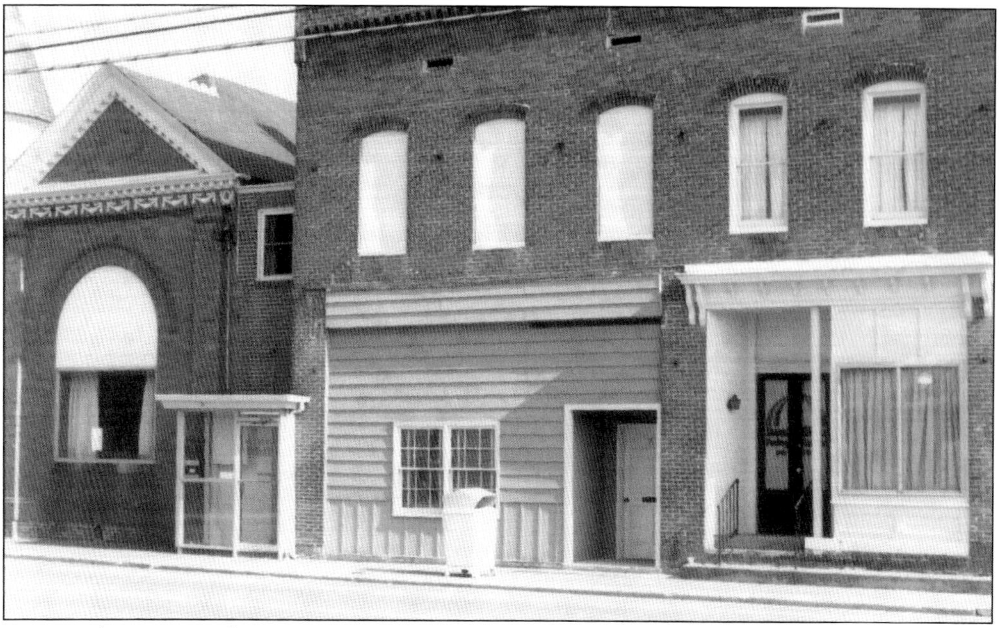

In town, the amount of restoration necessary depended not only on condition but also on how much the building had been fixed up. Some buildings only needed a good scrubbing and an appropriate paint job. The L. L. Dirickson Private Bank building, above left, was improperly modernized in the mid-1960s. The window was redone and partially covered, and an aluminum and glass rear entrance installed. The Ayres Building, above right, was probably built after the fire of 1901. It has two storefronts, the larger being built for the Ayres brothers' general store and the smaller for the Ayres sisters' millinery shop. In the 1950s, the brothers' storefront was removed, a pseudo-Williamsburg facade constructed, and the floor lowered to street level. The sisters' shop frontage remained undisturbed. In 1987, three Berlin natives bought the property and using the millinery shop's facade as a pattern, restored the brothers' store facade to its original appearance, below.

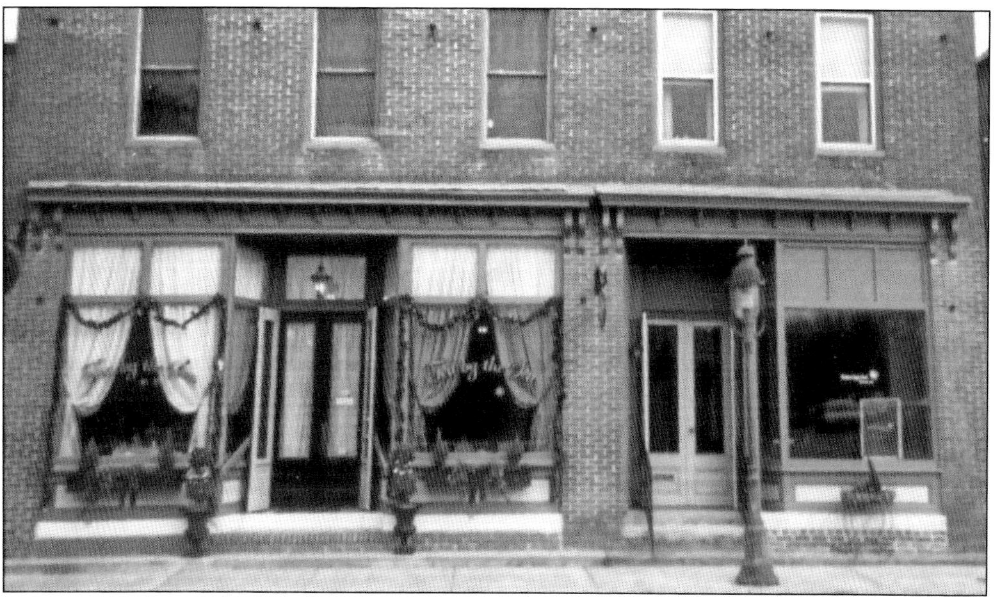

The L. L. Dirickson Private Bank building, pictured before restoration on the left in the top photograph on the previous page, is shown here after restoration. The aluminum panel and inappropriate entrance were removed and the windows restored.

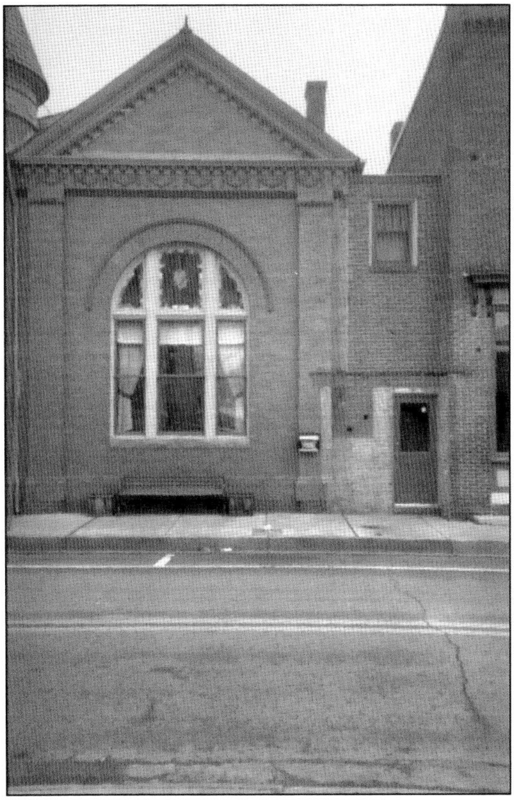

Paran Lodge No. 64 was constructed in 1902 by the Independent Order of the Odd Fellows, a popular men's fraternal organization. It was built on the site of the 1854 Armory, which had burned in the 1901 fire. Paran Lodge was a typical Odd Fellows building consisting of two storefronts leased to businesses and a large second-floor meeting room. The Odd Fellows built lodges employing the same general plan in rural areas across the country. It was bought by local businessmen in 1983 and required little restoration.

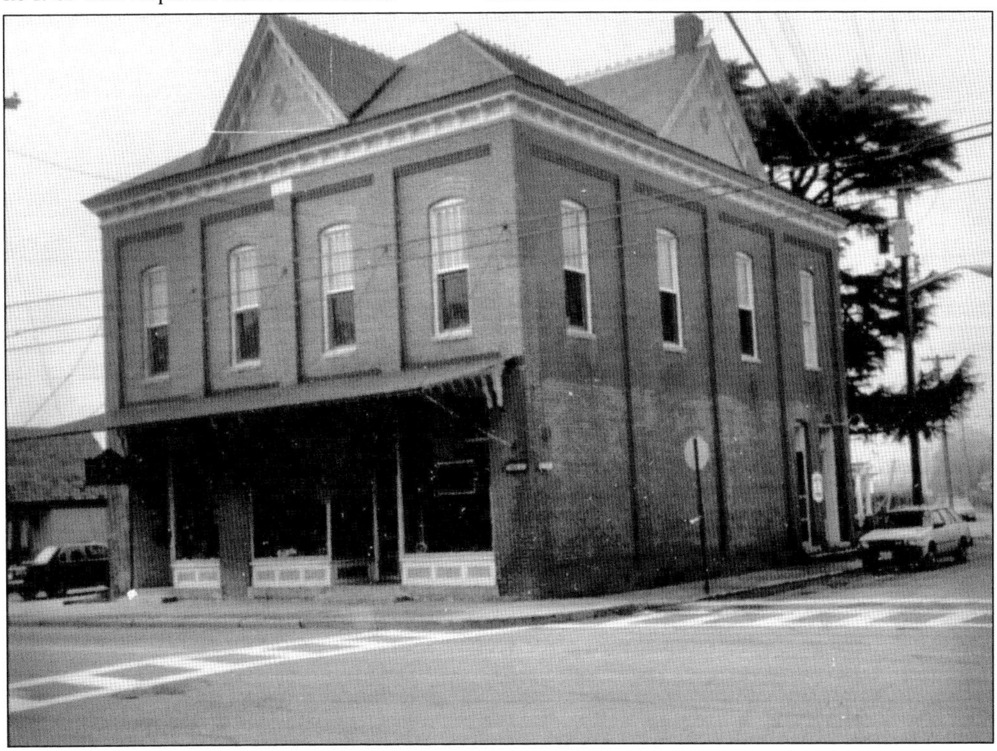

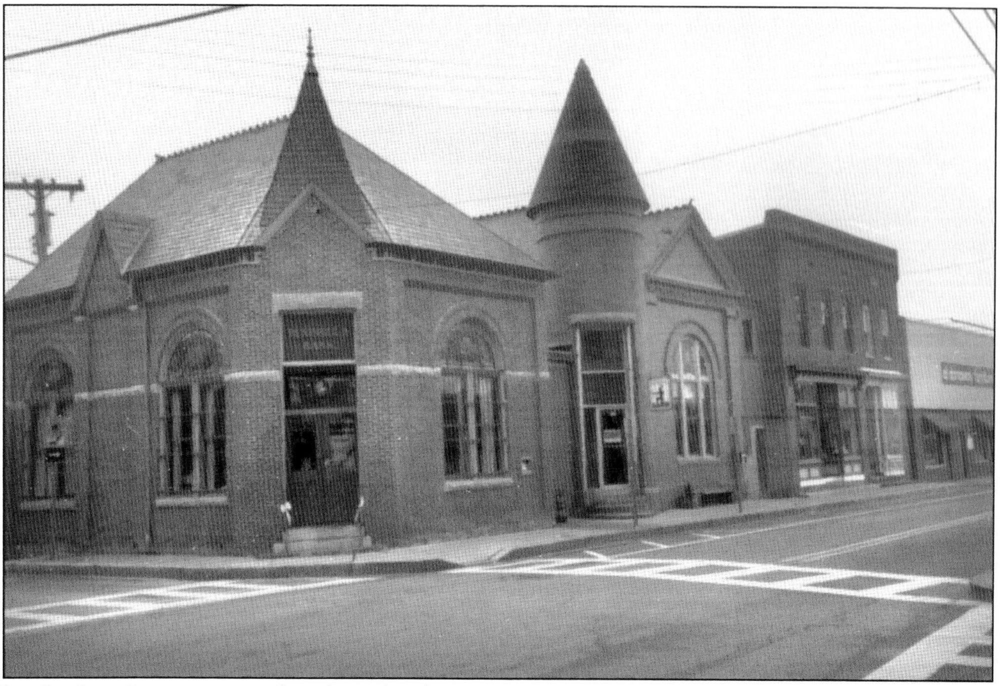

Look what the restoration has done for the streetscape. Attention to detail and color is vital to historic preservation. During the restoration of downtown and the Calvin B. Taylor House, art history professor Page Hammond provided essential advice on such matters.

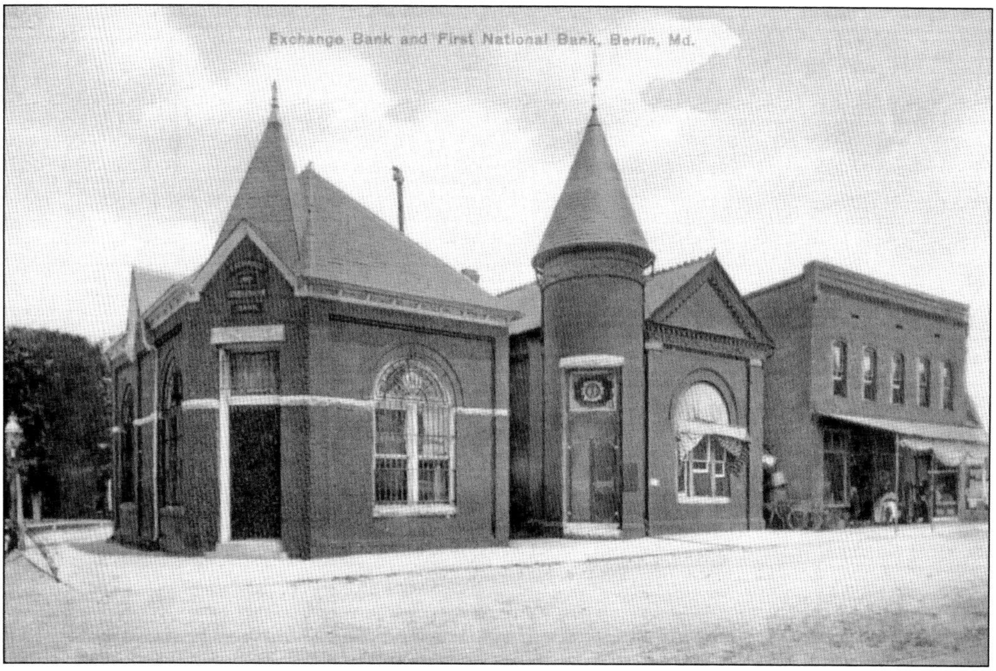


This is the same streetscape, taken in 1905. All that's needed today is the awning and window over the door of the L. L. Dirickson Bank. The more things change, the more they stay the same. (Mabel Rogers Collection.)

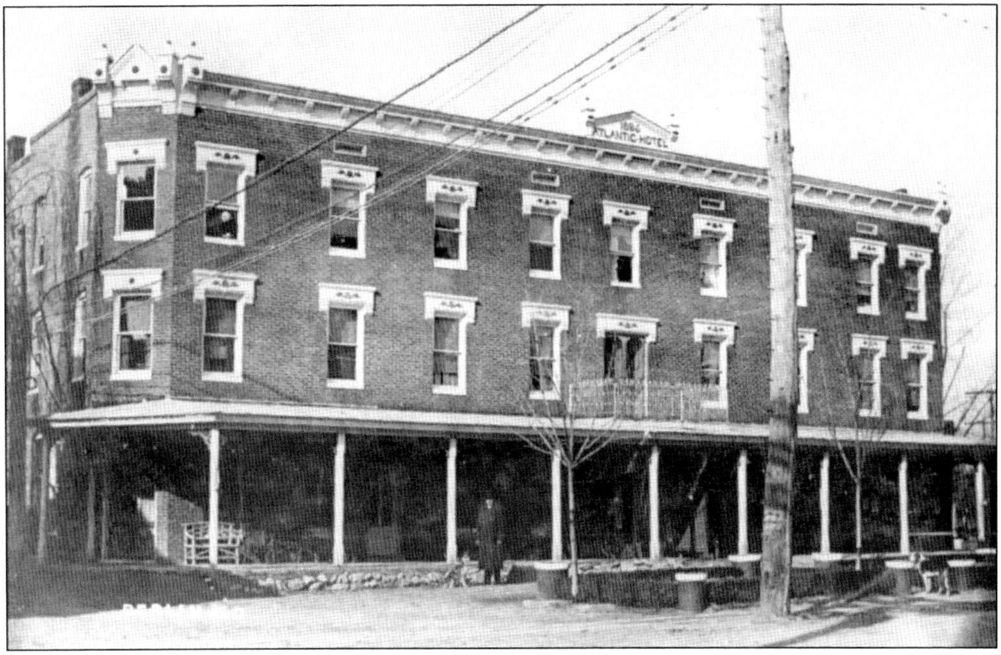

The Atlantic Hotel, built in 1895 after the 1895 fire destroyed its predecessor, was owned and operated by Horace and Virginia Harmonson. Mr. Harmonson also owned the livery stable behind the hotel. It was a salesman's hotel, catering to gentlemen arriving by train, but with a fine dining room. In 1946, an addition was built on the front, pictured below, virtually obscuring the original facade. As commercial practices changed, and the automobile became the choice mode of transportation, the hotel went into a decline. The dining room closed. Next, like the rest of downtown, the stores inside began to suffer and become marginal. The hotel hiding behind the brick and Formstone became a flophouse. Something had to be done. Ten native couples resolved to change things at the hotel and were determined to restore it. With only a hope and a prayer and no thought or motive of profit, they bought it.

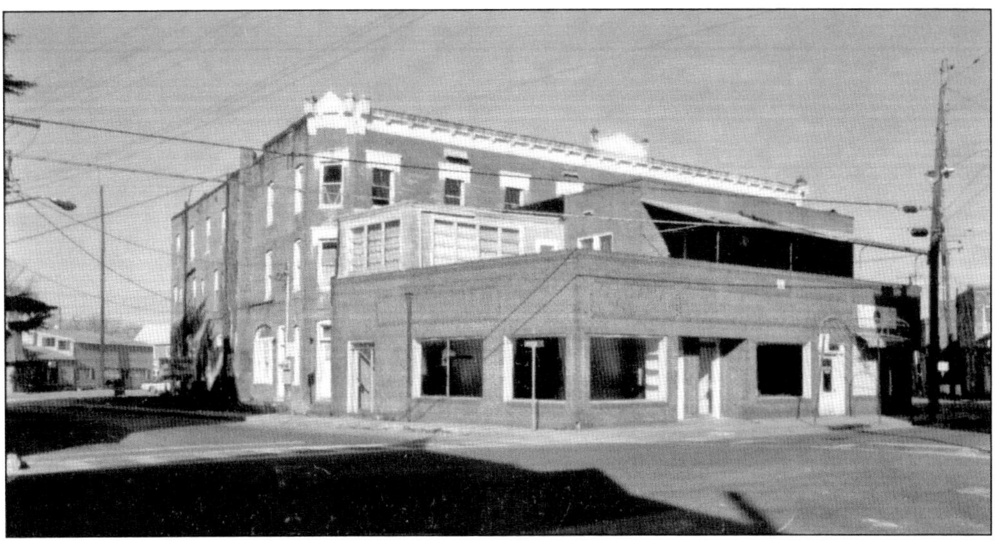

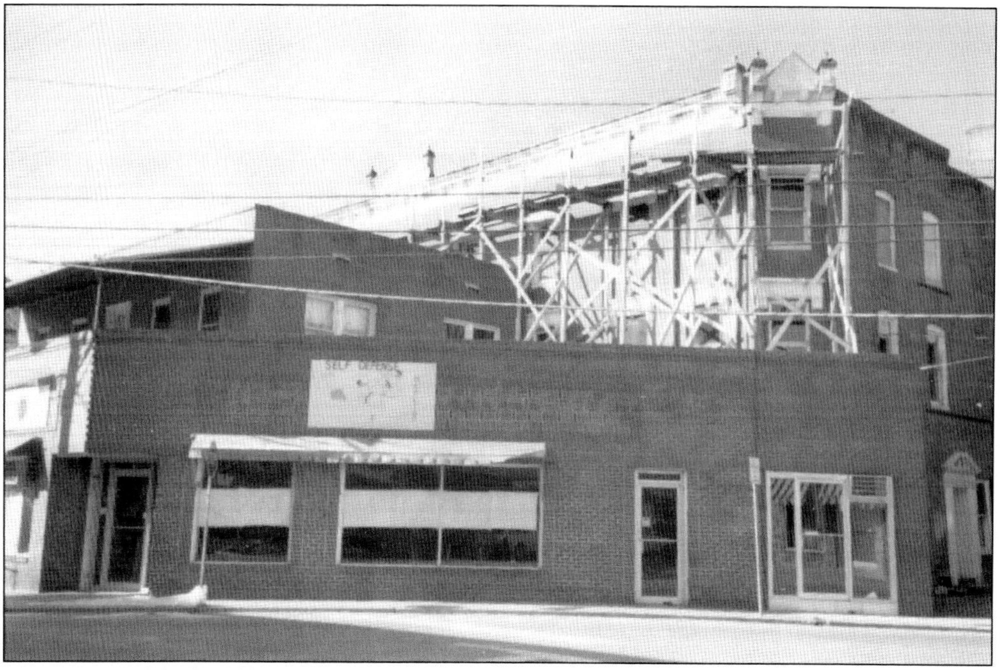


Restoration of the hotel began in 1986. The partnership hired Larry Widgeon, a local contractor, to execute the restoration. While the plans for the interior provided for comfortable rooms with private baths, unlike the original layout, the plan for the exterior was a collection of vintage photographs. The instructions were simple: "Larry, make it look like it did originally." When restoration started, the building was in such poor condition that one could stand on the first floor and see the sky through the third-floor roof. Three inches of water stood in the dining room. The brick walls bulged. Larry commenced tearing out; the partners wrung their hands. Larry tore more; the partners wrung harder. Finally, however, he started putting back.

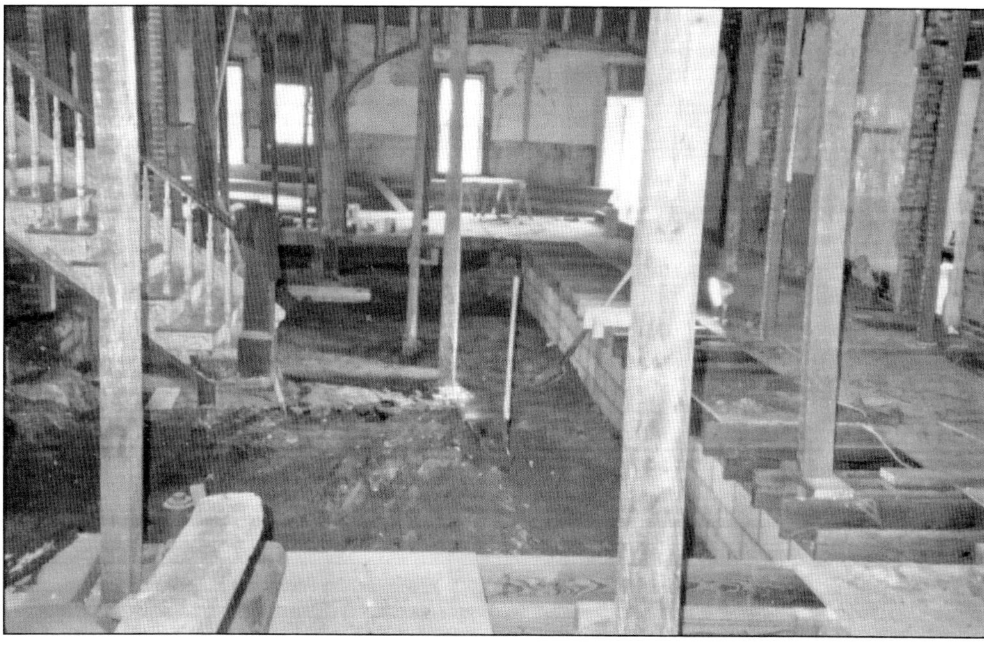

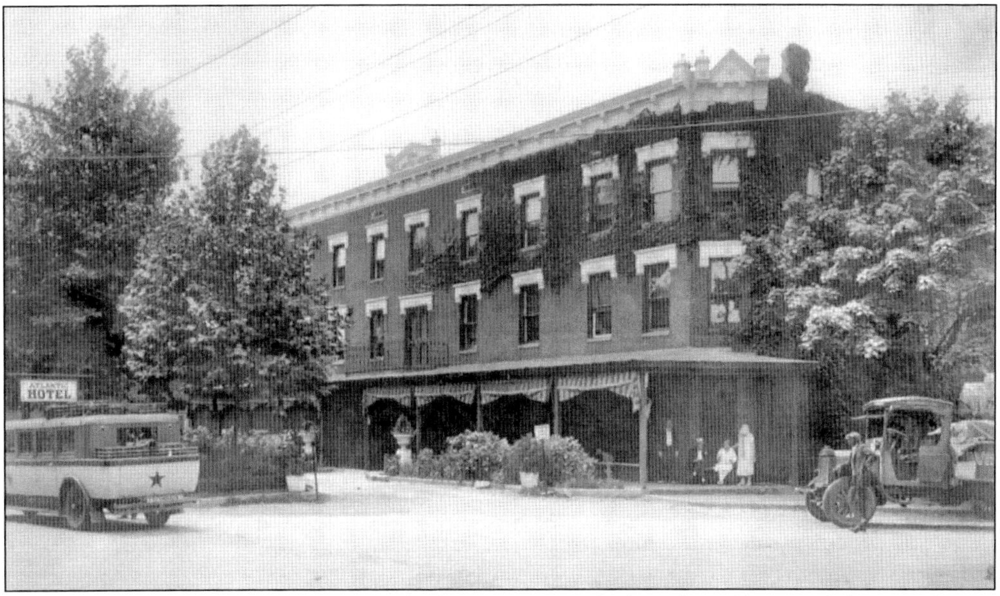


The Atlantic Hotel is shown as it looked in the 1930s, before the addition of the storefronts. Note the Red Star bus on the left.

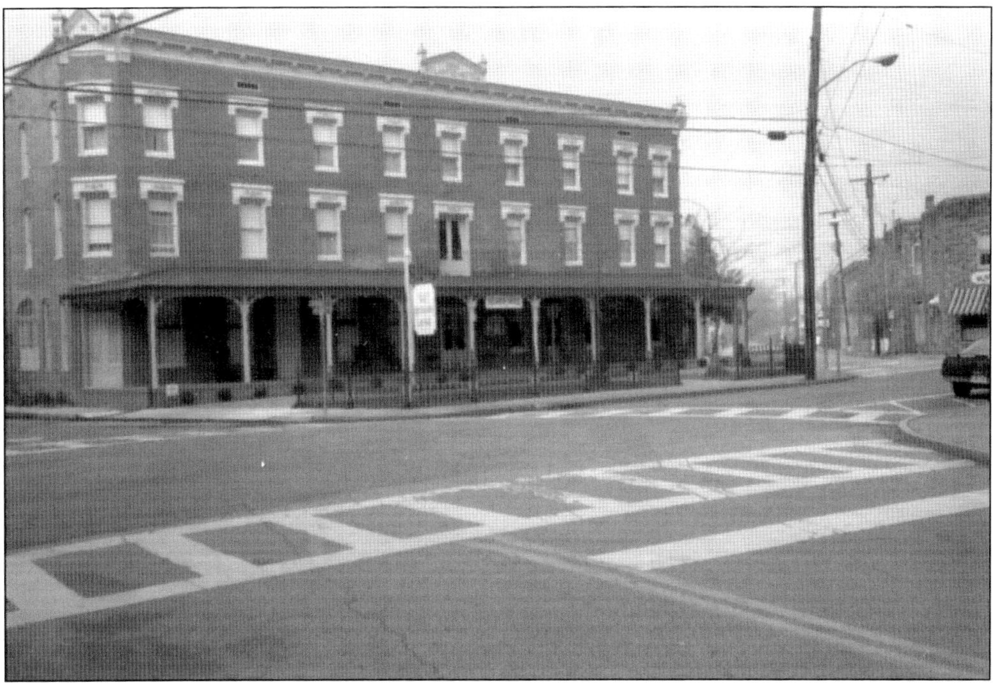

In 1992, the restoration of the Atlantic Hotel was completed. The result is magnificent. The plans and specifications for the facade were clear. The restoration won the State Preservation Award.

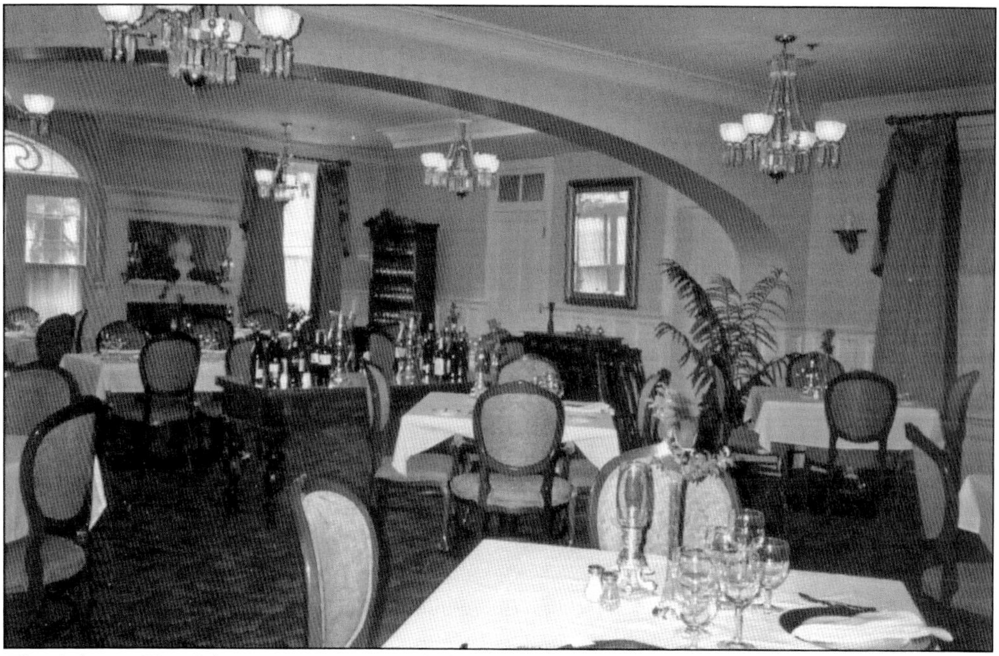

The Atlantic Hotel dining room, pictured after restoration, provided a gourmet dining experience for its patrons. A smaller Drummer's Café was located to the right of this formal dining area and provided a simpler fare.

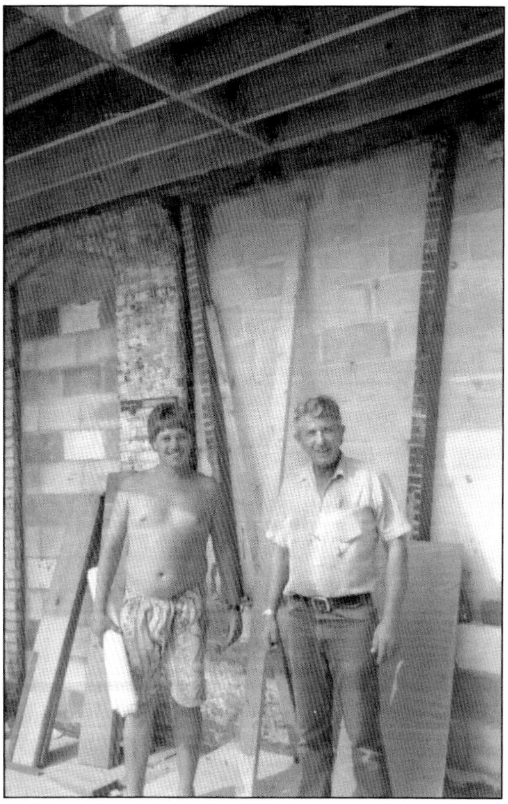

Without Larry Widgeon, downtown Berlin would never have been properly restored. His understanding of the restoration and the quality of his execution were unsurpassed. Above all, his problem-solving ability and resourcefulness put him at the top of his profession. Here he is at the commencement of the Atlantic Hotel project with his son, Shawn, a master cabinetmaker, at a very young age.

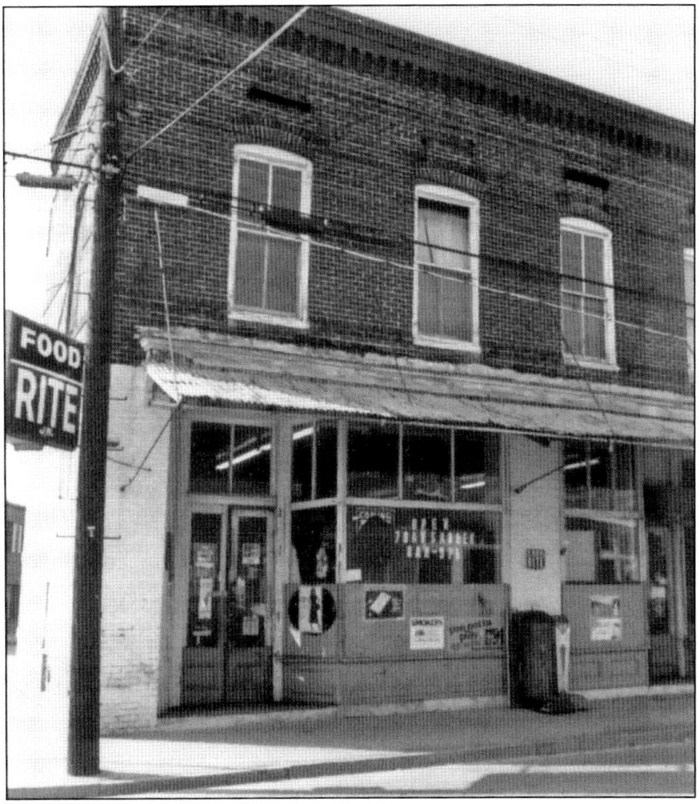


The Eagle Hotel, located at the corner of North Main Street and Commerce Street, formerly known as Lovely Lane, was built after the fire of 1895 and originally consisted of two storefronts and seven guest rooms sharing one bath. It was a place of lodging for people just passing through and the more thrifty salesmen who came to town. It has been used as a cobbler's shop, a hardware store, a clothing store, and a food store. Now Victorian Charm, it was used as the bridal shop where Maggie bought her dresses in the movie *Runaway Bride*. The building was restored by a group of locals in 1984.

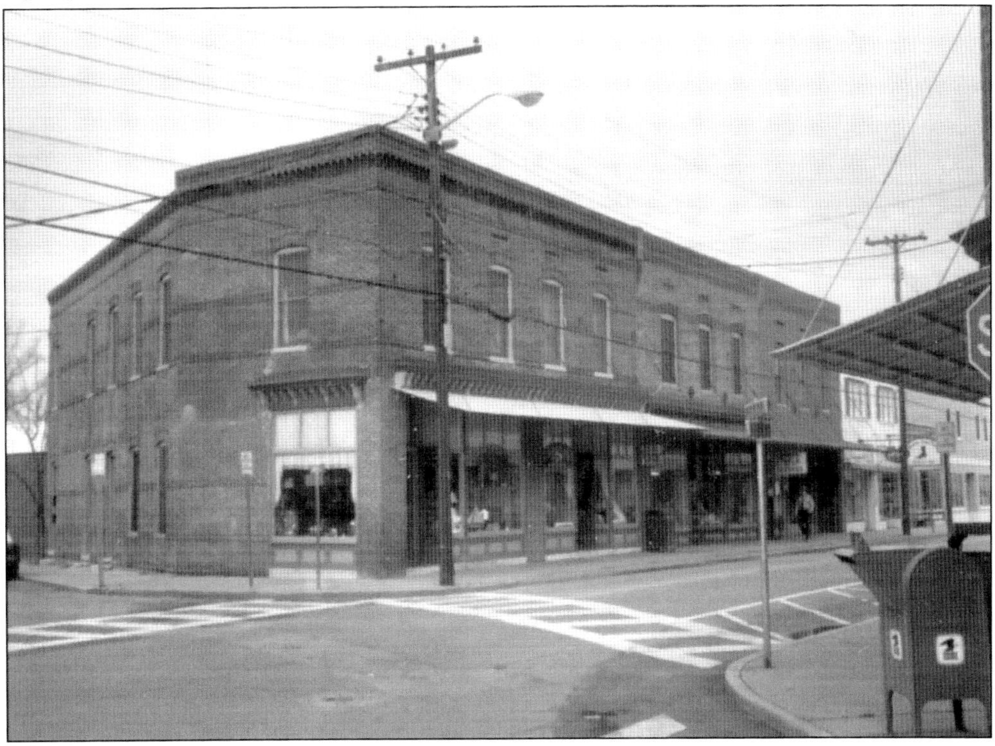

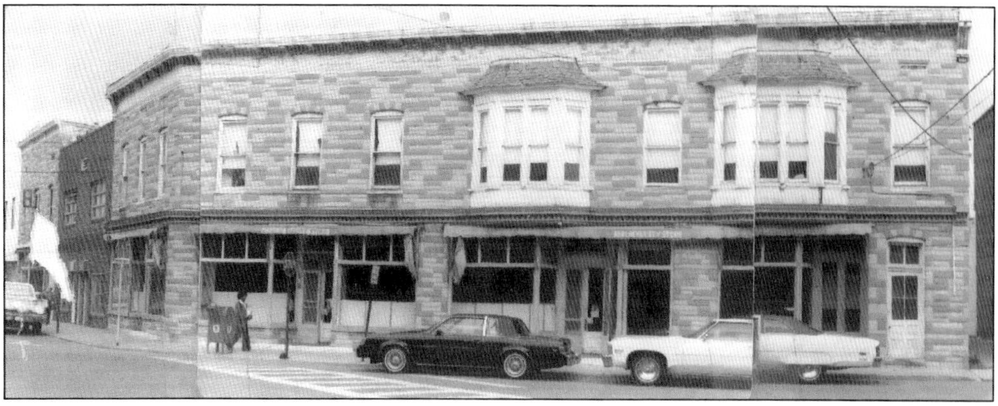

In 1981, two local couples, Mr. and Mrs. James Barrett and Mr. and Mrs. William Freeman, purchased the Berlin Variety Store and hired contractor Larry Widgeon. Citizens watched intently as the new owners threw money at the old building. It was renamed Renaissance Plaza and won the State Preservation Award. In the restoration of Renaissance Plaza, the owners and contractor were faced with the first attempt in Berlin to remove Formstone, a masonry product applied to the exterior. It had been popular in the late 1940s when five downtown buildings and several houses were subjected to the installation of this architecturally disfiguring process. Fortunately, on Renaissance Plaza, the Formstone was applied over wire lathe, and this was relatively easily removed. The Formstone has been removed from many downtown buildings. (Above, Nancy Barrett Collection.)

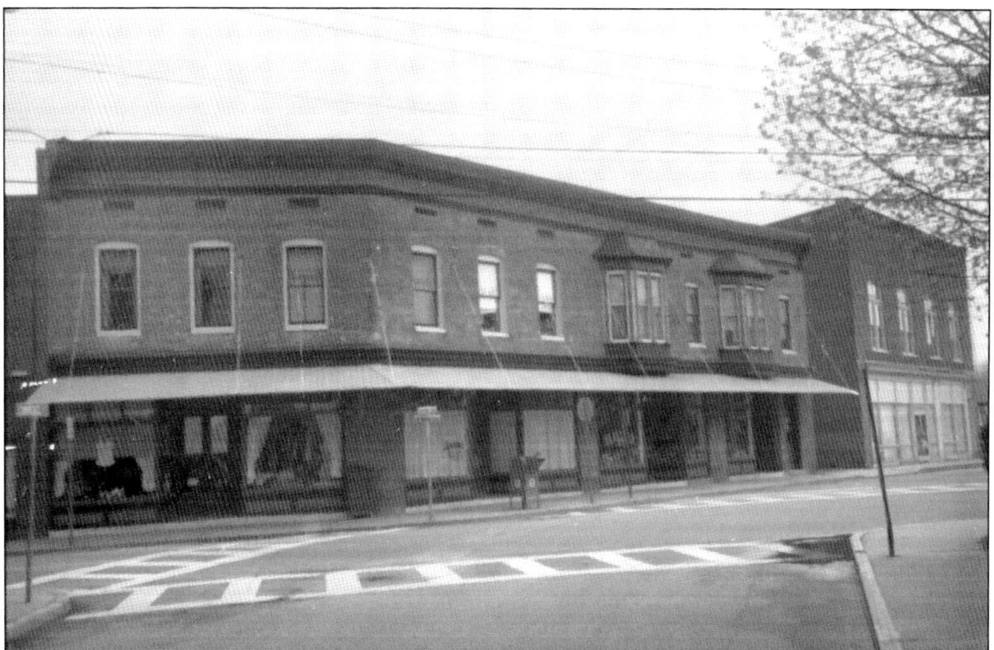

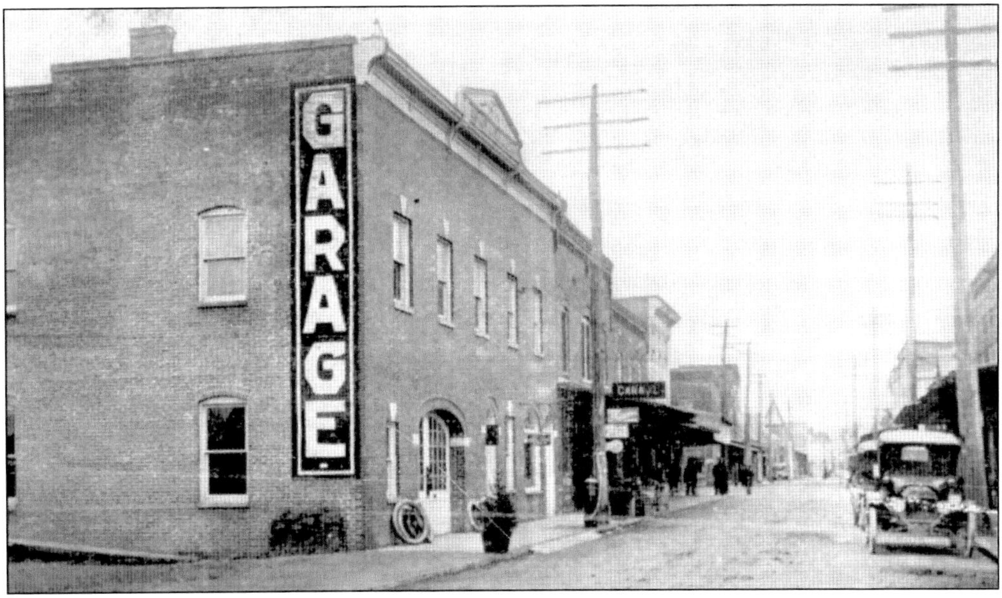


The Barretts and Freemans weren't finished. Down the street from Renaissance Plaza stood the Dollar General Store. It had originally been two automobile dealerships, Jess Taylor's and Walter Murphy's. Jim Barrett's father, Gil, had purchased the property in 1951 and moved his family here from Annapolis, Maryland. The top photograph is from before construction of Murphy's garage. In the bottom photograph, the building has become just another generic storefront found in "Anytown, U.S.A." (Above, Taylor Bank Collection; Below, Nancy Barrett Collection.)

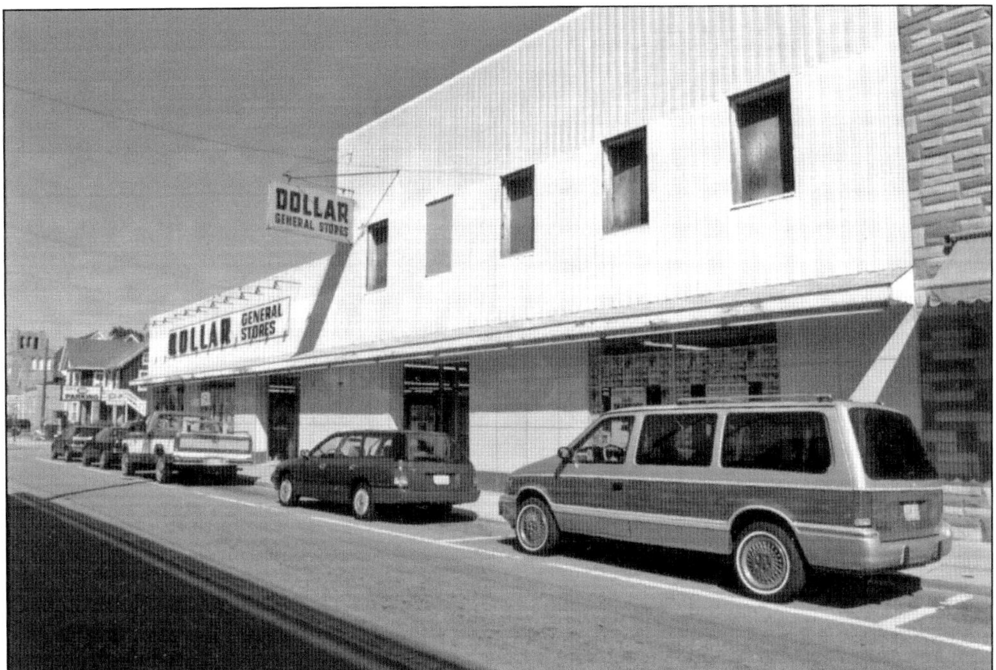

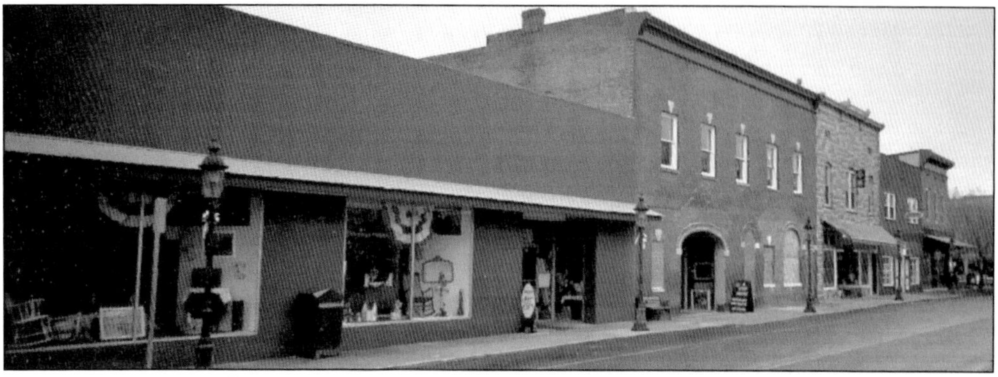

Once again, Larry Widgeon was turned loose in historic Berlin. As usual, he did a superb job, paid careful attention to what was there, and used old photographs as guides. This is how it turned out. Today's storefronts are, from left to right, Town Center Antiques II, the newly renovated Masonic Hall, the studio of Patrick L. Henry, and the Church Mouse. (Nancy Barrett Collection.)

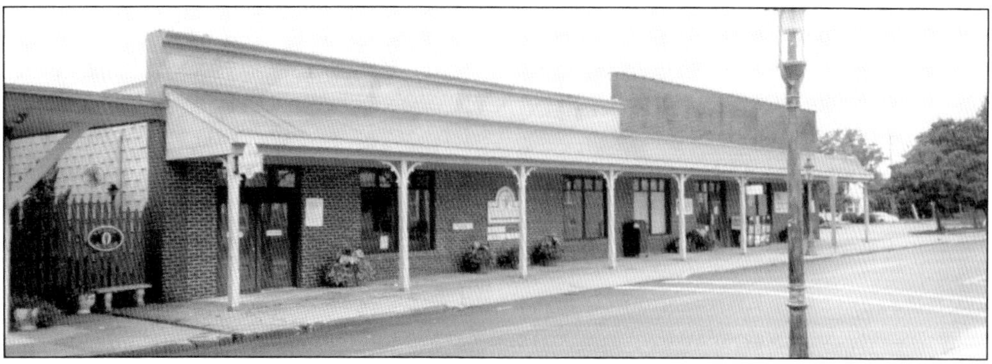

Next, the Barretts and Freemans completed their third major project, the remodeling of the ubiquitous 1960s Acme Market. No one felt the urge to photograph the Acme, but most readers can imagine what it looked like. This is what the building looks like today. (Nancy Barrett Collection.)

In the fall of 1998, all of the hard restoration work paid off. Berlin was selected to become the town "Hale," the location of a Paramount movie to be known as *Runaway Bride*, starring box office stars Julia Roberts and Richard Gere. The time period set for the movie was the present, so very little was required of the set designers. Hollywood wanted an all-American small town, and they got one—Berlin.

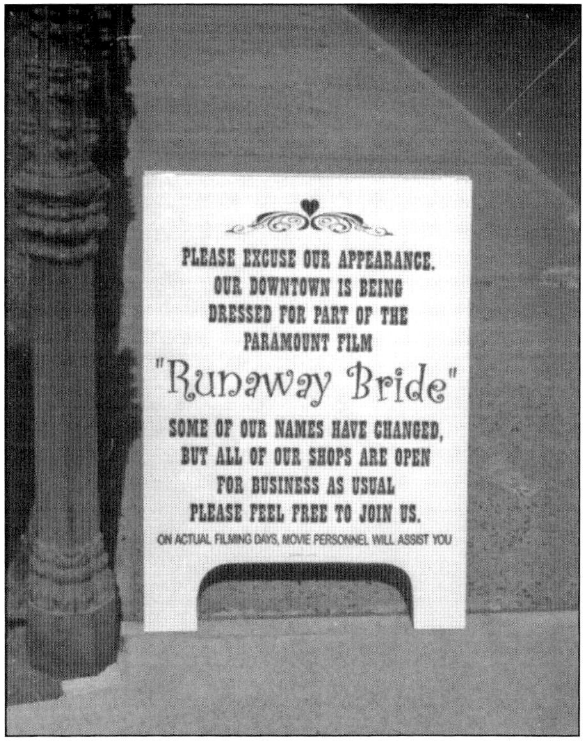


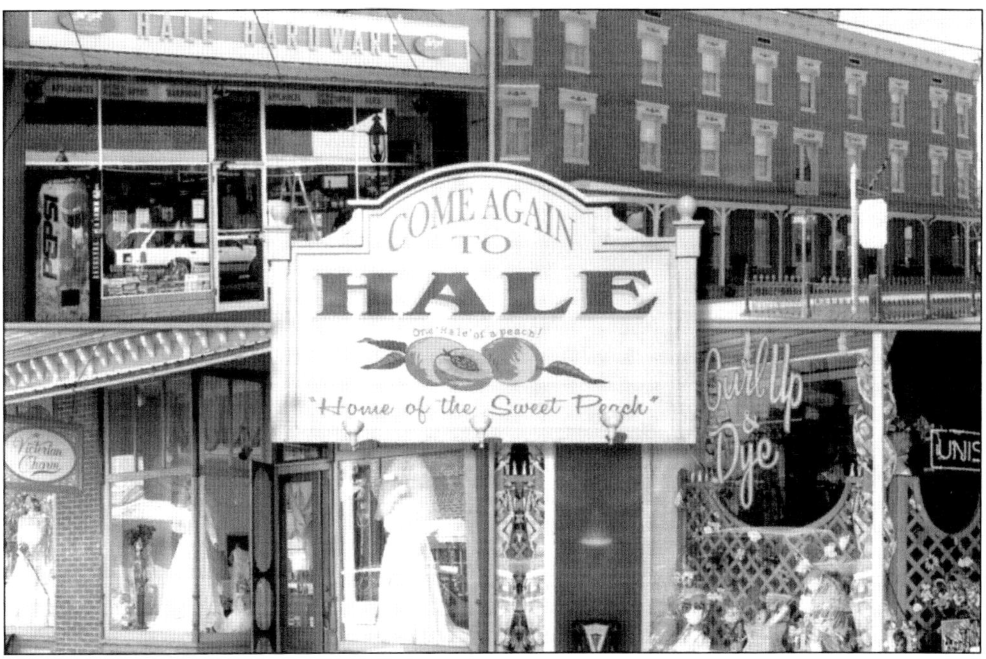


The downtown was featured in the movie with numerous scenes filmed on Main Street. Several buildings including the Atlantic Hotel, Berlin Hardware, Victorian Charm (the Eagle Hotel), and the Hair Shop were used extensively for both indoor and outdoor shots. Many local extras became Hale residents for a day or two. The Paramount staff was pleasant and respectful and director Gary Marshall delightful.

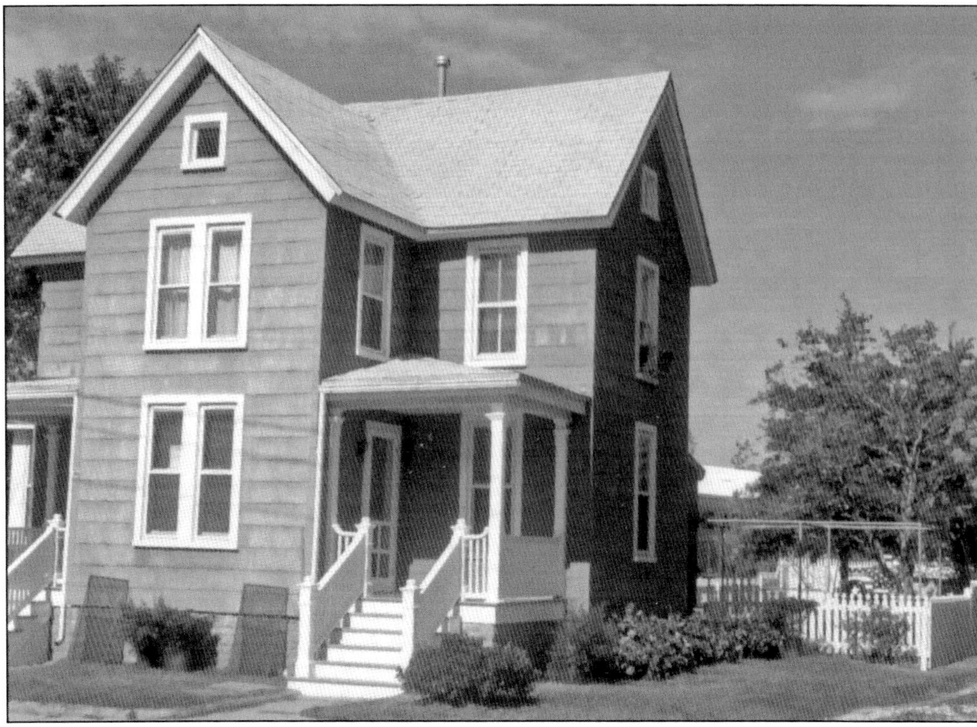

Maggie, the heroine and runaway bride in the film, lived in this modest house on Baker Street. The dwelling was used extensively inside and out. She worked, however, at Hale Hardware (Berlin Hardware). When filming was not actually in progress, stores were open for business while still "dressed." In the hardware store, certain items "for sale" were in fact props and temporary signs advised "not for sale." Maggie purchased one of her many wedding dresses next door at the Hale Bridal Shop, which was actually Victorian Charm. Main Street was the star of the show. One Washington movie critic criticized the film because no town could look that good. Residents agreed on three things about the experience: the people were very nice; the crew was very efficient; Julia Roberts was even prettier in real life than on film.

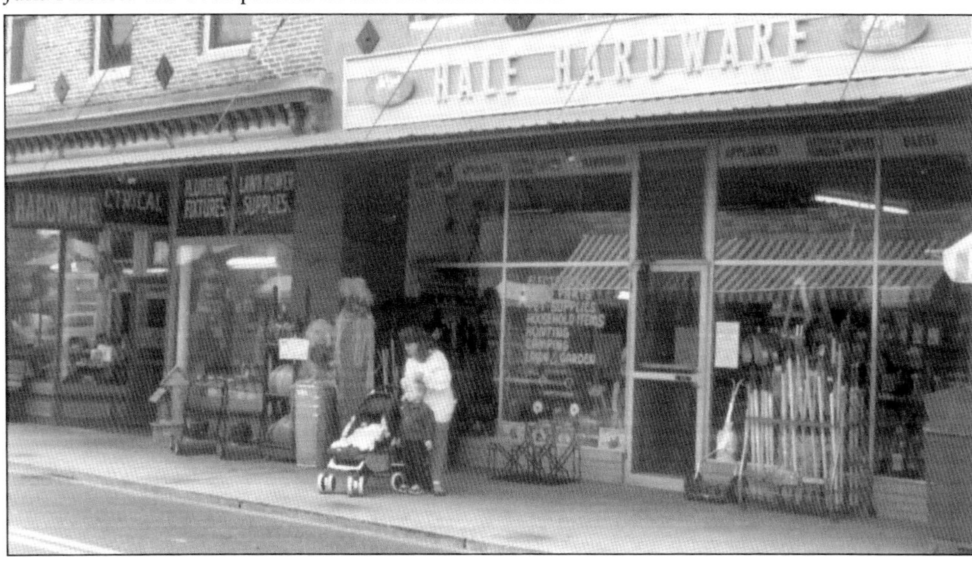

In the spring of 2001, Disney came to town, and Berlin became Treegap. This movie was quite different from *Runaway Bride*. It was set in 1910. The film was *Tuck Everlasting* starring Alexis Bledel, Jonathan Jackson, Sissy Spacek, Ben Kingsley, and William Hurt.

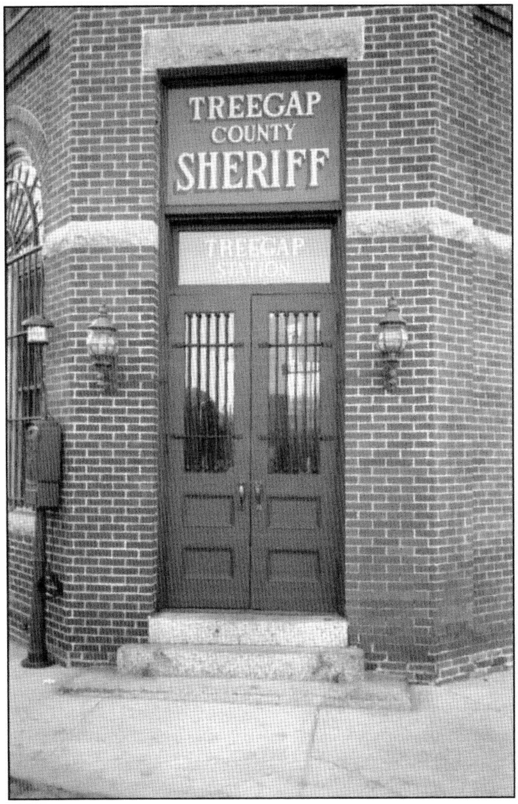


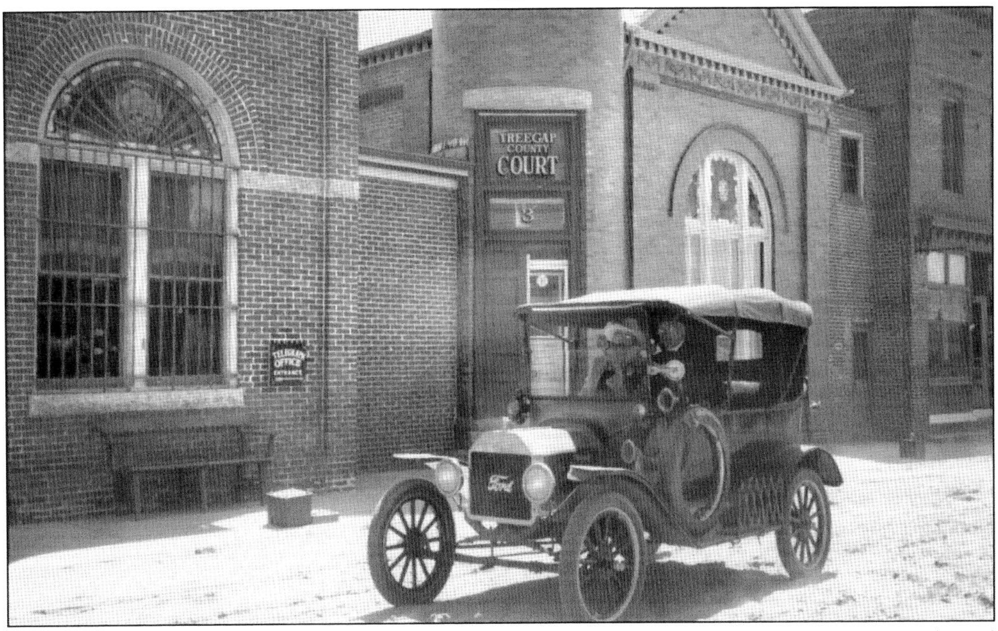


The streets had to be returned to their 19th-century condition by adding layers of materials and dirt. Antique automobiles came to town; horses and mules showed up. It was a dusty time. Faye Jarmon, head housekeeper at the Atlantic Hotel, was heard to remark, "People think this looks quaint but they don't have to sweep it up."

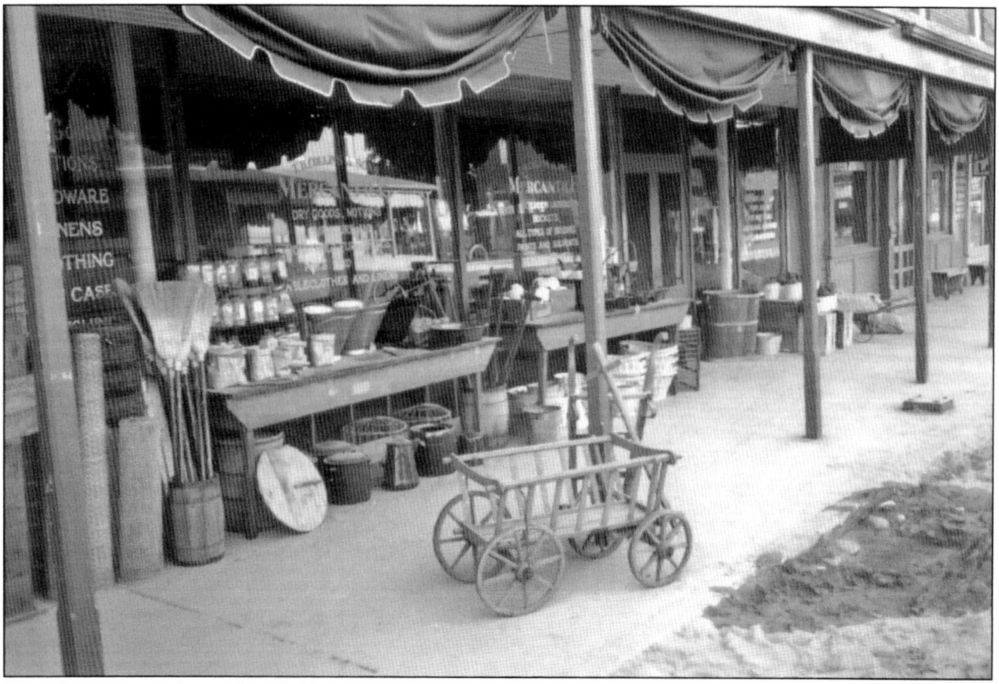

Storefronts were dressed and all manner of early-20th-century merchandise placed on the sidewalks. As with the prior movie, the crew was quite friendly, and the townspeople were given free access to Main Street during filming, much of which was done at night with bright lights.

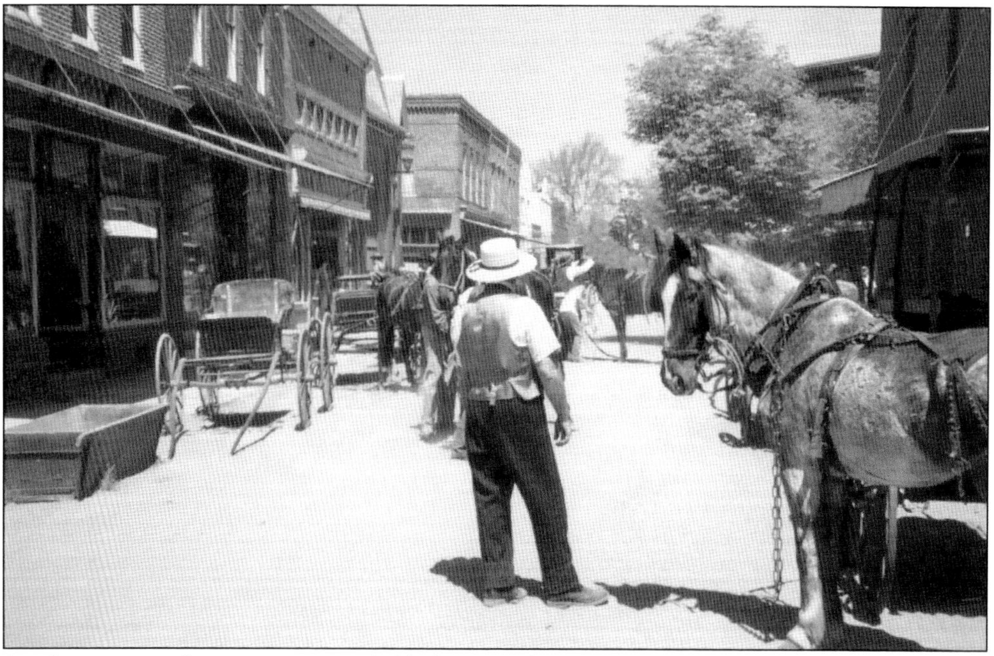

Set designers made extensive use of old photographs in the collection of the Calvin B. Taylor House Museum for ideas. Many historic shop signs were copied faithfully for this film, including the Joe. Hollins sign, which hung in front of Mr. Hollins's store 100 years ago. As in the case of Paramount, the Disney crews were efficient, polite, and friendly.

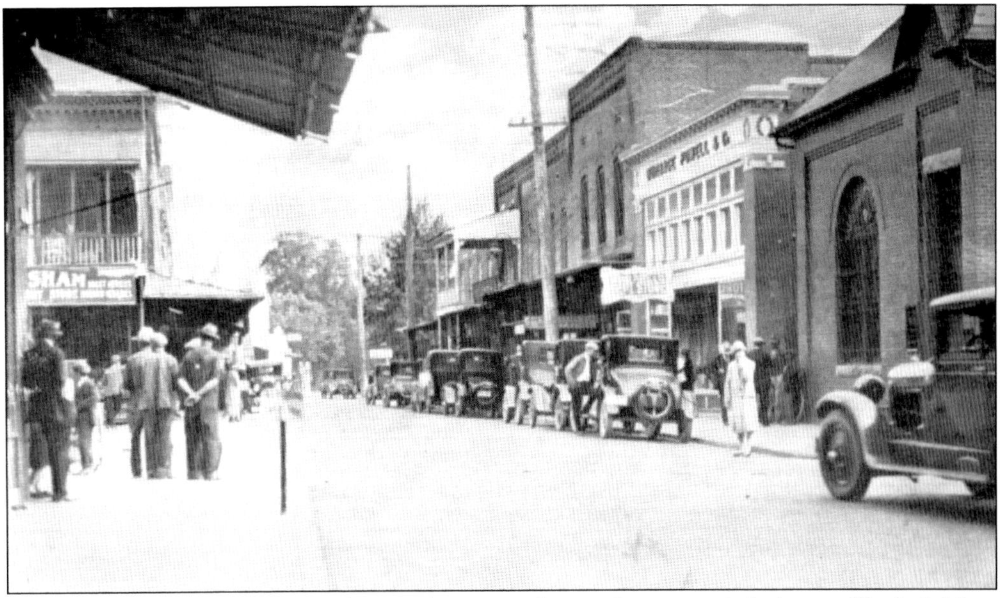

Although this photograph was taken in the 1920s, change the cars and clothes and Berlin's Main Street retains this historic character. (Mabel Rogers Collection.)

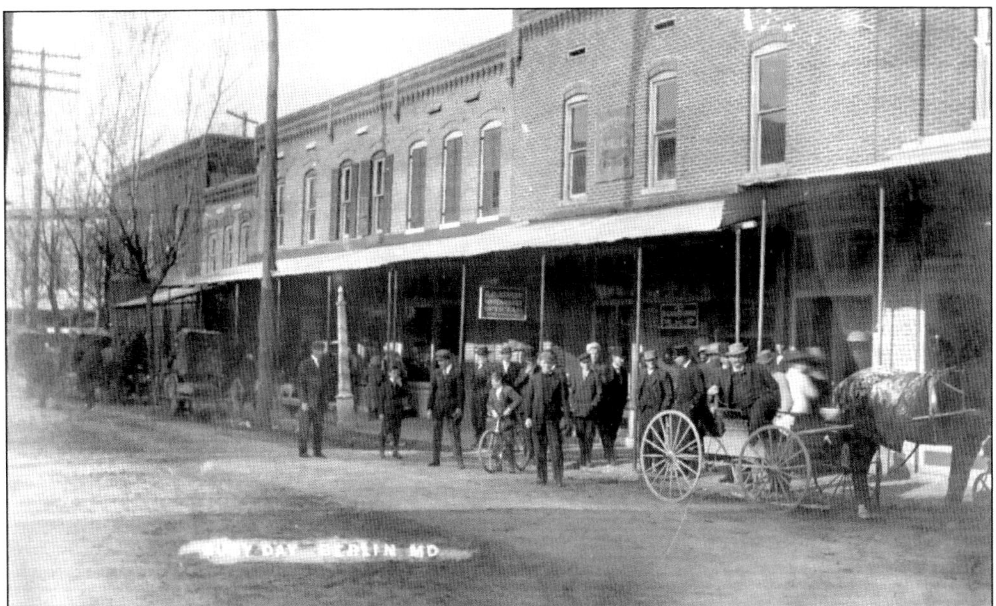

People do not come to town in horse-drawn wagons today, but they still come. The good life lives on in Berlin. Come see us. Make our past your present. (Ellis Wainwright Collection.)